To E. L. Schenbux

With best wishes of

Choirs of

First Baptist Church

Bloomington, Ills.

October 26, 1956

Billy Graham

Billy Graham

The personal story
of the man,
his message,
and his mission

by Stanley High

McGraw-Hill Book Company, Inc.
New York Toronto London

For Tim
whose gift
is an
understanding
heart

ACKNOWLEDGMENT

It was on assignment as an editor of *The Reader's Digest* that I first met Billy Graham at his home in Montreat, North Carolina, in May, 1954. Over the two succeeding years, at home and abroad, my repeated contacts with him and my opportunity to observe, firsthand, his "Crusades" and their consequences were almost wholly due to similar *Reader's Digest* assignments and resulted in five articles which have appeared in that magazine.

There are many to whom, for help in assembling the material for *Billy Graham*, I am indebted: to Ruth and Billy Graham for their wholehearted approval of and cooperation in this undertaking; to Mel Larson for his painstaking research; to members of the Billy Graham Team; to my associates, Dorothy B. Gardner and Mary Allen Thompson.

But my first and, by all odds, greatest indebtedness is to *The Reader's Digest* and to DeWitt Wallace, its editor.

Stanley High

Contents

Illustrations

Introduction:
The great succession

IF, AS IS POSSIBLE, the big story of mid-twentieth-century America turns out to be religion, then, on the human level, the big name in that story is likely to be Billy Graham. This, if it happens, will not be for statistical or intellectual reasons, but for others of greater moment.

Statistically, the success of Billy Graham, important and impressive as it is, is only one among many indications that, by every quantitative measurement, religion in the United States is booming. By that measurement, his ministry is an unprecedented phenomenon in an area where much seems, at present, to be unprecedented.

Moreover, if it should happen again that religion stands in need of intellectual defenders—as it did not many decades ago —it is not likely that Billy Graham would be recruited or that, in such a cause, he would offer his services. This would not be because of what would be held to be his intellectual limitations—which he would be among the first to admit, even to magnify. A more important reason would be the fact that his

1

entire ministry has been an expression of the conviction that for any generation and for all kinds and conditions of people, for Nicodemus quite as much as for the Samaritan Woman, the discovery of the reality of God is not chiefly an intellectual, but an empirical achievement. He is sure faith can be bolstered by reason—as his own faith increasingly is. But with him, as with most, the vitality of that faith is a product less of argument than of experience. He would say, as Martin Luther did, "To believe in God is to go down on your knees."

In his relatively short ministry, Billy Graham has probably preached, face to face, to more people than any spokesman for the faith in all Christian history: by the end of 1955, no less than 20,000,000. It is probable, also, that more people, under his ministry, in his Crusades and through his radio and film ministries, have made "decisions for Christ": an estimated 1,000,000.

But, amazing as these figures are, I do not believe that his is likely to be the big name of this religious era chiefly for quantitative, but rather for qualitative reasons. The biggest difference his ministry may make is not of numbers, but of kind. He will never add significantly to theology's arguments for God. The more important possibility is that he may add significantly to the number of Christians who, beyond argument, have found Him. From such a leaven there could be restored to the church something of its earlier zeal for making that kind of Christians and something of its one-time knowledge of how to go about it.

Many churchmen honestly doubt and some will vehemently deny that any such consequences as these are in prospect from the ministry of Billy Graham. But one fact, I think, can be made clear even to Billy Graham's critics: the man and his ministry are in the revival-producing tradition. Moreover, the potential significance of his ministry can hardly be understood apart from some understanding of revivals and revivalists.

It is a striking fact about revivals that, whenever they come,

2

they are essentially so much the same. For one thing, they do not come by human calculation or planning. Neither is their coming predictable. What can be said about them—and it can be said, I think, about all of them which have had great significance—is that, as Dr. Alexander Whyte pointed out in the mid nineteenth century, "There is a divine mystery about revivals. God's sovereignty is in them."

Whether or not such a revival is now in the making and whether or not Billy Graham will be its instrument, it is also true that for every revival there is such a human instrument. In his book, *Wesley and His Century,* Dr. W. H. Fitchett says, "A great revival is usually linked with a single commanding figure." In connection with almost every spiritual awakening, says Dr. Charles T. Cook, "it would seem to be God's purpose to choose a man who will sum up in himself the yearnings of his time—a man divinely gifted and empowered to interpret to his own generation their deepest needs, and to declare the remedy."

On the face of it, of course, the church should be the adequate instrument of revival and the minister its evangelist. Whatever the place of religious need, some church—with plant, personnel, and program—is within at least physical reach of it. Whatever the kind of religious need, the church is committed—and no less than once every seven days reaffirms the canons of its commitment—to a Gospel adequate to meet it. Further than that the basic doctrines—the statements of faith—of almost every Protestant denomination contain that same unqualified commitment.

If the available resources, material and spiritual, of the church were being made adequately available, then revivals, as something stirred from without the church's normal operations by someone outside its conventional ministry, would be —save, perhaps, as a special exercise for the devout—unnecessary and unlikely. Revivals are a result of the fact that the available resources of the church are not being made ade-

3

quately available. An authentic revival is not artificially induced. Neither does it create its own fuel. Its fuel is a widespread religious need: a need within reach of the church but which the church is not reaching.

There is, I think, something heartening in this. If, left to themselves, people were no better than they are sometimes said to be, then it would follow that this falling off of the effectiveness of the institution aimed to inculcate and extend the faith would lead to an increase in the ease with which increasing numbers of people settled down well satisfied with an inadequate faith or none at all. That, instead of such an increase of contentment in disbelief, there is an increase of the dissatisfactions from which revivals come indicates that, as nature abhors a vacuum, human natures seem to abhor a spiritual vacuum. "Thou has formed us for Thyself," said St. Augustine, "and our souls are restless till they find rest in Thee."

The revival which, in the early eighteenth century, swept through New England was begun by the preaching, from his rural pulpit in Northampton, Massachusetts, of Jonathan Edwards. No preaching, before or since, ever made Hell so hot or imminent. But Jonathan Edwards did not set out to contrive a revival. A revival ensued from his preaching because, as the religious zeal of the earliest period began to be swallowed up in concern for the material upbuilding of the colonies, the church in New England had fallen into sterility, religion into "deadness." But it was this apparent unpropitiousness of the times which for a revival made the times propitious.

Later, the fires of evangelism caught on in New York and spread southward through the Colonies as far as Georgia in what has been called the Great Awakening. The foremost evangelist of the Great Awakening was George Whitefield. Its fuel was the same need: a need for a vital religion which the agencies and spokesmen for religion were not adequately supplying.

It was the same in England. The church there was in league

with aristocracy and the new industrial rich, and almost totally unconcerned for the masses who were desperately poor. "Religion seemed to be dying, if not already dead. It was an age of a confident and triumphant deism. Unbelief had seized all classes."

Out of this came the Evangelical Revival—the most significant religious upsurge in the modern history of the church. John Wesley was its evangelist. This was not because he set out to be, but because beneath the surface of so much disbelieving there was a widespread yearning, a restlessness of soul, for something more satisfying than disbelief, which something Wesley himself came to possess and was empowered to transmit.

Fifty years ago, Dr. Robertson Nicoll, famous British churchman, wrote in the *British Weekly:* "The Church can only live in the world by successive individual transferences from the natural to the spiritual kingdom, in other words, the Church is always dying, always being raised again. That is why we speak of revival Christianity. For it is by revivals of religion that the Church of God makes its most visible advance. When all things seem becalmed, when no breath stirs the air, when all worship seems to have ended but the worship of matter, then it is that the Spirit of God is poured upon the Church, then it is that the Christianity of the apostles and martyrs . . . keeps rising from the catacombs of oblivion."

Therein is another particular in which, in their essentials, revivals are the same. The social and intellectual qualifications of great revivalists differ greatly. Their religious qualifications are essentially the same. Their manners of presenting the Gospel do not have much in common. The Gospel they present and the results they aim for have almost everything in common.

Superficially, two men, each the great evangelist of his time, could hardly have been less alike than John Wesley and, a century later, Dwight L. Moody. By family background and parsonage birth, Wesley belonged to the religious aristocracy,

5

was raised a High Church Anglican, became an Oxford Don, carried a Greek Bible in his saddle bags and sprinkled Latin phrases through the pages of his famous *Journal*.

Moody was a layman of the humblest rural American origin. His formal education ended when he was thirteen—which, to the perennial delight of his critics, resulted in his lifelong disregard for some of the fine points of the English language. So meager was his formal religious training that, at seventeen, when asked to read to a group a passage from the Book of Daniel he confessed not knowing where to look—whether in the Old or the New Testament.

More important than these differences are the matters in which they were the same. Both before they became evangelists were in the church, one as a minister, the other as an active layman. Both found that the conventional requirements of the church did not suffice. Neither was satisfied with what he had. Both were looking for something more than the traditional minimum. Wesley, returning from a missionary journey to the New World, cried out, "I went to America to convert the Indians; but Oh, who will convert me?" For Moody, though much younger at the time of his conversion, the uncertainty of his Christian conviction was such that after he had attempted to testify publicly as to his faith, his pastor suggested, "in all kindness," that he could probably better serve the Lord in silence.

Both found what they were looking for: Wesley at the meeting in Aldersgate Street in London; Moody in Boston, Massachusetts, in the back room of the shoestore where he was employed and where his Sunday-school teacher, a devout layman, one day sought him out.

Wesley wrote in his *Journal* the familiar paragraph:

"In the evening I went very unwillingly to a society in Aldersgate Street where one was reading Luther's preface to the Epistle to the Romans. About a quarter before nine, while he was describing the change which God works in the heart through faith in Christ, I felt my heart strangely warmed. I felt

6

I did trust Christ, and Christ alone for my salvation; and an assurance was given me that He had taken away my sins, even mine, and saved me from the law of sin and death."

That paragraph—and particularly the phrase, "I felt my heart strangely warmed"—became, for many evangelical generations, descriptive of "the people called Methodist"; the origin of their commonest supplication: for a "heart-warming experience"; one reason why annual revivals were not only expected of Methodist preachers but prescribed by the Methodist Discipline; one explanation for the sometimes held-to-be-untoward Methodist enthusiasm, particularly the enthusiasm with which in less inhibited times and in their other-than-Gothic churches Methodists sang their rollicking Gospel hymns, one of the most Methodist of them, directly in the Aldersgate Street tradition, being:

"Blessed assurance, Jesus is mine,
Oh for a foretaste of Glory Divine."

Moody's experience—his conversion—was no less conclusive than Wesley's and throughout his life the certainty did not diminish. Many years later he said, "Some day you will read in the papers that D. L. Moody of East Northfield is dead. Don't you believe a word of it. At that moment I shall be more alive than I am now . . . I was born of the flesh in 1837. I was born of the spirit in 1856. That which is born of the flesh may die. That which is born of the spirit will live forever."

Of that day in 1856 in Boston, he wrote: "I thought the old sun shone brighter than it ever had before. I thought it was just smiling upon me. As I walked upon Boston Common and heard the birds singing in the trees, I thought they were all singing a song to me."

This is much like the conversion testimony of Jonathan Edwards. "God's excellency, His wisdom, His purity and love seemed to appear in everything; in the sun, moon and stars; in the clouds and blue sky; in the grass, and flowers and trees, in the water and all nature." Similarly, George Whitefield, after his conversion, found that "wherever he was he could not refrain from singing Psalms."

Thus like other great evangelists, Wesley and Moody—dissimilar as they outwardly were—received like credentials from a like experience and were thereby qualified to speak with the same revival-stirring authority.

"Conversion"—save for purposes of historical allusion—is no longer a familiar word in many churches; a reflection, no doubt, of the fact that converting has become an unfamiliar practice. One of Wesley's church-approved biographers is so careful lest he run afoul of the prevailing mood that he introduced the Aldersgate Street story with this qualifying sentence: "Within a few days of each other, John and Charles Wesley passed through an experience which it is usual to describe as conversion."

But whatever our reluctance to use the word or to risk the experience, two facts about it seem inescapable. The first is that every great Christian evangelist, in so far as his own testimony can be believed, had it. It came to St. Paul on the Damascus Road, to St. Augustine in his mother's garden in Milan, to St. Francis on a pilgrimage to Rome, to Erasmus during his translation of the Gospels into Greek, to Jonathan Edwards while reading one day in the Scriptures, to George Whitefield during a protracted illness.

The second fact is that for every great Christian evangel, this experience was—by the record of what subsequently happened—the turning point, religiously, from the mediocre to the preeminent, from the ordinary to the extraordinary, from the modestly to the historically effective.

This introduces what is the most important of the likenesses between Wesley and Moody—as well as with others of the revivalist tradition: the likeness of what they preached.

Nowadays, the Bible as a more-than-human document has widely gone the way of conversion as a more-than-human ex-

8

perionoo. From fifty years of paring away, its status is less Source than sourcebook. To some who are pleased to call themselves modern, treating the Bible as Source—as something possessing a potency which does not inhere in words—is called "biblicism" or "bibliolatry."

Of this alleged error both Wesley and Moody, like all the others in this succession, were guilty—though the biographer quoted above is careful to point out that, in Wesley's case, an unqualified belief in the Bible was possible only because such belief was "never exposed to his critical faculty."

Just as their confidence and dedication derived from religious experience, so their authority derived from the Bible. Both, in the currently disparaging phrase, were "Bible-preachers."

Wesley wrote:

"I want to know one thing—the way to Heaven; how to land safe on that happy shore. God Himself has condescended to teach the way: For this very end He came from Heaven. He hath written it down in a book. O give me that book. At any price, give me the book of God. I have it: Here is knowledge enough for me. Let me be 'homo unius libri.' "

Moody, too, was a man of one book. "His Bible got to be at his finger tips. Vivid appreciation of the facts of Scripture was the greatest source of his pulpit power." Many things in the Bible were difficult to understand, but "there was so much he could grasp: The power of sin, the redemptive power of the Gospel, the love of God." He once said, "Ministers will not fill their churches until they get back to preaching all the Bible."

Billy Graham wishes that Moody had said what no doubt he believed, namely that "ministers will not fill their churches with *dynamic Christians* until they get back to preaching all the Bible." It is true that in America's present upsurge of religious interest many preachers preaching less than all the Bible have full churches. It is also evident that such preaching has not produced from churches thus filled the evangelical stirrings which

9

are the herald of religious revival. The bread which increasing numbers of people seem to be seeking from the church too often proves, when they get there, to be a stone.

The second fact about the preaching of great revivalists is that they preached a personal Gospel. It has been customary, of late, in discussing periods of religious awakening—i.e., revival—to treat them in terms of and to find their chief meaning in their collective consequences, their effect on the social and economic and international order. This, no doubt, is largely due to the ascendance of the so-called social Gospel and the tendency of its exponents to preach the evangelizing of the social order, not as a result of the evangelizing of the individual but as a substitute for it.

It is, unfortunately, true that concern for the salvation of society does not, *ipso facto,* follow from concern for the salvation of the individual. Many of these churchmen, ministers and laity, who are most burdened by the presence of sin, when it is on the individual level, are least aware of it on the collective and corporate level. As, for some, the social Gospel serves as compensation for their lack of a personal Gospel, so, for some of these, exclusive emphasis on a personal Gospel serves as insulation against the social, economic, and political implications of a social Gospel. What seems to be lacking in both cases is a whole Gospel.

From the preaching of St. Paul, which planted in the Roman Empire a leaven that proved more powerful than Rome, to that of John Wesley, which aroused England's social conscience and, according to the historian Lecky, saved the nation from social disruption, to that of Dwight L. Moody, which gave the church in both Great Britain and America a more acute social concern, the socially transforming effects of every great revival movement have been unmistakable. They are, I think, a measure of the authenticity of such a movement.

But it would be a mistake to conclude that revivals start with the social Gospel or that the saving of society has been,

10

for great evangelists, their first concern. In their wake, some things inevitably happen to society. But their starting point is people: not people in the collective, impersonal "they" sense, but people in the individual, personal "me" sense.

The first revival meeting in Christian history began at Pentecost. St. Peter was the preacher:

"Repent ye, and be baptized, every one of you in the name of Jesus Christ unto the remission of your sins and ye shall receive the gift of the Holy Spirit."

What began at Pentecost did turn the world upside down, thereby bringing it more nearly right side up. But the early Christians had no such externally revolutionizing purpose on their agenda. The message of the early Christians was not "reform," but "Christ is risen."

Troublesome though the Roman authorities regarded him, there is no definable subversion in the preaching of St. Paul; little to offend the devout reactionary, considerable to reassure him. The social consequences which began in the wake of St. Paul's preaching were not due to any society-improving program sponsored by the early Christian church. They were due to the fact that the early church was so largely comprised of Christians whose personal religious experience was too real and vital to be personally contained. It transformed them, not in a few, but in all their relationships.

"If any man is in Christ," said St. Paul, "he is a new creature; old things are passed away; behold all things are become new."

It was not only the paganisms of the flesh that passed away in this re-creation but, eventually, a whole pagan society. But the new creature of Paul's preaching was a person and the newness he preached "in Christ" was a personal experience.

What John Wesley preached, says a church historian, "was no new message. It had most of its roots in the teachings of St. Paul and Luther. Men were sinners, deserving condemnation and punishment. They might be saved by an act of faith in Christ. They might have an inner knowledge of such salvation,

11

leading to a joyful life. If they persisted in living right lives they might finally come so under the sway of right motives—love of God and one's fellows—that they could be said to have obtained perfection in Christian character. Inner religion would show itself in outreaching forms of service. This was the message that proved able to transform the lives of hundreds of thousands."

This was the revival message of Dwight L. Moody. Like Wesley, he preached a Gospel of sin, repentance, and salvation. He preached it at a time when the church, "dying of respectability," had widely lost its evangelizing power. He preached it to change men's lives: completely and now. He had a single yardstick for his preaching: what transpired at the altar where he preached. Because of what did transpire there, "the population of Hell was reduced by a million souls."

No great evangelist of Christian history has preached a different Gospel; nor is there any record of a great revival from a different kind of preaching.

That there is, at present, a shortage in the church of such preaching is no reason to doubt that a great revival may be in the making. Such a shortage and the spiritual undernourishment which is its consequence have always been the fuel for great revivals.

Neither is the reluctance in some church circles to concede that Billy Graham stands in this reviving succession a necessarily valid reason to doubt that he may stand there. It may be reason to believe that he will—since such reluctance, or worse, has been the lot of every great evangelist.

Jonathan Edwards was berated for his revival preaching. The General Convention of Congregational Ministers in Massachusetts published in 1743 a "Testimony" denouncing the revival which his preaching started. In America and England, George Whitefield was the object of "violent opposition." Both Harvard and Yale, then citadels of the faith, published "Testimonies" against him and a meeting of clergy in Connecticut re-

12

solved that "it would by no means be advisable for any of our ministers to admit him into their pulpits or for any of our people to attend his ministrations."

The opposition to John Wesley was more violent—centering, in considerable part, on what was described as the "enthusiasm"—"emotionalism" would be the current word for it—stirred in his meetings. Dwight L. Moody, in his day, was put down as "a ranter of the most vulgar type."

All of which points up the fact—already evident in the ministry of Billy Graham—that what a great evangelist helps to bring to pass among the clergy and lay leadership of the churches may be fully as significant as his ministry to the more recognizably unsaved.

Unless there is substantial evidence that he does stand in the succession of great evangelists and that his ministry does hold a promise such as was fulfilled in theirs, there would be no adequate reason at this stage in his career to write, at length, the story of Billy Graham. But I do not believe that any observer whose prejudices were not insurmountable could make a close-up, protracted study of the man and his ministry and fail to find such substantial evidence.

For many months, in America and abroad, I have made such a study. The result is the conviction that the ministry of Billy Graham gives substance to the hope that the present unparalleled turn to religion can be turned to authentic religious account; that out of this reviving religious interest there may come an awakening which will merit the name because by the standards of Christian history it is, in fact, a revival of religion.

That conviction is the reason for this book.

1: What manner of man?

REPORTING ON Billy Graham's All-Scotland Crusade in the Kelvin Hall, Glasgow, in the spring of 1955, a distinguished British commentator wrote:

"What is happening in Kelvin Hall is very mysterious to me."

After many months of inquiry, at home and abroad, there remains, for me, something mysterious, not only about Billy Graham's meetings, but about Billy Graham. The facts about Billy Graham add up to an extraordinary story. But they do not add up to an explanation of Billy Graham. They are not as extraordinary as that.

Neither did the facts, extraordinary as they were, about George Whitefield, John Wesley, or Dwight L. Moody add up to an explanation of what transpired from their preaching. There was an additional something which could not be explained any more than it could be escaped.

"I believe," said the writer quoted above, "that within this mystery is the redeeming energy of the Holy Spirit."

No doubt there are more popularly acceptable words for it. But I think I know what that writer meant. As my own fund of information aimed to explain the Billy Graham phenomenon has increased, so has my conviction that the ultimate explanation will have to be found in some Power which, however real it may be, is beyond the reach of ordinary journalistic probing.

I once heard a newspaper reporter ask Billy Graham: "How do you explain your success?"

"The only explanation I know is God."

"But why," asked the reporter, "did God choose you?"

"When I get to Heaven," said Billy Graham, "that's the first question I am going to ask Him."

Whitefield, Wesley, and Moody, on their arrival in Heaven, may have asked the same question. What, on the earthly level, appears more important is the fact that, as human calculations go, they seemed abundantly to justify the choice. Whatever answer Billy Graham gets as to why God chose him, there are certain facts, within the range of terrestrial reporting, which seem to justify his choice. And whatever, ultimately, God has chosen him for, there is no mystery about Billy Graham's determination to live, now, in such a way as to prove that that choice, too, has been justified.

There is a sense in which, as the political saying goes, Billy Graham "runs scared." He does not take the visible signs of his success as evidence that—as God sees it—he has necessarily succeeded. On the contrary, the more convincing these visible signs of success seem to be, the harder he seems to work to ward off what—in God's appraisal—might be counted failure. The fear he lives with is not that, outwardly, he may fail but that, inwardly, he may fail the Almighty.

Against this fear he goes armed with Paul's statement in I Corinthians 9:27: "But I keep under my body and bring it into subjection: lest that by any means, when I have preached to others, I myself should be a castaway."

"Billy Graham is not remarkable for his gifts," says the editor of the Church of Scotland magazine, *Life and Work*. "He is remarkable for what he is making of God's gift."

Billy Graham would agree with that estimate of his gifts. But

16

he would say that what he may be making of God's gift is wholly God's doing and that only God can continue to do it.

"No one," he says, "ever called me a great preacher. There are thousands of better ones. I'm no great intellectual. The Bible has been my Harvard and Yale. If God should take His hands off my life my lips would turn to clay."

He might not, he says, know the exact time. Everything, outwardly, might seem the same. Momentum would probably carry him along for a while. But that would run out and when it did, what remained would be "ashes."

For an awesome case history of how this has happened and might happen to him, he goes back to the story of Samson. Samson, he says, was used "mightily" of the Lord. Time after time he went up against the Philistines and "smote them hip and thigh." Then he sinned against the Lord, and Delilah "caused his locks to be shaved" while he slept. "And his strength went from him." When he awoke, however, everything seemed the same. He was as tall as ever. His muscles were as thick as ever. He said, "I will go out as at other times before, and shake myself. And he wist not that the Lord was departed from him."

"That," says Billy Graham, "could happen to me."

To a group of us, team members and friends, sitting early one evening in his room before going out to a Crusade meeting, he suddenly said, "I've been asking myself, sitting here: 'Billy Graham, are you filled with the Holy Spirit?' My only claim to power is the Holy Spirit. Without that, whatever I do is of the energy of the flesh and will be burned up before the judgment seat of Christ. I don't care how big the crowds are and how big the reported results are; it's all 'sounding brass and tinkling cymbal' unless I am filled with the Holy Spirit."

"One of Billy Graham's drawbacks," a newspaper reporter once wrote, "is his appearance. Tall, handsome, athletic, he has all the physical attributes and charm of a potential film star

17

—a glamour boy in fact. The question is at once asked: 'Is he genuine?' "

To those to whom a "glamorous" appearance may be religiously suspect, it is, I suppose, a drawback that Billy Graham, instead of being notably short and thin as John Wesley was (five feet four inches—125 pounds) or bearded, short, and corpulent as Dwight L. Moody was or shiny-bald as Billy Sunday was, is tall, trim, and with a head of wavy hair so thick he frequently has to have it thinned as well as cut. At least a shorter, fatter, balder Billy Graham would have been spared —only, no doubt, to have suffered from worse—some of the descriptions his appearance has given rise to, among them: Gabriel in Gabardine, Barrymore of the Bible, Hollywood John the Baptist, Matinee Idol Revivalist.

Billy Graham, shoes off, stands six feet two. Beginning at the time of his 1956 mission to India, he has regularly followed a rigorous regime of daily exercise. But he is no "young giant" with "muscles rippling under the gabardine." He is a lanky 180 pounds; subject to an occasional stomach upset, and, under tension, to insomnia. In every long Crusade he loses from 10 to 15 pounds, which reduces him to the point of gauntness. His hands are long and narrow; his face thin; his hair a sunburned blond; his eyes blue, deep-set and, as a script writer would put it, "piercing," not the kind of eyes given easily to tears.

Sitting, he likes to slouch, legs stretched in front of him. On a straightaway, he walks with a spring which you are sure— trying to keep up—will break any minute into a lope. He shakes hands vigorously—without any muscle-moving technique. His speech comes within the category of a Southern drawl—but not the slow, dragged-out you-all drawl of the Deep South.

Once at a luncheon where Billy Graham spoke I sat at the same table with a woman who is internationally known—pro and con—as a professional party-thrower. After an address

18

that stirred a vast audience, her comment was: "He is so eloquent and *so* handsome. Isn't it a shame that he isn't in politics?"

To which I heard Ruth Graham reply: "Maybe the Lord thought politics had its share and decided to give the ministry a break."

Though, as in the case of the reporter quoted above, Billy Graham's good looks may give rise to the question "Is he genuine?" there is remarkable agreement with the answer which that reporter found: "I have never heard anyone doubt his integrity."

Philip Santora, in the first of four striking articles in the New York *Daily News* about Billy Graham and his ministry, wrote, in 1954: "Millions of persons want to know if Billy Graham is sincere, if he's as dedicated to the Cause as he seems. They wonder if he isn't taking advantage of a situation to make himself a million dollars on the side while he preaches humility and abject surrender to Christ. . . .

"To understand Billy Graham you should spend a great deal of time with him, examine him under a magnifying glass, then step away from him for a few days so that he can be reexamined coldly and logically. . . .

"After all this you reach the conclusion that this young man who has had such influence on the more than 13,000,000 persons who have gone to hear him is exactly as he purports to be: a dedicated person who believes in what he is teaching, whose aim in life is to harvest as many souls as possible. . . ."

Few religious leaders have more freely invited critical scrutiny than Billy Graham, and probably none has ever had more of it. Only a man whose life actually is as he often says his must be—"an open book"—could have survived it with his reputation intact. Only a near-totally honest person would invite such total exposure.

Once, a number of years ago, when his fame was not so great or his crowds so large, he, with his associate evangelist,

Grady Wilson, was conducting a meeting in a middle-sized Southern city. A veteran revivalist, an old friend, attended their meetings and imparted "a word of advice from an old hand."

"You are telling the newspapers," he said, "the exact size of your audiences. That won't do. The bigger the crowds people think you are getting, the bigger the crowds you will get. If you think you've got 2,000, raise it to 3,000 for the papers. There's nothing really wrong about that. Everybody does it."

"I've seldom seen Billy so startled and shocked," says Grady Wilson. "He was speechless. He turned to me when the old man had left. 'Grady,' he said, 'God being my helper, I'll be honest all the way through or this isn't God's business and I'll get out of it.' "

Today, newspapermen are often startled when Jerry Beavan, the public relations member of the Billy Graham team, goes to considerable pains to grade down to the exact figure the frequent overestimate of the size of Billy Graham's crowds or the number who have made "decisions for Christ."

Wherever he goes nowadays, the newspapermen—notebooks and cameras in hand—are there. Most of them are responsible, but all of them are on the lookout. I have seen him baited, jabbed, and pried at by the most cunning and unscrupulous reporters of the Western world's most irresponsible press. They invariably get some things they do not particularly like and some things they certainly do not understand, but of dissimulation, evasion, or cover-up—which would really make their mouths water—what they invariably get is zero. Many of them, too, go away mumbling reluctant tribute to his sincerity. And though, his job being what it is, he had to give a derogatory twist, even the columnist of the Communist New York *Daily Worker* could not quite escape mentioning it: "He speaks with an arrogant humility which is terrifying."

Few Americans were ever so hounded by so hostile a press as Billy Graham when he arrived in England on the eve of the Greater London Crusade early in 1954. The almost complete turnabout which, within a few weeks, came to pass was not due to his eloquence or the crowds he drew or any other public aspect of his ministry. It was chiefly due to the straightforwardness with which he withstood personal inspection.

"After we'd watched him for a while like hawks," one London reporter said, "we finally had to admit that when it came to honesty he lived up to the advance notices."

A correspondent for the *Manchester Guardian* wrote: "Mr. Graham has been a great personal success. He has impressed a wide range of people, from the Archbishop of Canterbury to those perspicacious evangelists who run the *Daily Mirror* by his sincerity and humility. I, myself, supping with him in a party of four, found him one of the most likeable people I have ever met. He has a holy simplicity. . . ."

There is, however, something more to Billy Graham's sincerity than the fact, important as it is, that it has survived such scrutiny. There seems to be, even among his critics, something that amounts almost to a compulsion to mention that, however low he may otherwise be rated, he is sincere. In fact, adverse comments almost always start with something like this: "Of course I don't doubt his sincerity, but. . . ."

Here are a few recently published illustrations of what I mean:

"I am not doubting Billy Graham's sincerity," but "with him, religion is a show." "He did not strike me as in any way insincere," but "he preached the same old Bible-thumping stuff." "I am sure he believes what he says," but "his theology is incredible." "The press commentators were not much impressed," but "they have all acknowledged his sincerity." "We still don't know what it is he's got," but "we're sure by now that he's the real thing."

There is an explanation for this which, I think, will be questioned only by those whose contact with Billy Graham has been very limited. Experienced observers who are accustomed to

21

appraise, if only for precautionary purposes, the sincerity of public figures, but who seldom, thereafter, may mention it, invariably mention the sincerity of Billy Graham because, with him, it is not a passive, but an active characteristic. It is not negative: something which is true merely because, having passed the insincerity test, it is found not to be untrue. It is something positive: one of the things about the man which, like the loud neckties he once preferred, but, growing in dignity, no longer wears, cannot be missed and cries out to be mentioned.

The British newspaper *Truth* called it "dynamic sincerity." "Blazingly sincere," said Beverly Nichols in the London *Sunday Chronicle*.

The London *Spectator* said: "That is something—the sincerity of one dedicated Christian witness made manifest to over a million people."

I am sure that Billy Graham's temptations run the usual human gamut. But the one he confesses he wrestles with most vigorously is pride. He gets an earthy assist in this from Grady Wilson who, in addition to being his associate evangelist, is his oldest and closest friend. Against the threat of pride, Wilson, the practical joker of the team, often serves, for Billy Graham, something of the same purpose once served by those lackeys whose function it was to run, ringing a small bell, behind the chariots of Rome's conquering heroes to remind them they were human. "If the Lord will keep him anointed," says Wilson, "I'll keep him humble."

But Billy Graham does not leave this temptation to any such uncertain ministry. He wrestles with it by prayer and by Scripture. In fact there are three passages of Scripture any one or all three of which—but particularly the last one—he is likely to quote whenever his "successes" are seriously discussed: "Pride goeth before destruction"; "A man's pride shall bring him low"; "I am the Lord; that is my name; and my glory will I not give to another."

22

It is not for the music—he is not notably musical—but because it expresses his own sense of dependence that the theme song for every Billy Graham Crusade is "To God Be the Glory, Great Things He Hath Done." It is the pervasiveness of that same feeling which explains why, among the articulately devout, especially ministers, the phrase "To God Be the Glory" comes to rank in his meetings as an expression of reverent enthusiasm, along with such words as "Amen" and "Praise the Lord." And it is for the same reason that Cliff Barrows, Billy Graham's song leader, always concludes whatever foreword he writes for each Crusade songbook with this verse from the Ninety-eighth Psalm:

"O sing unto the Lord a new song: for He hath done marvelous things; His right hand and His holy arm, hath gotten Him the victory."

From Boston he wrote of the signs of religious awakening and the size of the opportunity—too large for any one man to encompass: "The _____ Hotel had to put on an extra operator to handle the long-distance calls for me personally. It is almost unbelievable. It's fantastic. The opportunity is beyond anything I had ever dreamed. The average Christian leader across America does not realize the open doors at this moment. My constant prayer is that God will raise up other evangelists to whom these doors will be opened. The harvest indeed is plenteous but the laborers are few."

I have seen newspaper reporters snicker and then, after longer contact, concede that he means it when Billy Graham says something like this, as he frequently does: "Every time I see my name up in lights, every time I am patted on the back, it makes me sick at heart, for God said He will share His glory with no man. So if you want to stop my ministry, pat *me* on the back."

After the opening meeting of one of his Crusades, he wrote to Ruth, his wife: "The television lights were beaming right in our faces. The television and newsreel cameras were whirring,

23

and I wondered as I walked up the stairs how much of this was of the flesh and how much of the Spirit. I will be so glad when the press gets all of its stories written and the publicity dies down so that we can get on with the message."

On the eve of the Greater London Crusade he said, "I have one fear and that is that you may be looking to a man to bring revival. No man can do that, only the Holy Spirit of God. We are here to glorify the Lord Jesus Christ."

On the eve of the All-Scotland Crusade, he said, "Much has been said about a man. But the thing that matters is the message. The important thing is that we do not become so absorbed in a human instrument that we fail to get the message God is sending us. At the outset, I must openly and completely transfer any glory and honor that may have been given me over to Jesus Christ, to Whom belongs all praise and glory."

In Glasgow's Hampden Park, before 100,000 people—the largest congregation ever gathered in the history of Scotland—he said, in the concluding message of the All-Scotland Crusade:

"This is a sight we will remember all through our lives and talk about all through eternity. It is Christ who has been lifted up these weeks in Scotland and not Billy Graham. Our name, we trust, will now be heard less and less and His name, which is above every name, more and more.

"And I want to tell you that there have been thousands of unsung heroes in this Crusade—praying and working men and women whose names never got into the press. But I am sure if there are newspapers in Heaven, it's their names and not mine you'll find on the front page."

Early in 1955, before a distinguished gathering at Valley Forge, Pennsylvania, Freedom's Foundation gave Billy Graham a special national award: "In the ebb and flow of human life, few men in recorded history have so captured the spiritual interest of the multitudes. . . ." His reply was: "I accept this award only temporarily. Someday I shall hand it to the Person Who is responsible for all our activities: the Lord Jesus Christ."

Of the luncheon that followed the ceremonies that day, he wrote: "I had the privilege of sitting at the table with Secretary of Defense Wilson. Another person at our table was Dr. Kirk, the president of Columbia University. It was very interesting to hear these men talk. They are great men and I came away with a profound respect for both of them. I tried to put in my two cents' worth on spiritual things from time to time. They seemed interested."

"A great speech," someone said after he had addressed a gathering of laymen in New York City. "I didn't want it to be 'great,'" he wrote in his diary, "only Christ-glorifying." Then he wrote out in full, as if to underscore that single-mindedness, the first two verses of the second chapter of Paul's first letter to the Corinthians:

"And I, brethren, when I came to you, came not with excellency of speech or of wisdom, declaring unto you the testimony of God. For I determined not to know anything among you, save Jesus Christ and Him crucified."

Late in 1952 Billy Graham made a speaking tour of the war front in Korea and of American military posts in Japan. While in Tokyo en route to Korea, he spoke one night to 750 Christian missionaries of all denominations—said to have been the largest gathering of missionaries not only in Japan but on any mission field. After his address that night he wrote:

"That evening was a memorable one in my life. Never have I felt less worthy to stand before an audience. These are the true warriors of the Cross. These men and women have left their homes and loved ones to battle on the front lines of Gospel endeavor. I was anxious that I glorify none save Christ, and I cried to God for a message.

"It was my privilege to speak for well over an hour. We wept together; we laughed together; we prayed together, and together we were challenged by the Holy Spirit. When it was over, I knew that God had begun to speak to my heart, and that I could never be the same again after that evening."

"There is one doubt I have," he told me when we first discussed this book. "I know there has to be a lot of Billy Graham in it. But do you think you can write about me so as to write past me, so that the people who read it will see past me and be drawn, not to Billy Graham, but to the God Billy Graham tries to serve?"

I have observed Billy Graham in large gatherings, small gatherings, and alone in a good many places and under a good many different conditions: on a holiday in Florida and one in Scotland, fishing, on the golf course, driving across country, in his home, at all kinds of eating places, in hotel rooms that were good and not so good, before and behind the scenes in several Crusades.

Though I hope it is to my credit as a journalist that I have tried, I have never yet found him—in his zeal for things of the spirit—in an off season. He seems, on occasion, to shake off some of the almost unbelievable pressures that bear down on him. At least he wears the garments of relaxation and, with every evidence of enjoyment, does the things relaxed people are supposed to do. Spiritually, however, he lives under a perpetual alert. That pressure appears to be congenital.

It has been so with every great evangelist. To his friend Benjamin Franklin, George Whitefield once wrote: "I find that you grow more and more famous in the learned world. As you have made pretty considerable progress in the mysteries of electricity I would now humbly recommend to you diligent and unprejudiced pursuit and study of the mysteries of the New Birth. It is a most important and interesting study and when mastered will richly answer and repay all your pains—you will excuse this freedom. I must have *aliquid Christo* [something of Christ] in all my letters."

After listening one morning while Billy Graham effortlessly turned a visit to the office of a prominent American newspaper publisher into a discussion of personal religion, I asked him

26

how he explained the ease with which he uses almost every occasion as an opportunity "to bear witness" for Christ.

"Don't you think," he said, "if I had known President Eisenhower intimately, for a long time, it would be the most natural thing in the world to talk about him. Well, I know Jesus Christ far better than I will ever know the President or any other human being. To me, above all earthly rulers, He is King of Kings and Lord of Lords. How can I help talking about Him?

"Moreover, I have a duty to talk about Him. They tell me the American Embassy in Moscow was formerly near Red Square and that the rulers of Red Russia, looking out from the Kremlin, could see the U.S. flag flying from our Embassy staff every day. But suppose our Ambassador said, 'I don't want to wear my patriotism on my sleeve; it might offend the Russians' —and took down the flag. Don't you think the President would recall such an Ambassador for having betrayed his trust?

"I can't forget that the Apostle Paul said, 'Now, then, we are Ambassadors for Christ.' "

He once told an old friend, "I meet so many people and yet I reach so few of them. Too often, I leave a person and before I have gone ten steps I say, 'O God, I left him nothing. I joked with him, chatted with him, told him my latest story, but O God, forgive me, I didn't tell him what You gave me today in my early morning devotions.' "

Billy Graham flies his flag in some unusual places. One evening, with his wife and several members of the team, he was my guest in Paris at one of Europe's oldest and most famous restaurants. I doubt if, in its 200 years, such a thing had ever happened there before, but, before we ordered our meal, and while two bedecked and astonished waiters stood by, he asked, "Do you mind if we say grace?" His quietly spoken grace was: "O God we thank Thee for this good fellowship in this beautiful place. Amen."

After a press conference aboard the *Liberté* in New York harbor he wrote in his diary: "Fifty reporters were there and newsreel cameramen. I gave them a talk. I tried to give them enough of the Gospel so that any one of these reporters could have been converted right there."

Describing the drive from Plymouth to London, he wrote to Ruth, his wife: "We stopped for lunch at Bournemouth. . . . A delicious meal. Several people recognized us in the restaurant and when I went into the rest room a man followed me in there, saying he needed God. It was a joy to pray with him and give him some of the Gospel and get his promise that he would be at our Wembley meeting and also listen over the relay system. . . ."

From Glasgow he wrote to Ruth: "Every move we make people are staring at us or taking pictures or asking for autographs. I don't like it. But an autograph is really so little one can do. However, when I give an autograph, I always try to leave a little word of witness behind and make them promise they will go to church next Sunday."

In Glasgow, two businessmen gave a luncheon in his honor for some 300 leaders of Scotland's business and industrial community. He wrote: "I have decided in businessmen's luncheons to go all out for the Gospel. I am not going to give a talk on world events or give them sweet little lullabies. Today, the Lord wonderfully blessed and gave great liberty in the speaking."

In mid-May, 1955, during his seven-day series of meetings at London's Wembley Stadium, Billy and Ruth Graham were invited to have tea at Clarence House with Queen Mother Elizabeth and Princess Margaret. He wrote in his diary: "Ruth and I were with them exactly forty-two minutes. Our entire conversation revolved around spiritual matters. As we sat there, they put us right at ease and I lost all fear and began to talk freely concerning the Gospel. It was a privilege to outline to them God's plan of salvation."

One Sunday morning in the spring of 1955 he preached at the National Presbyterian Church in Washington, D.C. The President of the United States and Mrs. Eisenhower, many members of the Cabinet, the U.S. House of Representatives, and the Senate were in the overflowing audience.

"Strange to say," he wrote, "all nervousness and fear had left me. I felt perfectly calm and confident. I felt the Spirit of God in my heart and I knew He had given me a message for that hour.

"During the entire service I did not see the President once, though I knew where he was sitting. In fact, I forgot all about the fact that he was in the audience. I preached the Gospel as straight and as clearly as I have ever preached it. I felt that there was power and authority in the message. As soon as I was through, I gave thanks to God for the power He had given."

Billy Graham's urge to turn every situation to God's account is something which extends to and encompasses his critics.

"I am not going to answer mud-slinging with mud-slinging," he wrote to Ruth after a series of particularly vicious attacks. "I am going to take the position of Nehemiah who refused to take time out for his enemies, saying, instead, 'I am too busy building the wall.' We are too busy trying to win souls to Christ and helping to build the church. . . ."

Many of his critics, he once wrote to me, "remind me of the verses in Luke 9: And John answered and said, Master, we saw one casting out devils in thy name; and we forbade him, because he followeth not with us. And Jesus said unto him, Forbid him not; for he that is not against us is for us.

"What we need today is more love and less bickering, strife, and fighting. It is said that one day Lord Nelson came upon two of his men fighting on the deck of his ship. He stopped and said, 'Gentlemen, there is your foe,' and he pointed to the enemy's ships on the horizon. The enemy we face is materialism, sin, social injustice. Why should we be fighting each other?"

During one of his Crusades, someone brought him a report of a series of articles by an extreme U.S. fundamentalist, charg-

29

ing that, by having fellowship with churchmen of different theologies, he was betraying "the faith once delivered to the saints." This report stirred him deeply and aroused in him such resentment that he found himself unable to carry on his preparation for that night's sermon. Finally, he went to his room, locked himself in, and an hour later appeared and dictated a letter to the author of the attacks in which he told how he had felt and what he did about it: "I got on my knees and asked God to give me love in my heart. I had the greatest peace flood my soul and the Holy Spirit seemed to flood my heart with a peculiar love for you. Beloved friend, if you feel led of the Spirit of God to continue your attacks upon me, rest assured that I shall not answer back . . . I shall hold my peace. My objective is to glorify our Lord Jesus Christ by the preaching of His Word to sinners. He has seen fit in a small measure to honor the ministry of His Word through me. I am totally unworthy of this little service the Master has assigned me. If, by being attacked by friend or foe, it can be used to advance His Kingdom and glorify His name, I gladly offer myself and rejoice that I have been counted worthy to suffer in His name. . . ."

These facts about Billy Graham—his contagious sincerity, his humility, his commitment, his constant unequivocal witnessing—do not explain Billy Graham. They bring us back, rather, to the conclusion with which this chapter began: that, in explaining him, something more than facts—the kinds of facts, at least, with which journalists are accustomed to deal— is involved. For me, at any rate—after prolonged and close-up observation—there is no other conclusion. Others have reached the same conclusion.

Coming away from an interview, an Atlanta newspaperman wrote: "Sitting at ease in a nearby chair, he looks like any successful businessman who likes a splash of color in his clothing. His manner is cordial, his flow of language fluent, his attitude gracious. Yet, somehow, there is a difference which you don't fully grasp until you are on the elevator descending to the street. That's it . . . a glow. It surrounds him and is of him. And maybe that explains why during the conversation between you two, you had the unmistakable feeling that there were three persons in the room."

It has been said that the greatest single religious meeting ever held in New England was the day, in the spring of 1950, when in a pouring rain, Billy Graham spoke on Boston Common. Grady Wilson, all that morning, had tried to persuade him, in the face of the downpour, to call off the meeting altogether.

"It won't do anybody any good, getting soaked," said Wilson. "Besides, nobody will come, and if they do they won't stay."

Billy Graham was adamant. "The Lord's going to be there," he said, "and so am I."

Those who came and stayed that day numbered 50,000 people. A newspaper reporter summed it up: "Some people may go to hear Billy Graham out of curiosity. But 50,000 do not stand in the rain to see any man. Those people were drawn by the power of God."

"The only power Billy Graham has more of," says a prominent Scottish minister, "is the power of God. Nothing less could turn the vast, often ugly halls where he preaches into a sanctuary or make his unlikely texts come so alive or give his uneloquent preaching such force and meaning for so many people."

The editor of the Church of Scotland magazine, *Life and Work,* has written: "The spirit of God was speaking through him; using him, by-passing him, turning even his mistakes to account, all the time reminding him that this was not his doing, but God's."

"There are many things that Billy Graham is not," says a writer in the *Christian Century.* "There is one thing that he is—a man of God. Plainly he is being used as a channel of communication. There is no other explanation."

31

The Moderator of the United Free Church of Scotland has told this story: "A minister was asked recently: 'Does Dr. Billy Graham have something which the average minister does not possess?'

"The reply given was: 'No! I do not think he has. The success of his campaign is due to the fact that every two or three generations God lays His hand on some man, and He has laid His hand on this man—Billy Graham.' "

Of Joshua it is said: "On that day the Lord magnified Joshua in the sight of all Israel." Considerable as his abilities are, Billy Graham is not a self-made man. A greater power has reached down to this North Carolina farm boy and magnified him. It is too soon to estimate all that may accrue to our age as a consequence of that choice. But I can say with certainty that he lives as though he knew that, every day, the choice was being reviewed by the Almighty.

Living that way has produced in him the kind of personal conviction which, better than his eloquence, speaks for the faith he publicly proclaims. He sums it up in the concluding sentences of his book, *Peace with God:*

"What a prospect! What a future! What a hope! What a life! I would not change places with the wealthiest and most influential man in the world. I would rather be a child of the King, a joint-heir with Christ, a member of the Royal Family of Heaven.

"I know where I've come from, I know why I'm here, I know where I'm going—and I have peace in my heart. His peace floods my heart and overwhelms my soul."

2: How can he be so sure?

SOMEONE ONCE WROTE Billy Graham: "Why is it you try to impose your views on others? How can you be so sure? You are making the same mistake Jesus made."

So far as the last sentence is concerned, the propagation of "the mistake that Jesus made" is, I think, Billy Graham's life work. As for imposing his views, he often says, "This isn't my message. I'm only the messenger boy. I can't decide what you do about the message when you get it. I can only try to make sure you get it." And few phrases are repeated oftener in his sermons than these: "I didn't say it; Jesus said it"; "This is not man's opinion; this is God's opinion." "It's not important what Billy Graham says; here is what the Bible says."

As for the second question—How can he be so sure?—that, I believe, is a good one. How can he?

Like many other questions about Billy Graham, the answer to this one involves inquiry in an area to which preachers, presumably, are acclimated but where the secular observer, obliged to do his observing with something less or at least other than the "eye of faith" and make his report in the vernacular, may be somewhat handicapped. I can only try to do what two earlier reporters did:

"Speak the things which we have seen and heard."

For Billy Graham, himself, there is no doubt where his certainty is rooted or when it began to grow—any more than there was for Paul, Augustine, and Erasmus, or for Whitefield, Wesley, and Moody. As for them, his certainty is rooted in an experience and it began at a specific date: the same experience and at a date as specific as theirs. There seems to me to be no more reason to doubt his testimony on this than there is to doubt theirs. There are the same reasons to believe it, namely, as with them, what happened to him at the time and, more convincing, what has been happening, as a consequence, ever since.

This is not the place to discuss what Billy Graham means by "conversion." The word, like the experience, has pretty well dropped out of the working lexicon of many churches which, historically, are still called and once were "evangelical." It is hard to know how much the response to the conversion-weighted ministry of Billy Graham may be due to the failure of the church's modern synonyms to prove synonymous. For him, however, there is no doubt that his certainty began with his conversion.

Billy Graham, at the time, was seventeen. An old-style, hell-and-damnation evangelist, Mordecai Ham by name, had opened a three-month assault on sin in the Graham home town of Charlotte, North Carolina. There was nothing notably sinful about Billy. He was a high-school baseball and basketball star, popular with the girls. He had no very definite idea what he wanted to do with himself unless, as he sometimes hoped, he could make the major leagues as a first baseman. He was the well-thought-of, nonsmoking, nondrinking, churchgoing son of devout parents.

He had, however, no special interest in the church and something of the aversion often found in high-school-age boys as well as in high-school-minded adults toward the overt expression of religious concern. What he did, churchwise, was out of deference to his parents, and no more, if he could help it, than

34

the minimum. As for being a preacher, he rated preaching, according to one of his high-school friends, as "the one job in the world worse than being an undertaker."

For the first several weeks, Ham's assault on sin in Charlotte left him untouched, since, despite some not-too-subtle hints from his parents, he kept himself out of reach. When one night he finally went out to the revival tent it was with a group of his high-school friends whose ideas on what else to do in Charlotte on a midsummer night had run out.

What he saw amazed him and, no doubt, stirred his imagination: the size of the crowd—more than 5,000, filling every seat, filling the bare-planked wooden platform, sitting on chairs, benches, and boxes beyond the tent walls; the long, sawdust-carpeted aisles; the unpainted pulpit; the "great choir," the women in white dresses, the men in shirt sleeves; most of all the scene when choir and congregation stood and sang together—basses and altos coming in with a booming volume on the chorus downbeat:

> "When the Trumpet of the Lord shall sound
> And time shall be no more
> And the morning breaks eternal, bright and fair,
> And the saved of earth shall gather
> Over on the other shore
> And the roll is called up yonder I'll be there.
>
> When the roll is called up yonder . . .
> When the roll . . ."

What he heard from "Brother Ham" impressed him less—although when, half through the sermon, the preacher pointed a finger straight at him and thundered, "You're a sinner," Billy, to avoid a direct hit, ducked behind the hat of a woman in front of him. A night or two later he went again, this time with his friend Albert McMakin. They went together several times thereafter. Under this nightly hammering, a few things began

35

to take shape in Billy's mind: the Heaven he could choose, the Hell he might be headed for, most of all, he says, a sermon on John 3:16: "For God so loved the world that He gave His only begotten Son, that whosoever believeth in Him should not perish, but have everlasting life."

The next night, with another friend, Grady Wilson, he sat in the choir where, though unable to carry a tune, he figured he could escape the evangelist by being behind him. The evangelist's first words were: "There's a great sinner in this place tonight." Billy at once concluded: "Mother's been telling him about me." That night, when the invitation was given, Billy turned to Grady and said what thousands since have said in Billy Graham Crusades: "Let's go."

He climbed down from the choir and, with Grady close behind, made his way to the altar. There were no tears, no blazing vision, no gift of tongues: "Right there I made my decision for Christ. It was as simple as that—and as conclusive."

His testimony has the same "joy and gladness" ring of others I have quoted in a previous chapter: "Have you ever been outdoors on a dark day when the sun suddenly bursts through the clouds? Deep inside, that's how I felt. The next day, I'm sure, I looked the same. But to me everything—even the flowers and the leaves on the trees—looked different. I was finding out for the first time the sweetness and joy of God, of being truly born again."

On the way home that night the two friends, Billy and Grady, made a pact: having gone so far, finding it so good, they would, to the best of their ability and with God's help, "go all out." They eventually found a text which ever since has served them both to keep their pact intact, Philippians 1:6:

"Being confident of this very thing, that He which hath begun a good work in you will perform it, until the day of Jesus Christ."

Recently, during a Billy Graham Crusade in an American city, the police sergeant in charge of the detail assigned to the

36

auditorium came up to Billy Graham at the end of an evening meeting and said, "I wish you'd tell me how to start being sure you are a Christian."

"That's what I try to tell every night," said Billy Graham. "It's no magic formula to be said and then said over and over. The nearest I can come to it in one word is the word 'surrender.' You can't be sure of Christ until He is sure of you. He can't be sure of you until, by the surrender of your will for yourself to His will for you, your life is committed to Him."

For Billy Graham, the answer to the question—How can he be so sure?—began in the revival tent of Mordecai Ham that night in Charlotte as it did for Paul on the road to Damascus, for Wesley in the meetings in Aldersgate Street and for the young layman Dwight L. Moody in Boston in the back room of his employer's shoestore.

But Billy Graham does not believe that religious certainty comes all done up, delivered, and complete in a conversion package. It did not come that way for him. He has had to work at it. He still works at it. In fact I gather that the surer he thinks he is the harder he works at it lest, I suppose, the Almighty regard his assurance as self-assurance. What he says is: "When I let up, God seems to let up, too."

The two practices which he does not let up on or, if he does, he feels he suffers for are Bible study and prayer. The Apostle Paul, speaking of his own persistence in such matters, frequently used the phrase "without ceasing." He prayed "without ceasing"; gave thanks "without ceasing"; remembered "without ceasing." In Billy Graham's Bible reading and prayer, his practice of what has been called "the presence of God," there is something which, though short of ceaseless, is not very far short. In this he stands in the succession of the great Christian evangelists. They, too, were "men of the Book" and of prayer.

In one pocket or another, he always carries a Bible or a pocket Testament. He wears out one a year. Given two or three uninterrupted minutes, out it comes—like, for some of the rest of us, a paper-backed who-done-it in which he had just reached the payoff episode. Neither is his praying limited to morning and evening devotions. I once asked Ruth Graham about that. She said, "If you see your wife all day you don't have special times to talk to her and then talk to her only at those times. With Bill it is 'pray without ceasing.' "

Others have borne witness to that fact. On the last day of the All-Scotland Crusade, in the spring of 1955, the columnist for the Glasgow *Daily Record* wrote a farewell message to Billy Graham in which he said, in part:

"Dear Billy:

"Sorry you are going. In some ways we saw so little of you —and that will seem queer to the folk who said they couldn't look at a paper without having to suffer your photo.

"But really there was so little of you.

"I'm glad it was like that in some ways. I suppose the secret of Billy Graham must be those morning and afternoon hours when *nobody* can keep you from God in prayer and Bible reading. Maybe it is just that your priorities are a little more sensible than most of ours.

"You always have time for God. Maybe this is your biggest lesson for bustlin', hustlin' Glasgow.

"I have listened to some of the suggestions. About easily influenced adolescents and emotional appeals and all that. But on the whole the facts don't bear that out and I don't really have enough faith for that theory.

"No, here's one man who has seen God at work through you, Billy.

"When are you coming back?

"Yours aye,
"Robert McMahon."

For Billy Graham, the Bible, from cover to cover, is the divinely inspired Word of God. Early in his ministry, he says, "I was doing a lot of preaching, but there was little power in it.

Then one day I got down on my knees and I said, 'O God, I have got to get out of the ministry unless I can find a message with power.' As I prayed, I accepted the Bible, by faith, as God's Word. From that moment, my ministry has been different."

He is not, however, a word-by-word literalist. In fact, some extreme fundamentalists are not at all happy at the evidence they see of his departure from what, by their rigid prescriptions, is the orthodox treatment of the Scriptures. They also object to the fact that, instead of regarding the Word of God as having been delivered once and for all to the saints in the King James version, he frequently makes free to use the Scriptures in modern translation. He regularly recommends some of those translations to converts as "easier to understand."

Unlike the extreme fundamentalists, some of whom seem more concerned for their views about the Bible than about the Bible and who make it a book of controversy and division, to Billy Graham it is an instrument, an indispensable instrument of faith.

"One can be a Christian without reading the Bible," he says, "because it is faith in Christ which makes one a Christian, and not reading the Bible. But no one can be an intelligent and instructed Christian—and very few, I think, are Christians of any kind for very long—without the constant study of the Scriptures."

To new converts, he says, "To the Christian, the Bible is no longer just a holy book to be placed on the shelf in solitary state. It is a mighty weapon to take hold of with both hands and to be used in defeating the enemy. You would not expect to lead a healthy physical life unless you ate your meals regularly. Show the same amount of common sense about preserving your spiritual life in a vigorous and healthy state. Daily Bible reading is an essential part of our spiritual diet."

The power which he finds in the Bible is something more than the ordinary power of the printed word—however extraordinary, as in other great literature, the words may be. It was that more-than-ordinary power, he says, which Jesus recognized and made use of when, during His temptation in the wilderness, His answer to each of Satan's lures was a verse from Scripture: "It is written . . ."

This strange quality about the Book is even revealed in reverse—Billy Graham debits this to Satan—for, he says, "Is there any other book about which people are so painfully self-conscious? Many church people who don't hesitate to put almost any other kind of book on the table in the living room would hesitate to let their neighbors find the Bible there. Commuters riding trains to and from work read newspapers and magazines of all sorts, without embarrassment. How few of them—even active church members—could, without great embarrassment, get out a pocket Testament and, in the presence of their fellow commuters, read their way to work in it?"

Driving with me one day in Florida, he took out his Bible and laid it open under his hand on his knee. "It's a strange thing about this book. There are many things in it I don't understand and can't explain. Some of the questions I have about it I am sure will never be answered this side of Heaven. But I know one thing: it contains enough that is so clear that he who runs may read. It contains a mysterious power to direct and impel people—all kinds and conditions of people—into changed lives, and it helps to keep them changed. Inside these covers, on these printed pages are the guides and signposts to the answers to all man's deepest needs. That is not what I suppose to be true. That is what, in the actual lives of actual people, I have seen to be true. That is why I can open this book in front of you or before an audience of people and say, 'This is the Word of God.' "

He believes that the Bible has this power over men's lives and the answers to their needs because, in it, Jesus Christ is revealed as the Son of God and through that revelation God's plan of salvation is made plain and accessible.

One morning in the summer of 1955, when Billy Graham had stopped between trains in Washington, D.C., en route from Europe to his home in North Carolina, he received an unexpected call from the White House. The President and Mrs. Eisenhower, he was told, would appreciate it if he could call on them at their Gettysburg farm that afternoon. A car, the White House informed him, would call in two hours.

For the first of the two hours, Billy Graham sat alone in his room. A friend who looked in saw him sitting in a chair, a Bible open in his lap. At the end of an hour he came out.

"Now," he said, "I'm ready."

"Weren't you ready?" someone asked.

"Not enough," he said. "Suppose the President or Mrs. Eisenhower should ask me this afternoon for spiritual advice. I had to be sure."

Since, to him, the Bible has Divine authority he preaches it without equivocation or apology. His often-repeated phrase, "The Bible says," is the Billy Graham equivalent for the prophetic declaration, "Thus saith the Lord." While preaching he carries an open Bible back and forth across the platform, gestures with it held aloft in his hands.

"He is all the time letting the Word of God speak," writes a Scottish minister, "instead of, as so many of us do, speaking about it. He stands with the Book in his hands, not as a symbol (though he likes it to be that) but because it is the Book that is speaking, not he."

The hundreds of counsellors at every Crusade meeting, the choir members and ushers are all expected to bring their Bibles. Everyone else is urged to do the same. In this modern era when, for many preachers, the Bible is a point of departure and, often, of "no return," and for many church members a closed book, it is an unusual, not to say stirring experience to hear—in the moment when Billy Graham waits after giving the Scripture passage from which he is to preach—the wave of sound that sweeps through the auditorium as thousands of people, swishing the pages, find the place in their Bibles.

In his personal life, the Bible is an unfailing restorative, inspiration, and guide. He has memorized great portions of it. Before one Crusade where he planned to preach a series of sermons on the Beatitudes, he memorized—as part of his "training program"—the entire three chapters in Matthew's Gospel of the Sermon on the Mount. He seldom spends less than an hour each day, sometimes much longer, in Bible reading.

There are frequent entries in his diary like this one written in his room in a New York hotel: "Had a wonderful time in the Bible this afternoon. Sometimes when I am reading it I have to stop. I become so full I can take no more." Again, he writes to Ruth: "Have just finished reading Colossians in the Williams translation and notice how much emphasis Paul puts on putting to death the old man in our life and putting on the new self which Christ gives. I feel that in my own life I come so far short of living the thrilling Christian experience as outlined in the New Testament."

On Good Friday night, 1955, Billy Graham spoke from Glasgow over the entire TV and radio network of the British Broadcasting Corporation to what was officially said to have been the largest TV and radio audience, save that at the Coronation, in the history of British broadcasting, and far and away the largest audience ever addressed by a preacher. On that day he wrote to Ruth:

"This is Good Friday. Tonight I am to speak on 'The Cross' on BBC television and radio. For two days I have been agonizing before the Lord that He would give me the message that would glorify Christ and make the Gospel so simple that the smallest child might understand. Now all day I have been resting and reading and rereading the story of the Crucifixion of our Lord. When I read of His suffering and death by crucifixion, it overwhelms me. I have knelt down more than once during the day, feeling my own unworthiness and sinfulness."

The other part of the practice by which it is possible for Billy Graham to "be so sure" is prayer. He believes that the power of God in his Crusades is a result of the power of the prayers by which they are supported. His first great Crusade success was in Los Angeles in the fall of 1949. The meeting there was at first scheduled to run three weeks. It ran eight. His tent auditorium had a seating capacity of 6,000. It had to be enlarged to 9,000. More than 2,700 made "decisions for Christ."

Numerous factors helped to account for this outpouring. Billy Graham is certain that the one factor back of all the factors was prayer. For it was in preparation for the Los Angeles meeting that, for the first time, members of the Graham team and local ministers organized an advance "prayer Crusade." Weeks before the Crusade itself began, several hundred prayer groups were meeting regularly all over Los Angeles to pray for its success.

"The only difference between that Crusade and all the others we had held up to then was more prayer. But that made all the difference."

His Crusades have never lacked for praying since. More than 500 prayer groups in Scotland, another 500 in England, Northern Ireland, and Wales were meeting regularly weeks before the 1955 Crusade began in Glasgow. Every night during that Crusade from 100 to 400 persons gave up their hard-to-get tickets in order to join in prayer in an improvised "Upper Room" in Kelvin Hall for the success of that night's meeting. Reports were received of scores of prayer groups, recruited by church papers and through Billy Graham's radio broadcasts, in the Christian churches of Korea, Africa, and India as well as throughout the British Commonwealth and Empire. There were "tens of thousands" of regularly praying people in the United States.

"Because of the triumphs of modern communications," Billy

43

Graham said at the opening meeting, "Glasgow tonight is probably the most prayed-for city in Christian history."

A Scottish minister, standing one wet night with Billy Graham while the thousands streamed into Kelvin Hall, remarked, "What a miracle."

"It is no miracle," said Billy Graham. "It would be a miracle if they didn't come. What is happening is the inevitable and natural result of God answering prayer. This is God in action."

To new converts he gives this counsel: "Learn the secret of prayer. Christ's prayer life was one of the most amazing and impressive features of His earthly ministry. Throughout the days of His life He was a man of prayer. He prayed with His disciples. He prayed in secret. Sometimes He spent all night in prayer. If He, the holy, sinless Son of God, could not live His earthly life without constant fellowship with God, you certainly cannot do so."

For those who are uncertain how to go about it, he says:

"Perhaps you say, 'But I don't know what to say when I pray.' God does not mind your stumbling and halting phrases. He is not interested in your grammar. He is interested in your heart.

"I have a little boy only two years old. He stumbles and falters trying to express himself to me; but I think I love his little words that I cannot understand even more than I will appreciate his correct grammatical sentences when he grows older.

"Have a secret time to pray each day. Make it a habit— vital and necessary as your daily food. Learn to 'pray without ceasing'—that is, live through the day breathing a prayer to God. Another thing: make a prayer list of people and subjects to engage your prayers.

"Above all, be sure that your motive in praying is always the glory of God."

Praying, he says, "does not always mean getting down on your knees. There is nothing Scriptural about kneeling or standing or bowing. Attitude of heart—not of body—is the important thing."

His diary and letters reveal what praying means to him.

"Received a long letter from Jerry Beavan this morning. It was so thought-provoking that I fell on my knees immediately in prayer." Before the overflow meeting in Madison Square Garden: "I spent almost the entire afternoon in prayer." After the meeting: "We immediately boarded the train for Washington. The first thing I did was to thank God for the victories of the evening. As I go to bed, I am shouting His praises."

Before an important interview in Philadelphia: "We knelt on the train and prayed that He would lead us." On shipboard, en route to Scotland with the members of his team: "Grady and I had a very delightful time of prayer and so did Lee and I today." On another day: "We had a delightful prayer meeting of the entire group."

Of the journey from London to Glasgow, he wrote to Ruth: "A number of reporters got on the train with us and tried to interview me in the corridor. I said good night and went back to crawl into bed. Then I felt a great burden of prayer. So I got on my knees beside the little bed as the train was rolling through the outer edges of London and prayed for our meetings in Glasgow. I prayed particularly for the press conference the next morning, that God would give great wisdom. The verse kept coming over and over as having an immediate personal meaning for me: '. . . and guided them by the skillfulness of His hands.' I had had difficulty resting the last few nights, so I also prayed the Lord would give me a good night's rest. I had no sooner prayed and crawled into bed than I went sound asleep."

After meeting with several members of the team on the eve of the Glasgow Crusade, he wrote to Ruth again: "We had dinner in my room and then we started to pray. As we were praying, it seemed that we could hear the rushing of the wind. I have never had but one or two spiritual experiences like it. It was

45

so wonderful, so thrilling, so sacred that I cannot even tell about it. It was almost like a Pentecostal experience."

The certainty which such close to ceaseless practice of the presence of God has produced in Billy Graham is centered in the person of Jesus Christ. He once said to me, "If there were no historical evidence for Jesus Christ, if there were no Bible to tell His story, I would still believe in Him because—beyond history and outside the Bible—I have come to know Him by personal experience. He is as real to me as any living person. That's why I don't argue about Him or try to make Him seem plausible by intellectual defense. I only say 'Seek Him,' 'Try Him.' There is no other way to be sure."

In his diary and letters Billy Graham writes of Him as one might write of a close friend, confidant, and trusted companion.

After attending and addressing a large banquet in Chicago with his wife, he writes: "The Lord certainly knew what He was doing when He chose her for my wife and number one advisor." He describes an old friend: "He loves the Lord with all his 300 pounds." After prolonged discussion of a vexing problem: "We still don't know just what to do. But the Lord will give the answer." Again: "Had an especially good time in devotions this morning. The Lord was very real."

Before the opening meeting of one Crusade: "Many people have an idea that we should not give an invitation the first night. However, as the day has gone along, the faith is increasing in me to believe the Lord is going to do a great thing this opening night. I can already sense His presence here in the room."

When, in the winter of 1955, he was interviewed by Washington, D.C., newsmen on the TV program *Meet the Press,* he wrote: "This was probably my biggest ordeal. I did not know one question they were going to ask me. The perspiration was in the palms of my hands and I think a little was on my brow. But I had made this a matter of prayer and I knew the Lord was going to help me. The questions gave me a great opportunity to witness concerning the saving grace and power of Christ. I am praying that souls may come to Christ as a result of this one program."

There is no record of how that prayer was answered. But Lawrence Spivak, the director of *Meet the Press,* said later that the mail received from that program was a near record for all the years it had been on the air. As a result, breaking the program's precedents, Billy Graham was invited to appear a second time in the same year.

To the question, How can he be so sure?, Billy Graham would probably give somewhat the same answer I once heard him give a reporter who had asked: "Why did you become an evangelist?"

"Let me ask you a question. Suppose I should discover a chemical which if taken by any person would make that person radiant and happy, give meaning to his life, and assure him of immortal life hereafter. Then suppose I should decide to keep that secret to myself. What would you say about me? You'd say, wouldn't you, 'Billy, you're a criminal'?

"If I didn't know, for sure, that faith in Christ is vital, transforming, that it gives direction to life and makes life worth living, I'd go back to my little North Carolina farm and spend the rest of my days tilling the soil. But I have seen too many lives untangled and rehabilitated, too many homes reconstructed, too many people find peace and joy through simple, humble confession of faith in Christ ever to doubt that He is the answer.

"I am an evangelist for the same reason the Apostle Paul was: 'Woe is unto me, if I preach not the gospel.' "

3: As one having authority

ONE NIGHT, during a Billy Graham sermon, a newspaper columnist sitting across the table from me in the press section passed over a note: "I can't figure this out."

I wrote back: "You're not the first."

At the end of the meeting we walked out together. The columnist had no further comment until we reached the exit and were ready to separate. Then he said, "Isn't there something in the Bible about its having been good for us to be here?"

"That," I said, "was Peter on the Mount of Transfiguration."

"Well," he said, "I still can't figure it out. But that's the way I feel."

No fact about the preaching of Billy Graham is more amazing than the number of those who, by ordinary analyzing, cannot figure it out and yet, their hearts strangely warmed, cannot lightly dismiss it. When he says, "I am no great preacher," other preachers generally agree. Yet he has been heard by more people than any preacher in Christian history; more people, hearing him preach, have made "decisions for Christ."

"Homiletically," said Dr. W. E. Sangster, one of England's foremost ministers, "his sermons leave almost everything to be desired. They are often without discernible structure. Sometimes there is little or no logical progression. Illustrations are few and far between and generally not of the best.

"Yet, in the wake of this 'poor' preaching I have seen things happen I never expected to see, things which I doubt any man has seen since the Day of Pentecost. To hear that preaching I have seen 100,000 people together in one place—most of them standing in the cold and rain. And at the end of it, I have seen 3,000 of them stream across the sodden turf to stand in the downpour before a crude, unpainted platform as though it were the very foot of the Cross. What am I to say of preaching such as that save 'Amen' and 'Amen'?"

Let us admit, writes the Reverend Tom Allan, a leading minister of the Church of Scotland, that Billy Graham's preaching "is not, by the accepted standards, of the highest order. His sermons were often without form. There were some quirks in his grammar. His few illustrations were never from general literature but invariably from the Bible or from life. . . .

"But for myself it was preaching in the New Testament sense of the word. It was 'proclamation' of the Faith once delivered to the saints, the central affirmations of the Gospel stripped of all irrelevancies, of all concessions . . . stark simplicity of utterance which allowed the facts of the faith to emerge without distraction. The verdict simply is: 'We understand what this man is saying.' And when, at his invitation, the people come, the evangelist, at last, stands back silent, forgotten. This is the moment of the Spirit of God."

Some observers who have undertaken to report on Billy Graham while aiming at the same time to keep their skepticism intact have been driven to offer some extraordinary explanations for the power of his preaching. Most of these explanations, it seems to me, put a greater strain on one's gullibility than those advanced by believers and would require, to give them substance, the "passing" of even greater miracles than those of faith. I have heard him accounted for by "his good looks," "the bobby-sox appeal," "the hypnotism in his eyes," "the mesmeric sound of his voice." Alistair Cooke, who observed Billy Graham one night in Madison Square Garden and whose report to the *Manchester Guardian* was as clever as it was indicative of the extent of his contact, summed it all up as "seduction." To J. B. Priestley—whose knowledge, he confessed, was derived from having once heard Billy Graham on television—the response to his preaching was "not hunger for religion," but "because what so many of us want now is a show."

I am sure that neither Mr. Cooke nor Mr. Priestley would have presumed to base such final judgment of any subject on such paucity of knowledge save on the assumption that most of their readers would be equally ill-informed. As explanations for Billy Graham, the "seduction" of his personality and "the show" he puts on could only be written out of ignorance for the benefit of others equally ignorant of the fact that 20,000,-000 people listen to his *Hour of Decision* sermon every Sunday afternoon in the seduction-insulated quiet of their homes, or of the fact that every night during the All-Scotland Crusade up to a million people assembled in churches, halls, and movie theaters in England, Scotland, Northern Ireland, and Wales to listen to his preachings piped in to them, totally unadorned with the trappings of showmanship, by telephone relay.

However much the plausibility of such appraisals as those I have quoted is derived from ignorance, I do not doubt they are a solace to that considerable number of people who, heretofore confident, not to say cocksure, in their religious unconcern, have been stirred into some uneasiness by the Billy Graham phenomenon. They are a means to escape the unpleasantly discommoding prospect of having to take him seriously. But it is significant that such "explanations" are only advanced by those who, like Messrs. Cooke and Priestley, have been unwilling to risk more than the briefest possible exposure to him or his preaching. I have found that objective observers generally agree with the famed English writer and

51

Cambridge University professor, C. S. Lewis, who remarked during Billy Graham's 1955 series of meetings in Cambridge, "I've noticed that those who really know Billy Graham and have heard him often invariably speak well of him; those who speak otherwise have generally seldom seen or heard him." I have met many skeptics who, having heard him, remained skeptical. I have not met one who, having mustered sufficient courage to hear him repeatedly, did not say that the explanations born of skepticism were not good enough.

I have sat through several dozen Billy Graham sermons. I have taken notes of many of them. Some of them flow point after point—one, two, three and, in one case, up to twelve points—in the smooth homiletical tradition of Sunday morning in suburbia. In others, there is little discoverable trace of organization. They always have a subject. All of them have —at some point or other in the discourse—a text. But, in these numerous instances, subject and text serve chiefly as a point of departure. From them the preacher took off and preached —letting the points, if any, fall where they might.

But in my notes I also recorded, after each sermon, the results. Unlike the results of some preaching, they were always distinguishable enough to deserve recording. But they often seemed to be in reverse ratio to the homiletical excellence of what had gone before. Those sermons which came out, in outline, as likeliest to rate among the experts' "Best Sermons of the Year" often appeared to rate less than average among the people who listened, whereas some of those which, in my notes at least, seemed to have little form or orderliness or climactic build-up seemed to have more power to stir people to leave the places where they sat and, in the sight of the multitude, walk down the long aisles to give what Billy Graham calls "a yes verdict to Jesus Christ."

Perhaps this is what Billy Graham had in mind when he once wrote: "I am convinced there is a vast difference between

52

liberty and power, that sometimes when you do not feel liberty, you have the greatest power."

At any rate, Billy Graham's preaching, though it never leaves me cold, often leaves me, like many others, puzzled. It is not too difficult to describe how he preaches and recount what he preaches. It is puzzling when one tries to describe why the how and the what of his preaching invariably produce such consequences. There is nothing in the script adequate to explain it.

Someone once asked George Whitefield, whose preaching in the mid-eighteenth century stirred colonial America into the "Great Awakening," for permission to publish his sermons.

"Certainly," said Whitefield, "if you will include the fire and the lightning."

Although, in the eighteenth-century sense, Billy Graham is no thunderer, the unmistakable fire and fervor of his preaching are beyond transmitting by the printed word. But even with the fire and fervor added, an explanation of the consequences of his preaching is not, I think, within the reach of technical analysis. Most of what happens is still unexplained.

In this, also, Billy Graham seems to stand in a notable succession. Beginning with Paul—whose preaching, to some, was "foolishness"—the triumphs of other great evangelists have seemed to be beyond ordinary explaining. Wesley's sermons, says one of his biographers, "do not help us to understand his power over the hearts of men." A Boston journalist, after listening night after night to Dwight L. Moody, wrote: "It is a marvel to many how the preaching of Mr. Moody produces the effect which evidently comes from it. He is not a learned man in doctrine or profound in theological study. He is not even strikingly original in thought or forcible in style of expression. He has few of the arts or graces of oratory and yet he brings people together in greater crowds and apparently produces more effect upon their thoughts and feeling and conduct than the most brilliant and cultured of popular divines. . . ."

After extensive observation, after trying out, without success, numerous other explanations, the conclusion has finally become inescapable for me that the single most convincing explanation of the power of Billy Graham's preaching is that he speaks "as one having authority." And the nearest I have come to explaining the consequences of his preaching is that he not only speaks with authority, but that, from sources not visible to the naked journalistic eye, he has been given authority for his speaking.

Sometimes the structure of what he says is oratorical. In fact, he has undoubted gifts as an orator and occasionally, particularly in his radio sermons, they are strikingly displayed. Sometimes, as my notes reveal, the structure of what he says is commonplace. But however he says it, the overtone of authority is never missing. There is authority in his voice and gestures. There is authority in the forthrightness of his declarations. There is authority in the total absence from his preaching of words of equivocation, of "if," "maybe," or "perhaps."

But these are merely the audio-visual marks of authority. They can be seen and heard and they might be calculated. But the oftener one hears Billy Graham preach and the closer one gets to the man, the more awareness there is that his authority is rooted in something deeper than anything seen or heard. I believe that that deeper thing is an authoritative, continually renewed experience of the presence of God. One's first inclination is to say, "He speaks as though he knows what he is talking about." Later, one is likelier to say, "He speaks *because* he knows what he is talking about."

"In short authoritative sentences," says a writer in the *Christian Century,* "the tall young man with the wavy hair and the Hollywood drape has spoken about God. It might be said that he is familiar with God. He knows God. He is sure."

In the spring of 1954, at the end of the Greater London Crusade, the London *Sunday Times,* after three months in

54

which to observe, gave its appraisal in a remarkable editorial reprinted, later, in the *U.S. News and World Report:*

"There are many puzzled people in Britain today. Three months ago a young American came to London. His arrival was greeted in some quarters with ridicule and hostility or with contemptuous silence. But religion has become front-page news and frequent articles have been printed either about Billy Graham or concerning the challenge he has brought to the churches.

"The people who thronged Harringay and Wembley are puzzled. Many went out of curiosity, expecting to find an exaggerated emotionalism or the raving of a Hot Gospeller. Instead, they heard a well-reasoned though forceful declaration of the half-forgotten fundamental truths of Christianity. To their surprise they discovered that these truths which they had imagined were out of date and irrelevant found a responsive echo in their own hearts and held out a possible hope in this age of despair. . . .

"Why has the preaching of this young man done for them what apparently the churches have not done? The answer seems to lie in this direction. The people want to know the truth. They want it declared with authority and conviction, dogmatically and without apology.

"Dr. Graham has appeared in the role of an Old Testament prophet or John the Baptist declaring 'Thus saith the Lord,' and thousands have responded to his message. Nineteen hundred years ago men were puzzled by the preaching of St. Paul, preaching which swept away the paganism of the Roman Empire and the dead ecclesiasticism of Judaism. The explanation which he himself gave is: 'The preaching of the Cross is to them that are perishing foolishness, but unto us which are being saved, it is the power of God.' Is not that the real answer to our questions today?"

Just where, precisely, Billy Graham can be assigned in the long and, on the whole, unhappy scale of theological opinions

55

as between liberals and fundamentalists it is difficult to say. He, himself, in an answer to that question in *Look* magazine has written:

"There are so many shades of fundamentalism and so many shades of liberalism that it is extremely difficult to point to a man and say he is a 'liberal' or he is a 'fundamentalist' without qualifying explanations. If by fundamentalist you mean 'narrow,' 'bigoted,' 'prejudiced,' 'extremist,' 'emotional,' 'snake handler,' 'without social conscience'—then I am definitely not a fundamentalist. However, if by fundamentalist you mean a person who accepts the authority of the Scriptures, the virgin birth of Christ, the atoning death of Christ, His bodily resurrection, His second coming and personal salvation by grace through faith, then I am a fundamentalist. . . ."

That answer, no doubt, puts Billy Graham to the fundamentalist right of center. How far right, however, is still an unresolved question and is likely to continue so. To theologically minded groups questioning him he says, "I am not a theologian. I can only tell you what I believe with what light I have." So far as his Scriptural literalism is concerned, that light—as is indicated in a later chapter—has undergone some modifying.

Still, no person who has been reared in the liberal theological tradition and accustomed to the kind of sermons which that tradition normally produces can, I think, fail to find in the preaching of Billy Graham doctrines which, on reflection, are both startling and difficult. What, however, seems to me of greater moment is the fact that his is not, essentially, doctrinal preaching. Its objective is not argument-inducing, but commitment-inducing. And the net consequence of his preaching is to create the conviction—even among many of those who strongly disagree with some aspects of his theology—that the commitment he pleads for is something which transcends theology and takes precedence over doctrine.

On this point, Dr. Leslie Weatherhead, distinguished Methodist minister of the City Temple, London, and author of numerous best-selling religious books, has written of Billy Graham:

"Theology is very important . . . But let us remember that a man can live a good life and be a devout follower of our Lord with very little theology. You do not need much theology to be a simple and humble follower of Jesus. . . .

"I have learned myself to accept the fact that there is such a variation in the way in which men's minds work that none has the right to deny the Christian loyalty of the other because of a difference in a theological point of view.

"I do not personally agree with some of Billy Graham's theology . . . but I certainly accept the value of Billy Graham's witness. He wisely realizes that men are changed by news, not views. He offered them the good news of Christ, and I should have thought that any minister who frequently preaches to small congregations might rejoice that Billy Graham is helping to fill our churches for us. We can teach theology when we have got somebody to teach. . . ."

Perhaps, in this, Billy Graham's "calling" does include theology. For it is his conviction that today's greatest revival need is for a revival *within* the church; that among both fundamentalists and liberals there are many who stand in need of being touched and changed by such a revival; that there is no greater challenge than to preach a Gospel which, whether they are fundamentalists or liberals, can reach, touch, and change those within the church who need changing. To be able to preach such an indiscriminately transforming Gospel is, I believe, the gift which Billy Graham most earnestly and devoutly prays for.

It is a matter of some regret to Billy Graham that he never attended a theological school. That he never did probably accounts for the fact that he is a bit in awe of theologians. "What a tremendous mind he has," he wrote after spending an afternoon with one. "We talked theology. He confirmed— from the theological point of view—some of the things I had been saying in my preaching which some ministers have criti-

57

cized. He gave me several extremely helpful suggestions. Again I say, what a tremendous mind."

No occasion makes him more nervous in anticipation than a speech at an intellectually "upper-bracket" theological assembly such as at Union Theological Seminary in New York City or before the students in theology at Cambridge University.

"If God used the service," he said, after speaking at Cambridge, "then I am thankful. But I have so little theological training I felt my own inadequacy in standing before so theological a group."

He is also aware that the inadequacies in such an encounter are not necessarily all his.

"It's surprising," he wrote to Ruth Graham after a question-and-answer session at one theological school, "how little theological students know about the Bible. They know about church history, psychology, pastoral theology and other things —all good—but they know little about the Bible. It is also surprising how confused theological students are, and yet, many times, how hungry. Sometimes I think theological professors make the mistake of being professors only. Every professor ought to be a preacher and an evangelist. He ought to come face to face with the hearts and the problems of men and women. Maybe then he could impart some warmth and conviction to his students."

But I have heard preachers, some of them equipped with the ultimate in theological education, question whether Billy Graham's lack in that regard is lack at all. "Not having gone to a seminary," said one minister with the highest credentials, "he has not been schooled in the complexities, the varying shades, the various alternatives. He has not, like so many of us, been tutored into uncertainty. He preaches as though nothing had ever come between him or, at least, had ever stood long between him and God—as though his faith were as clear and sure as it was on the day of his conversion." All Billy Graham would add is that, proving it daily for himself and seeing it so conclusively proved in the lives of others, his faith is clearer and surer than it was at his conversion and, as he once remarked, "is continually getting more so."

I once heard a professor of theology—gifted with above-average humility and humor—say that "theology is the art of reducing the obvious to the obscure." Whatever Billy Graham may have lost by not studying theology, the obscurity and uncertainty he might have found he has escaped.

"Sometimes people ask me," says Ruth Graham, "whether Bill ever entertains any doubt about what he believes and preaches. I always tell them, 'Of course he has doubts. But never for long because, you see, he never *entertains* them.' "

"I wouldn't know how to preach like Billy Graham," says a Presbyterian clergyman, a graduate of Princeton Theological Seminary. "For twenty years now I have been engaged, like most of our so-called modern preachers, in inventing logic, parable, intellectual forensics and everything but the words of the Bible to prove that they are not wrong.

"Here comes this fellow who says the Bible is right because he believes in God, and the Scriptures are God's words. That's simply it. No need to fiddle around with any more proof than that.

"Furthermore, I'd hate to admit it, but I think most of us have felt rather insecure about our congregations. We were afraid they would think we were old fuddy-duddies if we just opened the Bible and read from it and told a few Bible stories with complete belief. What Billy Graham has done is to give these words new dignity.

"And brother, in these times, how we need it."

Above the platform for every Billy Graham Crusade there is the same inscription:

"Jesus says, 'I am the Way, the Truth and the Life.' "

Every Crusade service uses, somewhere near the beginning, the same song: "To God Be the Glory, Great Things He Hath Done."

Every Billy Graham sermon is introduced by a solo by Beverly Shea, and Billy Graham begins with a prayer:

"Our Father and our God, may the people see only Christ tonight and not the speaker. We pray that there may be scores and hundreds here who will be born again, so that they will go back to the home, the office, the school, the factory to live and practice Christ. We pray that they will go from this place with Christ as their Lord and Savior. For we ask it in His name. Amen."

Every sermon has essentially the same message:

"Many of you here tonight are like a plane lost in a fog which has lost contact with the airport. You are circling round in the fear, insecurity, and loneliness of your lives. You can make contact with God through Jesus Christ. For your fear, the Bible says, 'Perfect love casteth out fear'; for your insecurity, 'He that overcometh fear shall inherit all things'; for your loneliness, 'Lo, I am with you always.'"

It is a mark of Billy Graham's preaching, as was said of another great preacher, that "he always cuts straight across country to Christ." Often, his opening words are these: "I want you to get a picture of Jesus." "Whatever subject he announces," says one minister, "whatever text he takes, every sermon has at its center 'Christ and Him Crucified.'"

"The invitation was a little more difficult last night," he writes to Ruth, "and fewer people came. The moment I walked down from the platform the Holy Spirit said to me, 'You did not preach Christ and the Cross as you should.' I looked back over my sermon and I remember that I had exalted Christ a little less, perhaps, and it was one of the few occasions that I did not touch on His death, burial, and resurrection as the heart of the message. The Lord taught me a lesson."

Although I have never heard him preach a sermon from that text, there is a sense in which Paul's testimony to Timothy is the text for all Billy Graham's sermons: "I know Whom I have believed and am persuaded. . . ."

Every Billy Graham sermon contains the same diagnosis:
"The Bible teaches that our souls have a disease. It is worse than dread cancer, polio, or heart disease. It is the plague that causes all the troubles and difficulties in the world. It causes all the troubles, confusions, and disillusionments in your own life. The name of the disease is an ugly word. We don't like to use it. But it is a word that the psychiatrists are beginning to use once again. In our desire to be modern, we had almost forgotten it, but once again we are beginning to realize that it is the root of all man's troubles. It is *sin*."

Sin is "anything which separates man from God." It is "transgression of the law of God." Or it is "iniquity—evil that springs from our inner motivations, those hidden things we so often try to keep from the eyes of men and God." Or it is "missing the mark—falling short of God's expectations for us and from our lives." Or it is "trespassing—the intrusion of self-will into the sphere of God's authority, the centering of affection in one's own being instead of reaching out, with all one's heart and mind and soul, to love God and to love our neighbor as ourself."

All men are sinners: "The Bible teaches 'all have sinned and come short.' " There is a real Hell, "an eternal judgment" toward which, aided by a real Satan, unrepentant man is headed. "Essentially, Hell is separation from God."

There is, in those definitions, plenty of room for the preaching of what is described as the social Gospel. And that Gospel undoubtedly has an increasing place in Billy Graham's preaching. He himself has said, "The Gospel is both vertical and horizontal. The vertical signifies our relationship to God. The horizontal signifies the application of the principles of the teachings of Christ to our daily lives. At least a third of my preaching is spent encouraging and teaching people to apply the principles of Christianity in their personal and social lives. . . . I would like to say emphatically that any Gospel that preaches only vertical relationships is only a half-Gospel; that a Gospel that preaches only horizontal relationships is only a half-Gospel. The message of evangelism must be for the whole man."

That declaration—which I doubt Billy Graham would have made ten years ago—is evidence, I think, that the social implications of the Gospel will be increasingly emphasized in his preaching. Those implications, however, are still considerably short of central to his concern. The righteousness he calls for with such authority in his preaching is still very largely a one-part matter of man's personally righteous relationship to his God, and not yet very insistently a two-part matter having, as its second part, man's socially righteous relationship to his fellows. His concept of sin is still very largely a Ten-Commandment concept which includes, it seems to me, too little of the beyond-the-Ten-Commandments sins which Amos, Hosea, and Micah—and Jesus most of all—cried out against. His idea of the Christian's social obligations is still too much limited to the charitable "cup of cold water"—a phrase he often uses—and extends too seldom to the Christian in his corporate, and communal, relationships.

"Every message that I preach," says Billy Graham, "carries with it social implications and social responsibilities." Inadequate and obscure though that emphasis may sometimes seem to be, no one can hear or read many of his sermons without being aware that it is on the increase.

Neither can anyone who has been familiar over the years with the social Gospel as it has been preached and written fail to recognize the truth in Billy Graham's belief that "much of this preaching puts the cart before the horse. The reason I have put first in my preaching the vertical relationship of the individual to his God is because the plain and Scriptural fact is that we cannot have a better world until we have better men. It is for me impossible to find any Scriptural basis for the belief that a righteously reborn social order can come in any other way save through the work of spiritually reborn men. That is because, as so much of history has tragically proved, the estab-

62

lishment of God's will on earth and among men is not possible for us in our own strength. It becomes possible in the home, the shop, the community, in the problem of race relations, in all these crucial matters only when our strength is lifted above the human norm by the in-dwelling of Christ."

Although in Billy Graham's preaching there may be some lack of some of those specifics which constitute what is commonly spoken of as the social Gospel, there is no doubt whatever that his preaching does invariably produce social consequences which must be rated as more than ordinarily significant. During and in the wake of every Billy Graham Crusade broken families are reunited, alcoholics are cured of their alcoholism, juvenile delinquents are brought within the influence of the church.

In the American South his insistence on nonsegregation in Crusade meetings has set an example not only for the churches but for entire communities. In scores of industrial plants in the United States and Great Britain employer-employee relations have improved as a result of prayer groups established during the Billy Graham meetings and maintained thereafter. In the field of international relationships it is doubtful whether any number of social-Gospel resolutions could match in practical results the contribution which, in his 1956 mission to Asia, Billy Graham made to East-West understanding and good will.

There has been, too, a considerable change which extreme fundamentalists may regard as dangerous deviationism in the specifics of Billy Graham's literalism. He is as sure as ever about the reality of Heaven and Hell, for example, but less sure about the literalists' blueprint of them.

Earlier in his preaching, Hell burned with a real, not a figurative fire. "The Bible says God has a fire—as when the three Hebrew children were thrown into the fiery furnace—that burns but does not consume." The Heaven he pictured then was straight from the drawing boards: "Sixteen hundred miles long, sixteen hundred miles wide, sixteen hundred miles high."

Since those early days his emphasis has considerably changed. As sure as he is of the existence of Hell, he now says that Hell's fire may be "the burning thirst for God of those who have been eternally banished from His presence." Hell's "outer darkness" may be "the total absence of light where God Himself is totally absent." But whether we take the Bible's words "to be literal or figurative does not affect Hell's reality."

As for Heaven, "the description in the twenty-first and twenty-second chapters of Revelation is beyond our understanding . . . gates of pearls, streets of gold, a river of life, a tree of life. What we can be sure of is that it is a beautiful place, that it is a happy place, and that it is a place where there is work to do and that God is there. . . ."

Satan, however, has undergone no such alteration. "Don't doubt for a moment the existence of the Devil! We see his power and influence everywhere. He is very personal and he is very real. And he is extremely clever."

At the end of a long day of conferences preparatory to opening the All-Scotland Crusade in Glasgow, he wrote in his diary: "Satan is very cunning. We recognize that on our way to Glasgow, as we are holding our meetings and planning our strategy and spending time in prayer that God will send revival, that Satan is also holding his councils, laying his plans to bring, if he can, God's work to nought."

Prior to his mission in Cambridge University in the fall of 1955, he wrote: "During the past week I have felt the tremendous opposition of Satan. I seriously doubt if at any time in my ministry I have so felt the powers of darkness. It seems as though the demons of Hell had concentrated against this mission."

Just as it always contains the same diagnosis, so every Billy Graham sermon offers the same cure. God sent His Son "that whosoever believeth in Him should not perish but have everlasting life." For our salvation, Christ died on the Cross: "Ye are bought with a price." By Christ's resurrection from the

64

dead, God's promise of our salvation is confirmed and validated. Through the "gift of the Holy Spirit," given at Pentecost, that promise is made available to all succeeding generations.

"For you who are hopeless, for a world that is desperate, there is Good News. That Good News is the Gospel of Jesus Christ. Those of us who know Him have no fear of the present. He is Lord of the present. We have no fear of the future. He is the key to the future.

"This faith in Christ that we are preaching night after night is not superstition or an empty theory or a means of livelihood or a meaningless creed. It is the power of God unto salvation. It is vital; it is transforming; it is empowering; it is stabilizing; it is comforting and it gives direction to life."

Man's cure, his "laying hold of the new life," requires his conversion: "I didn't say that; Jesus said it: 'Except ye be converted and become as little children, ye shall not enter the Kingdom of Heaven.' " Conversion requires that "you confess and repent of your sins; surrender your will to Christ; by faith receive Him as Lord and Master." "The Bible says, 'If we confess our sins He is faithful and just to forgive us our sins, and to cleanse us from all unrighteousness.' "

The "where" of conversion is not important—whether "in the quiet of your home, the hallowed sanctuary of a church, or at an evangelistic meeting." Neither is the "how" important—"whether suddenly, as with Paul on the Damascus Road or slowly over many months." What is important is "Who—the Person you decide for."

Just how it is conversion "happens," Billy Graham does not profess to understand. He knows it happened to him. He has seen it happen to all kinds and conditions of people—thousands who "for their dilemmas, problems, and frustrations found joy, hope, and peace." Like Nicodemus, he still asks, "How can these things be?"

"But neither," he says, "do I understand how a young man and a young woman fall in love. You cannot analyze it, dissect

65

it, or reduce it to a chemical formula. But there it is. And the fact that it cannot be explained does not make it any less real."

Billy Graham preaches every sermon "for a verdict." In fact, as was said of the preaching of Dwight L. Moody, every part of every sermon seems, from start to finish, to point to the altar and, often, he begins to make the invitation long before he is ready to ask for a response from the congregation.

There are no tear-wringing stories, no deathbed scenes, no hysteria-inducing endings. This—the absence of any extremes of emotion—is a fact which every objective observer notes, sometimes, in view of the assumptions of ill-informed critics, with astonishment.

Thus, in his column in the Toronto *Telegram,* Frank Tumpane writes: "I had thought Billy Graham was turning religion into an emotional exhibition. I never heard him in the flesh until the other night. My views changed radically. . . . The vast audience sits hushed, watching and hearing. There is little apparent emotionalism. A few say 'Amen' at various places throughout the sermon. But frenzy is completely lacking. The only outward emotionalism is on the platform."

Dr. Leslie Weatherhead, whom I have already quoted, has said:

"I found no emotion of the cheap, meretricious kind. There were no sentimental stories, no attempts to produce the easy tear. That being so, what is wrong with emotion? If Christianity is falling in love with Christ, has anyone ever fallen in love without emotion? . . . Human nature functions most potently when the will is fired by emotion. . . . Without some emotion no man has ever made such a profound choice as the choice to follow Christ."

Every conversion, says Billy Graham, has emotion in it. But the greater part is will. That is the way he preaches. That is why, among the many who stream forward every night during a Crusade, there is great soberness, but few tears.

In the actual invitation the words Billy Graham uses are always much the same:

"You can go out from here tonight with such peace and assurance as you have never known. . . ."

"You say, 'Billy, that's all well and good. I'll think it over and I may come back, I'll . . .' Wait a minute. You can't come to Christ any time you want to. You can only come when the Spirit of God is drawing and wooing you. I beg of you come now, before it is too late. . . ."

"I am not going to press you to make a decision. . . . This is not something between you and Billy Graham. This is between you and God. . . ."

"But you say, 'Billy, why must I get up in front of my friends, and come down these aisles?' It is true, coming down these aisles and standing here does not mean you are saved. But it is a seal upon your decision to accept Christ. And Jesus said that if we confess Him before men He will confess us before His Father Who is in Heaven. . . ."

"If you have friends or relatives, they'll wait on you. Whether you are young or old, rich or poor, white or colored, you know you need Christ in your life tonight. So now, while the choir sings softly, 'Just As I Am without One Plea,' you come and say, 'Billy, tonight I accept Jesus Christ.' "

Giving the invitation and waiting for the response, Billy Graham says, are the hardest part of his preaching; those few minutes take more out of him than the preceding forty. After the first meeting in Glasgow, he wrote to Ruth:

"Then came the moment of decision. There was a great hush and a great quiet. Would they come? Would they respond? At first, not a person moved. My heart began to sink a little. My faith wavered, but only for a second. Then it all came flooding back to me that millions of people were praying and that God was going to answer their prayers. Great faith came surging into my heart and I knew they would come even before the first one moved.

"I bowed my head and began to pray. When I glanced up people were streaming from everywhere. On the platform, I saw some of the ministers begin to weep. It had been a long time since Scotland had seen a sight like this: 14,500 under one roof and people streaming down every aisle to give their lives to Christ. Some were weeping openly. I knew that God was doing a genuine work.

"I went back to the Inquiry Room and spoke to them. They were so eager, so quiet and so hungry."

An editor of one of Scotland's largest newspapers said to me, "I'm a bit of a skeptic myself. But if I ever saw the light of God it was in the eyes of those people."

Watching from the press table, a British newspaper columnist wrote:

"It doesn't matter that he isn't a particularly good preacher. This is the ultimate spiritual energy that has always changed the world. And it made nonsense out of most of the speeches of the world's statesmen."

To his wife, Billy Graham's conclusion was a verse from the One hundred Eighteenth Psalm: " 'This is the Lord's doing; it is marvelous in our eyes.' "

4: Few are chosen

ON THE THIRD Sunday in May, 1940, twenty-one-year-old Billy Graham, ready for his graduation exercises from the Florida Bible Institute near Tampa, Florida, preached, as he regularly did, at a nearby trailer camp. Exactly fifteen years later, on the third Sunday in May, 1955, the British Court Calendar carried this announcement:

"The Queen and the Duke of Edinburgh attended Divine Service this morning in the private Chapel, the Royal Lodge. Dr. William Graham preached the sermon."

What his text was that morning at the trailer camp, Billy Graham cannot recall. His text in the Chapel at Windsor Castle was from the Book of Acts, Paul's words of reassurance to the crew of the gale-threatened ship in which he was a passenger: "Wherefore, sirs, be of good cheer; for I believe God, that it shall be even as it was told me."

As for the sermon, Billy Graham says it was essentially the same in both places, and I do not doubt it: "God's plan of salvation, with Christ and the Cross the heart of it." Essentially, he seldom preaches any other sermon and never, he says, effectively. And though Windsor is separated, not in miles only, by a great distance from Tampa and though his pulpit

69

manner before the royal family was considerably more sub-dued than anything his trailer-camp congregation was used to, it is safe to say that the quality which distinguished his preach-ing was the same in both places; he spoke "as one having authority."

To understand how he came by that preaching authority it is necessary to go back to his preaching origins. These origins could hardly have been humbler, intellectually, or more con-servative, theologically, or better calculated, spiritually, to produce the kind of preacher he is. The power he has today is rooted in those beginnings.

He was seventeen at his conversion, a senior in the Sharon, North Carolina, High School. His conversion did not result, for him, in a blinding revelation that he was called to preach. He was, in fact, slow to make up his mind—not slow by what is ordinarily expected of a seventeen-year-old, but slow when one considers what extraordinary expectations were centered in him. He still had a lurking idea he might play baseball—whetted by the few semipro games he actually played at $10 to $15 a game. But during that summer he never was for long beyond the reach of influences which made it unlikely he would ever go in for so secular a pursuit and unlikely that he could forget that preaching might be, in the devout and weighted phrase, "God's will for him."

Chief among these influences was the prayerful solicitude of his parents. His father had wanted to be a preacher himself. A quiet, gentle man, not given to pressuring or argument, his prayers at the family altar nonetheless left no doubt of the hope he held that his ambition would be realized in his son. Later, when his father saw that ambition being realized be-yond his expectations, he told how he had felt:

"In these recent months, my mind has been made clear on a matter which has bothered me for forty-five years. When I was converted I felt immediately a desire to preach. I prayed for years for a way to be opened. But never once was there the slightest encouragement from God. My heart burned and I wondered why God did not answer my prayer. Now I feel I have the answer. I believe my part was to raise a son to be a preacher.

"That dawned on me when a letter came to me from the editor of the Boston, Massachusetts, *Post* saying that no one, not even Roosevelt or Churchill, ever had drawn as many people in that city as Billy. After I finished reading that letter I felt that the Lord was with my boy. My burden to preach was lifted and I now felt God had used me to give Him a son."

Billy's mother, soon after his conversion, set aside a period every day for prayer devoted solely to Billy and the "calling" she believed was his. She continued those prayers, never missing a day, for seven years until the last uncertainty was resolved and Billy was well on his preaching way. She still continues them, though now her prayer—with a text drawn from II Timothy 2:15—is that what he preaches may meet with God's approval: "Study to show thyself approved unto God, a workman that needeth not to be ashamed, rightly dividing the word of truth."

Another influence turning Billy toward preaching was his friend Grady Wilson, who had followed close behind that night in the revival tent of Mordecai Ham. Grady, almost at once, had made up his mind to preach. Moreover, he started right off preaching, his platform manner and address and what theology he offered being carefully modeled on what he had seen and heard of Mordecai Ham. Some of Grady's early efforts did not stir in Billy any great urge toward emulation. On one memorable night—when he borrowed Billy's watch and wound it, as he preached, until the stem broke—he spoke on "God's Four Questions," taking a full hour on questions One and Two and, by dint of considerable telescoping, half an hour on Three and Four. But the fact that Grady knew what he was going to do with his life, and was so sure that nothing of comparable

71

importance with preaching could possibly be done with it, undoubtedly kept the issue alive and pressing in Billy's mind.

It was partly because of his meeting with three fervent Bob Jones students and partly because his parents "hoped" he would attend a Bible college that Billy in the fall of 1936 entered Bob Jones College in Cleveland, Tennessee—now located in Greenville, South Carolina, as Bob Jones University. In this school, the chance that a serious-minded young man with pious background could escape the ministry or the mission field was probably as remote as in any educational community in America. Its founder and head was the Reverend Bob Jones, a famed Southern evangelist. It was a place steeped in religion; a school of one book: the Bible. Bible reading, prayer, and practice-preaching were every student's daily diet. Billy, although still no candidate for the ministry, was quickly signed up for a "major" in theology.

But he did not stay long at Bob Jones College. In his uncertain frame of mind he found the religious rigidity of the place oppressive. Dr. Jones was a difficult taskmaster. There were rules and regulations galore; a too regimented social life; no intercollegiate sports. Billy, unfamiliar with such restraints and unhappy about them, was involved in an escapade or two which—though he eloquently talked his way out of them— left him marked as a possible "problem." He left at the end of the first semester.

Before he left, however, he preached his first sermon. It was in a small Tennessee town where, as in many areas of the South, the young, raw preacher is given a more than ordinarily sympathetic hearing. The date had been arranged by Billy's roommate, Wendell Phillips, a graduate of the Moody Bible Institute in Chicago who had been paired with Billy in something of the role of guardian. Since the school's rules prohibited the use of Wendell's car, the two went on foot—an eleven-mile journey—to the church.

Billy's sermon was in the best tradition of the inexperienced:

72

"If Christ Had Not Come, What?" Wendell Phillips gives this account of that first and, apparently, not altogether feeble effort:

"Billy started in the easy, casual way he always uses, but suddenly as he went along I realized I had heard this sermon before, or at least had read it. A few weeks earlier I had sold some Moody colportage books to several of the students and here, before my eyes, was one of these sermons coming to life. Billy went right down the line in the outline and sermon and did a terrific job. But in his desire to be dramatic he gave me an awful scare. He stood in that pulpit and declared as forcefully as he knew, 'The coming of Christ was foretold centuries before the Messiah came, by type, by symbol, and by prophecy. The smoke from every Jewish altar was an index finger pointing to the Lamb of God who would take away the sins of the world. One thousand years rolled by and still no Messiah. Two thousand years and still no Christ . . . Three thousand . . . Five thousand. . . .'

"Right there I began shaking my head from my front row seat. He saw me, looked a bit perplexed, and quickly switched to another thought. After the meeting he said to me, 'Wendell, why did you shake your head like that?' I told him, 'Billy, I was afraid you wouldn't stop, as you rolled the centuries back, short of fifteen to twenty thousand years, and those dear Bible-loving people—who put 6000 B.C. or so as the date of Creation—would never invite us back again."

The school Billy moved to from Bob Jones College was the Florida Bible Institute at Temple Terrace, near Tampa, Florida, now called Trinity College and located at Clearwater, Florida. Billy's choice of the Florida Bible Institute may have been partly due to a long siege he had with the flu, partly due to his love of baseball and the lure of being near the training camps of several major-league teams. The likeliest explanation is that Wendell Phillips, his roommate at Bob Jones, had gone

73

on ahead and sent back a stream of letters which were both evangelically and climatically aglow.

"I told him," says Phillips, "that his decision was a matter for serious prayer: that schools were not the primary thing, but that knowing God's will was of the utmost importance. In every letter I referred him to Proverbs 16:9: 'A man's heart deviseth his way: but the Lord directeth his steps.' "

Billy Graham is sure the Lord's directing hand was in his move to the Florida Bible Institute. It was there he made his decision to preach and there he began to lay hold of and, in practice, test the convictions which today give authority to his preaching.

By technical educational standards, it was not much of a school. It was located in a large, well-appointed tourist hotel frequented during the winter season by well-to-do visitors who favored for their holiday a place with a religious atmosphere. The students—of whom there were 75 when Billy enrolled—worked out their expenses as members of the hotel staff.

The school was surrounded by a beautiful championship golf course. Billy did a good deal of caddying—at anywhere from 25 cents to $1 for 18 holes. Between customers he learned the game himself. He learned to play with a strange, cross-handed grip which latterly he has changed to the great improvement of his game.

Billy's school job was dishwashing. He worked at it five hours a day at 20 cents an hour. That just covered the dollar-a-day cost of his board and room. As a dishwasher he was the fastest—"if not the best"—in the school. "With near-boiling water, plenty of suds, I'd send an armful of dishes through with little more than one swish." He, alone among the dishwashers, kept five driers going.

Head of the Florida Bible Institute was Dr. William T. Watson, minister of a Christian and Missionary Alliance church in Tampa. Preachers did all the teaching—aided, now and then, by visiting ministers and evangelists. The doctrines

74

of the school were Biblical fundamentalism. But it was fundamentalism which, for that period and locale, had considerably more than the average measure of tolerance in it. There were Methodists and Presbyterians among the preachers, as well as some of more rigid beliefs. Dissenting points of view were given a fair and friendly hearing. There was considerable emphasis on Christian social service, if not overtly on the so called social Gospel.

But the Bible was the one indispensable textbook. A personal religious experience, i.e., conversion, was regarded as the first of every Christian's credentials. Among the students, ambition was thought of almost exclusively in terms of ambition for some form of full-time Christian service. Even the regard of the girl students for the boys generally involved religious considerations.

This last fact soon involved Billy. Wendell Phillips, having gone on before, had spied out the land for Billy's benefit. The result was a girl—reputedly as devout as she was obviously beautiful. Billy fell hard and so did she. Before the end of the semester—during which she had had first lien on Billy's time, thoughts, and limited funds—they were unofficially engaged. Finally to put something of an official seal on it, Billy —when the time of the annual class party came around— instead of sending her the twenty-five-cent corsage customary for such occasions, went all-out and bought her one for fifty cents. It was love's lucre lost. She never wore it. Without warning, but with a highly feminine sense of timing, she used this occasion to tell Billy why, in words something like this, she had thrown him over for another:

Billy, she said, had shown himself, in the months she had known him, as something of a religious ne'er-do-well. He seemed to have no particular aim for his life, certainly no clear Christian purpose, and what aim he had he didn't work at very hard. He was pleasant, but irresponsible. All in all, she didn't think that he would ever get very far or be very important. Another young man—one of Billy's best friends, as it happened—had everything Billy lacked: he stood well in his studies, he was going into the ministry, he expected to attend a theological school. This young man—in whatever the campus language of the moment happened to be—was for her, and vice versa.

That, with the cosmic finality of undergraduate romance, "finished" Billy. To Wendell Phillips, home on sick leave, he wrote: "All the stars have fallen out of my sky. There is nothing to live for. We have broken up." Wendell was quick with consolation—framed, as one would expect, in a bracket which gave his words authority. "Read Romans 8:28," he wrote: " 'And we know that all things work together for good to them that love God, to them who are the called according to His purpose. . . .' "

For Billy, who had spent most of several previous nights walking off his "desolation" on a nearby golf course, that was a prescription he could accept and one he knew how to take. It worked—even beyond what Wendell Phillips had hoped. "I have settled it once and for all with the Lord," Billy wrote. "No girl or friend or anything shall ever come first in my life. I have resolved that the Lord Jesus Christ shall have all of me. I care not what the future holds. I have determined to follow Him at any cost."

Although this consequence of unrequited love was only one of many factors in the process of making up his mind to preach, there is no doubt that, thereafter, Billy acted as a young man headed for the ministry should act. He buckled down to his studies. Most of all, he buckled down to a class he was taking in practice preaching. Not content merely to outline a sermon and, then trusting the Lord for the right words for the right place, preaching it from notes, he took to writing his sermons in full and then reading them aloud.

Such rehearsing—even in a place so favorably inclined to all kinds of sermons at all kinds of hours—was not possible in

76

the congested dormitory. Billy's courage was not up to trying out in the chapel. He found his spot in a remote corner of the campus: a stump, well hidden by trees at the swampy edge of the Hillsboro River. There, hour after hour, he did his practicing. "If there were no kind words from the audience," he says, "neither was there any criticism." When he found a sermon in a book of sermons he copied that—with adaptations—and preached it. When visiting preachers came to the school he took notes of their pulpit mannerisms and tried them out—gesture by gesture, oddity by oddity—from his stump. From these services—invocation to altar call to benediction—he omitted nothing.

"Many times, surrounded by darkness," he says, "I called out from that cypress stump and asked sinners to come forward and accept Christ. There were none to come, of course. But as I waited I seemed to hear a voice within me saying, 'One day there will be many.' "

This went on for several months; Billy, meanwhile, increasing in preaching facility and discovering, also, that he liked it. After one such solitary sermon had ended with the usual unheard altar call, Billy suddenly found himself stirred by his own appeal. That night he walked the golf course again, "arguing with the Lord," sometimes out loud, against preaching: "I can't preach . . . I couldn't learn to preach . . . I don't want to preach . . . No church would have me."

"God," said Billy, "talked right back: 'I can use you . . . I need you . . . You make the choice, I will find the place. . . .' "

Finally, past midnight, Billy said, "All right, Lord, if You want me You've got me." Later that night he wrote a one-sentence letter to his parents: "Dear Mother and Dad: I feel that God has called me to be a preacher."

One man, meanwhile, had seen in Billy some possibilities above the ordinary. He was the Reverend John R. Minder, Dean of the Institute.

"If Dean Minder hadn't taken a hand in my life," says Billy Graham, "I'm not sure where I'd be or what I'd be doing."

Minder taught a course in preaching in which Billy was enrolled. His doctrine was straight-from-the-shoulder fundamentalism. Preaching, as he taught it, required speaking with authority. And, for the Christian preacher, the source of authority is the Bible.

This emphasis on the Bible supplemented and strengthened Billy Graham's devotion to the church—a devotion which was rooted in his upbringing and has grown with the years. Increasingly during and since that period of Florida preparation his ministry has been not only Bible-centered but also church-centered.

To the preparation of sermons, Dean Minder had a simple, three-part approach: Know your subject; believe your message; speak it with conviction. "Not knowing your subject is the source of half-baked sermons: sermons which, like Ephraim, are 'a cake not turned.' Believing it halfway or in part or with reservations may be the way to produce an essay; it's no way to produce a sermon. And if there's no fire in the preacher there's likely to be none kindled in the people." Moreover, great learning and great preaching are not, necessarily, "handmaidens." "Because you've hung a theological school diploma on the front of a pulpit doesn't necessarily mean that what's spoken from behind the pulpit is the Word of God. In preparing to preach God's Word, there is no substitute for preaching it." The best evidence that it is God's Word that is being preached is that people are being converted—"seeing sinners saved by grace."

That is about the sum total of the homiletics Billy Graham has been exposed to. I am inclined to think he believes it contains the essence of almost all that is needful to effective evangelistic preaching. At any rate, his first sermons there at the Florida Bible Institute were shaped by the Minder outline of what a sermon ought to be. That is still the way he preaches.

As for conversions as the test of preaching, he has never had any other. Fifteen years after he had graduated from the Florida Bible Institute he said to the students in theology— some 400 of them—at Cambridge University in England: "A minister is not a minister unless he is winning men for Christ. If theological students don't think they can do that, they should quit studying for the ministry."

The students, reported *Time* magazine, "applauded for three minutes."

But it was not Dean Minder's teaching, says Billy Graham, so much as "his Christian life—his kindliness, his patience, his availability, when things went wrong, at all hours of the day or night," that gave Billy the lift he was in need of. It was to Dean Minder that Billy went, in the middle of the night, after his fiancée had thrown him over. It was nearly daybreak when he left. Billy remembers—and cherishes—the Scripture passage which the Dean gave him at parting, II Corinthians 1:3–4: "Blessed be the Father of mercies and the God of all comfort; who comforteth us in our affliction, that we may be able to comfort them that are in any affliction, through the comfort wherewith we ourselves are comforted."

One Sunday, after he had preached at a United Brethren church in Tampa, Billy was given an envelope containing $2.25—his "pay." It was the first time he had ever been paid for preaching and he was deeply disturbed. "How," he said, "can I make a charge for the Gospel?" He carried the envelope with its "conscience money" for several days and finally took his problem to Dean Minder. For this, too, the Dean had an authoritative answer from Scripture—a long passage from the ninth chapter of I Corinthians, ending with the thirteenth and fourteenth verses: "Know ye not that they that minister about sacred things eat of the things of the temple and they that wait upon the altar have their portion with the altar? Even so did the Lord ordain that they that proclaim the

Gospel should live of the Gospel." Thus fortified, Billy kept the money.

It was Dean Minder who, having heard of Billy's solitary preaching in the swamp, began, with some regularity, to find him a place in a pulpit. On the first such occasion, Billy had gone with Minder to visit a Baptist church not far from Palatka, Florida. When the minister of that church asked Minder to preach for him that evening, Minder, with Billy at his side, replied, "No, Billy Graham is preaching here tonight."

Billy was shocked and frightened. "You don't understand," he said to Minder, "I've never really preached in my life."

"That," said the Dean, "is what we are about to remedy. If you run out of anything to say before the time is up, I'll take over."

Billy preached. "I knew four sermons pretty well," he says. "But I used up all four of them in ten minutes."

Minder has a different report: "He did a good job, beginning with a Scripture reading and following that with his own personal testimony. It is true, his sermon, by the clock, was under par. But when he finished he asked if there were any present who wished to accept Christ as Savior. Several raised their hands. Billy asked them, during the closing hymn, to come forward for prayer. One rough-handed woodsman who had raised his hand did not move. Billy left the pulpit and went down to talk with him. As Billy approached, the man said loudly, 'You don't need to think because you go to that school down there that you know everything.' Billy, surprised and embarrassed, backed away without replying. But that man and Billy's inability to say the right word troubled him for days." The Dean helped Billy see that perhaps God in this situation was taking him down a bit, after he had preached with such liberty, and giving him an early lesson in the sin of pride.

Thereafter, Dean Minder saw to it that Billy preached

often: at rescue missions in Tampa, in trailer camps, in country churches, occasionally on street corners. Then, for one six-week stretch during his absence on the West Coast, he asked Billy to take the pulpit in his Tampa church, at $6 a Sunday. In preparation for this assignment Billy leaned heavily on the printed sermons of famous evangelical ministers. He read them silently and then out loud. He outlined them with his own additions. He preached them in practice, from the outline. They were the basic elements in his sermons, but by Sunday morning he had his own message and was ready to go. For every point he had a supporting Biblical passage, sometimes several. He talked fast, excitedly, and with conviction. He strode the platform. He always concluded with an altar call. By the time Minder returned to his church word had got around about "the boy preacher from North Carolina" and a miniature revival was in progress.

After that the calls on Billy increased. Together with Minder he conducted a revival campaign in the north Florida town of Palatka. At the end of the first week's meeting, Minder said, "Billy, these people don't want to hear me. They're coming to hear you. You stay while I go back to the school. Let's see what you do on your own."

He returned a week later, on the concluding Sunday. The church was packed and a public address system had been rigged up to take care of the overflow crowd outside. As Minder came to the platform, Billy spoke to him. "I'm supposed to preach on the second coming of Christ and I'm scared. I've run out of sermons." "Let's sit down," said Minder —and during the half-hour song service with which the meeting began, they engaged in whispered conversation, Minder occasionally gesturing, Billy nodding his head and thumbing through his Bible. When sermon-time came, Billy had an outline, complete with Scripture references and, according to Minder, he preached with facility and fervor.

The church in which Billy Graham conducted this revival

—his first "Crusade"—was Southern Baptist. Billy was Presbyterian. In Charlotte, he belonged to his parents' church—the Associate Reformed Presbyterian Church. This, an offshoot of the conservative Southern Presbyterian Church, was not, on most doctrinal matters, far removed from the ultra-conservative Southern Baptist. On one matter, however, it was removed by what, to the Baptists, was a great gulf: immersion.

During a later Florida mission the rumor got around that "the Boy Preacher" had never been baptized by immersion. It was—despite what seemed to be God's blessing on his preaching—a damaging, not to say damning, report. Billy dealt with it Scripturally by confession and restitution. One night from the pulpit he confirmed the rumor: he had not been baptized by immersion. But, he said, at the end of the meeting—along with the revival's converts—he would be. On the following Sunday in a nearby lake he was. "A glorious experience."

It was also in this church at the revival's end that, having been immersed, he became a Baptist and—with the converts of the revival as his chief credentials—he was later ordained to preach by the St. John's Baptist Association of northern Florida.

When, in 1940, Billy graduated from the Florida Bible Institute, his religious faith was past the experimental stage; his commitment to what he believed to be God's will was unconditional; the Bible, from having been a book of reference, had become, for him, God's Word, and he was thoroughly at home in it; his preaching had many lacks, but—rooted in the Scriptures and his personal experience—a note of authority was not one of them.

Almost every day during his final year, Billy managed to get in a long walk—usually several miles. It was both exercise and devotion. As he walked, he prayed. The burden of his prayer was that God would make good use of his life. Sometimes he felt so sure of the answer, so sure that God would "do exceeding abundantly, above all that we ask or think" that, in broad daylight, he would drop to his knees beside the road and offer a prayer of thanksgiving.

"It is just as well I didn't know what was ahead. If I had known I might not have believed. What I did believe was that my times were in His hands. Since, there in Florida, I took those daily walks, praying as I went, I have never believed otherwise."

At graduation the entry under his picture in the school yearbook read: "Billy Frank Graham, Charlotte, N.C. Activities: President, Senior Class; Assistant Pastor; Chaplain, Tampa Trailer Court; Volley Ball, Swimming. Personal Aim: Evangelist. Favorite Song: Faith of Our Fathers. Favorite Scripture Verse: Jude 3: "I exhort you that ye should earnestly contend for the faith which was once delivered unto the saints."

He was twenty-one.

5: A long way from Palatka

WHEN IN LONDON in May, 1955, Billy Graham was announced as preacher before the Queen and the Duke of Edinburgh in the Royal Chapel at Windsor Castle, *Punch,* in the cause of British convention, had a word of counsel:

> " 'You are young, Dr. William!' the equerry cried,
>   'With procedural problems to grapple:
>   It may be all right to be Billy outside,
>   But *not,* if you please, in the Chapel.' "

Some British newspapers, unable to get any account of this unprecedented occasion from Billy Graham, made up their own account. One printed several paragraphs from his sermon —no part of which "quotation" he had said. Another told how he had put his hand on the head of young Prince Charles and remarked, "I've a little boy at home, just like you." Prince Charles was not at the service and Billy Graham never saw him, then or later. A third quoted "a member of the choir" as saying, "He shouted a lot. In the choir we were practically deafened." There was no choir.

Whatever might have been the verdict on what Billy Graham preached that morning, it can be taken for granted,

I think, that the way he preached, with hardly any gestures and in a voice that was not raised above the conversation level, would not have given offense to—would, in fact, probably have met with the approval of—not only *Punch*, but concerned clerics of the Church of England. He had come a long way from Palatka.

When he appeared on *Meet the Press* in the spring of 1955, someone asked Billy Graham about a statement he had made some years before describing Europe as well-nigh past saving. His reply was: "I said a lot of things five years or so ago out of immaturity which I wouldn't say today."

He also undoubtedly did some things out of immaturity he would not repeat. Once at the Chicago airport, when he was about to take off on a European mission with three colleagues of the Youth for Christ movement, he knelt by the ramp for an attention-getting farewell prayer service. I am sure he would not repeat that, even though, as he said then, he was supported by no less an authority than the Apostle Paul: "We kneeled down on the shore, and prayed. And when we had taken our leave one of another, we took ship; and they returned home again." Neither, I am sure, would he care to repeat the occasion when, after calling on President Truman, he let newspaper photographers persuade him to kneel for a word of prayer on the White House lawn.

He has also come a long way from Palatka in the manner of his preaching. I once listened to a recording of one of Billy Graham's sermons from his early days as a preacher. For me at least, what he preached was almost lost in the way he preached it. The way he preached was pretty much in the tradition of the "Hot Gospeller." His voice was strident. He was inclined to rant. The same sound effects in politics would, in most places, be called demagoguery.

It brought to my mind a picture of the Billy Sunday I heard preach in my youth: coat off, tie off, his face dripping sweat, down on all fours, peering over the edge of the platform

86

as into the fiery pit, shouting, in raw and rasping voice, his defiance of the hosts of Hell. The difference in effect on me may have been due to the difference between my age then and now, or perhaps to the lifetime of quiet, not often disquieting preaching to which I have been subjected. Or it may conceivably have been due to the difference between Billy Graham and Billy Sunday as actors.

At any rate, the shouting Billy Graham seemed to me not more, but less convincing. His drama did not seem very dramatic. In that earlier, more blood-curdling rendition, he left my blood uncurdled and me unstirred.

Others have testified similarly, among them such an unquestioned authority and uninhibited critic as Billy Graham's wife Ruth. On one of their first dates, Billy, as she expected he would, took Ruth to hear him preach.

"He put me right on the front row," she says. "He had hardly started preaching before he started shouting. I thought: 'How can I sit through this?' But I did, and when he gave the invitation I was glad I did. Five people came forward. There wasn't much I could say after that. But I still didn't believe it was because he shouted."

Ruth Graham likewise does not believe that the effectiveness of her husband's preaching is increased by histrionics. "You never especially liked my biographical sermons," he once wrote her after preaching one. "But somehow I like to preach them. They are so human and down to earth and fit so many people's case." The reason for Ruth Graham's lack of enthusiasm is that the biographical sermon, being episodic and anecdotal, tempts him to try to act it out. One of his—but not her—earlier favorites is a sermon, still preached but substantially modified, on Daniel:

"Daniel," he said in this earlier version, "was the prime minister of one of the powerful countries in the world and a pal of the boss—the King of the Medes and Persians. Some jealous guys were out to get him, so they trained their spyglass on him one morning when he was praying and had his Venetian blinds up. They tattled to the King. The King was on the spot, so he said to his lawyers, 'Find me a couple of loopholes so I can spring my pal, Dan.' They just couldn't find a loophole and the King just had to send Dan to the lions.

"So what happens? Old Daniel walks in. He's not afraid. He looks the first big cat in the eye and kicks him and says, 'Move over there, Leo. I want me a nice fat lion with a soft belly for a pillow, so I can get a good night's rest. . . .' "

"As an actor," says Ruth Graham, "I'm afraid he is pretty much a ham. When he starts that kind of acting sermon, I usually start to squirm. If I'm anywhere in sight he is sure to see me and know what's the matter. Afterward, I'll say, 'Bill, Jesus didn't act out the Gospel. He just preached it. I think that's all He has called you to do!' "

The noisier, more unrestrained manner of Billy Graham's earlier preaching was undoubtedly cut to the evangelical fashion favored by the Southern evangelists he heard and admired in his youth, and was in keeping with the evangelical mores which prevailed in the places where he first preached. A quiet evangelist in those times and places would have been so far out of the groove as to be ineffective, probably suspect. Gospel preaching, as Southern Baptists taught it, called for fire, and what better proof of fire than a fiery delivery?

Although noticeably moderated, Billy Graham's sermonic manner of speech is still a long distance removed from the calm, cool, and collected delivery of those who preach a calmer, cooler, more collected faith. In a Crusade meeting he moves almost continually. He crosses and recrosses the platform in long strides: forward and back, up, down, and across. The distance the average sermon takes him, terrestrially, has been clocked at a mile and a quarter.

I once remarked to him, after one of the first Crusade meetings I attended, that it was a little disappointing, after hearing the appeal he always makes for quiet—"nobody moving, nobody whispering"—to observe, as I had that night, how restless and unquiet, in his place on the platform, his song leader Cliff Barrows seemed to be. He suggested that, "to get a close-up of Cliff," I sit on the platform the next night, which I did. I soon saw, to my embarrassment, the reason for Cliff Barrows' "restlessness."

Just before the sermon, while Beverly Shea sang, Billy Graham hooked one end of a long electric cord into his belt and attached it to the buttonhole mike he wears, like an over-sized silver tie clasp, on his necktie. The other end ran to the radio control room. Between the control room and the pulpit were some fifty feet of extra line curled neatly on a chair beside Cliff Barrows. For the sermon's forty to fifty minutes, it was his exacting job to pay out that line and draw it in as Billy Graham—now fast, now slowly—advanced and retreated, to give him just enough line, but not too much, and all the time to keep it from getting entangled in his always moving, never predictable feet.

On the radio, Billy Graham once spoke at a Walter Winchell pace. Latterly he has slowed a bit. His staccato radio delivery was deliberately planned.

"Why shouldn't it be?" he says. "If God expects me to give thought to what's in my sermons, as I know He does, isn't it likely He expects me to give some thought as to how to deliver them?"

He listened, hours on end, to successful news commentators and radio personalities and finally concluded that, in so far as delivery had anything to do with it, radio ratings were probably helped by rapid-fire speech and, perhaps, a touch of Walter Winchell breathlessness. The development of that technique was not, for him, very difficult.

Neither, during his usual sermon, is there ever much pause between gestures. He moves from one to the next without interlude or breather. In the one that is most familiar he lifts up

89

the open Bible, first in one hand then in the other, sometimes with both, holding it aloft, as someone has said, "like a pizza from a hot oven." One observer given to statistics recorded during one sermon twenty-one gestures in the space of little more than a minute: "arms flailing, arms folded, arms akimbo, fists clenched, palms opened, slapping the Bible, the pulpit, the platform railing, finger pointing to Heaven, to Hell, at you. . . ."

But when, at the end of his sermon, Billy Graham gives the invitation to "make a decision for Christ," then he does not move or gesture. He stands in one place behind the pulpit, his arms folded, his head slightly bowed, his chin cupped in one hand. He does not plead or cajole or argue or call on his associates to witness to the numbers coming, as he once did. He speaks quietly, soberly, without excitement or emotion.

A great many influences have worked to moderate from its Florida beginnings his preaching manner, to subdue, somewhat, his voice, slow down a bit his speaking pace, and smooth the rough edges from some of his colloquialisms: among these influences—in addition to his wife—time and travel, his contact with other ministers of many denominations whose faith he has found to be no less sure for being more quietly expounded, his own maturing sense of the fitness of things.

He has also learned to suit his speaking manner to the place and the occasion. I have seen him, gowned and hooded, preach from a pulpit of upper-bracket dignity and, for forty minutes, not noticeably change his upright stance or gesture more than mildly or come any closer to shouting than such a congregation would be accustomed to—which would not be close. For a week, during the All-Scotland Crusade in Glasgow in the spring of 1955, he conducted early morning devotions over the BBC network. During those fifteen meditative minutes each morning, he never raised his voice above conversation level and he spoke so slowly that, to anyone accustomed to hearing him elsewhere, it sounded like hesitation—which, knowing him, I'm sure it wasn't.

When, early in 1954, he went to London to begin the Greater London Crusade, he had been billed by the press as a "Hot Gospeller" and the reporters who went the first nights to the Harringay Arena were looking for "a ranting, tearing show." Seldom has the press been more totally crossed up. Looking back on it, the London *Times*, archguardian of, among other things, British dignity, declared:

"It is important—and no more than fair to Mr. Graham— to say that if his lavish barrage of advance publicity has given rise to some suspicion that the Greater London Crusade would turn out to be lacking in taste, discretion and (not to strain the point) alien to the British way, the event was most demure.

"There are preachers already at work in Britain, particularly, perhaps, in Nonconformist connections, who are not only overswept by more passion but who command more of the demagogic parts than Mr. Graham."

Eighteen months later, in England in the fall of 1955, Billy Graham, on the invitation of the 400 undergraduate members of the Cambridge Inter-Collegiate Christian Union —CICCU, popularly called "Kick-You" by both its friends and foes—conducted a week's series of meetings at Cambridge University.

"It was one of the most difficult and hardest weeks of my life," Billy Graham wrote to Ruth. "History may say that it was one of the most profitable."

The meetings were held in the University church. The crowds overflowed and filled several other churches tied in by telephone. Five hundred students—more than twice as many as during the still-remembered meetings there of Dwight L. Moody—made decisions for Christ. "Indifference has been broken down and at least for a few days all Cambridge has been talking of Jesus Christ. As I go to bed tonight, I go with

91

peace in my heart and a great joy overflowing me for the privilege of serving Him this week."

During that week a correspondent of the United Press cabled this description of the Billy Graham whom Cambridge saw and heard:

"A new Billy Graham changed from serge suit to cap and gown and tried out his commonfolks preaching on the intellectually elite this week. The meeting of minds was polite, but enthusiastic.

"The evangelist came with his North Carolina drawl and dog-eared Bible into the big-brain country of Cambridge University. His style has changed, his listeners have changed and his surroundings have changed. The effect has been the same.

"Conservative and intellectual Cambridge turned out wholeheartedly. Congregations packed Great St. Mary's Church from the first night and overflowed into extra seats in the aisles. The listeners filled two other Cambridge churches. The wire network carried his talks to 15 other universities throughout England, Scotland, and Ireland.

"This wasn't sweaty Harringay where Graham attracted 12,000 Londoners nightly for weeks in 1954. It wasn't vast Wembley where he drew hundreds of thousands last year. This was cloistered Cambridge and Graham adapted his style to fit. He changed to academic robes. He spoke quietly. He came without ballyhoo. The pitch of his voice is lower. The content is more intellectual.

"But the message of Christianity was unaltered."

Billy Graham once took me to his study in his former home in Montreat, North Carolina. It was a comfortable, pine-paneled, second-floor room, supplied with a work desk, typewriter, dictaphone, and tape recorder. Several shelves were stacked with his sermons—he has several hundred in outline—in black looseleaf notebooks. The room was well stocked with books, none of them recent fiction; few nonreligious, save a secondhand edition of Shakespeare, several other standard classics, and a number of biographies. There were scores of books of devotional bent and religious experience and of sermons by preachers ancient and modern—the modern ones being chiefly sermons of evangelists. Nearest at hand were a Concordance and the Bible in several translations.

He was spending, then, four to five hours a day in his study. But studying is a practice he pursues, I think, less from pleasure than from apprehension. He told me that, several years before, he had come upon a statement by the late Senator William Edgar Borah that William Jennings Bryan would have been President of the United States "if he had read more and spoken less."

"That hit me with a terrific jolt," he said. "I suddenly realized I was speaking more and reading less. Maybe I was starting to coast a bit mentally. Since then I've spent more time in this study and got in more hours of reading on my trips."

There is little tangible evidence in his sermons that he reads a great deal outside the Bible, and some magazines. Almost every radio sermon on his *Hour of Decision* begins with —or has somewhere near the lead—a news peg on which, to start off with at least, he hangs his theme: the figures on juvenile delinquency, the suicide of a film star, the explosion of a hydrogen bomb, comments on the state of the world by Eisenhower, Churchill, Eden, J. Edgar Hoover, Toynbee, Niebuhr, even the Pope. But quotes or illustrations from current books or literature in general are few and far between. He has had, up to recently, no help in research, the gathering, classifying, and filing of sermonic material.

In addition to newspapers and magazines, most of his non-Biblical illustrations are either drawn from his own recent experiences—the stories of converts, comments of persons, often ministers, he has lately met, travel items—or are of the home, the family, and the home-town variety. When, as he often does, he used his wife and children to illustrate a point in a sermon he was preaching in his home church in North Carolina, his daughter Ann, five, whispered to her grandmother, "Why doesn't he keep all that to himself?" If he did, quite a few of his sermons would lose quite a bit of their humor and warmth. Balshazzar, the family's Great Pyrenees dog—so named because, like his namesake, he is inclined to gluttony—also serves an occasionally illustrative purpose. So, in sermons I have heard, do North Carolina sunrises, sunsets, and watermelons, his father's dairy farm and the 3 A.M. milking, the goat he had as a boy, his golf game, a country club near Asheville "that's harder to get into than lots of churches."

Some illustrations he uses repeatedly. One of them is on faith:

"Suppose I were driving along the road at fifty miles an hour and I came to the crest of a hill. Would I slam on my brakes, stop my car, get out, walk to the top of the hill and look over to see if that road continues? No, I wouldn't. I would trust the highway department of that state. I would continue at my normal rate of speed, secure in the knowledge that the road went on even though I couldn't see it. I would accept it on faith. So it is with saving faith in Christ."

Another concerns the "surrender" required for conversion.

"I heard about a man some years ago who was rolling a wheelbarrow back and forth across the Niagara River above Niagara Falls on a tightrope. He put a 200-pound sack of dirt in the wheelbarrow and rolled it over and then rolled it back. He turned to the crowd: 'How many of you believe I can roll a man across?'

"Everybody shouted. One man in the front row was very emphatic in his professed belief. The performer pointed to him. 'You're next.'

"Well, you couldn't see that fellow for dust. He actually didn't believe it. He said he believed it; he thought he believed

94

it. But he didn't believe enough to get into that wheelbarrow.

"Just so with Christ. There are many who say they believe in Him, that they will follow Him. But they have never actually committed their lives, surrendered themselves 100 per cent to Him. They've never gotten into the wheelbarrow."

At least half a dozen times in the course of one Crusade, I have heard him use the platform on which he stood as an illustration of the need for making an open decision for Christ. He stepped down and pointed at it. "Now this looks like a good platform." He shook the railing. "I believe it's a well-built platform." He put his foot, tentatively, on the step. "But I have to step on it before I know. I have to trust this platform enough to try it. You may think that Christ is all the Bible says He is. But you'll never know until you decide to try Him. That's what we are going to ask you to do right here, tonight."

Not in illustrations only, but in the way he phrases his ideas, there is repetition in Billy Graham's sermons. He says often, "If you can commit a sin and get away with it, I'll close this Bible, quit preaching and go back to a North Carolina farm." Not many of his Crusade sermons go by without this: "The Bible teaches you have a body. Your body has eyes, ears, nose, hands, feet. The Bible also teaches you have a soul. Your soul has certain attributes such as conscience, memory, intelligence. Your soul is the real you. Your body goes to its grave. But your soul lives on. The Bible teaches your soul will live on forever in one of two places: it will live on in Heaven or in Hell."

Charles H. Spurgeon, the famous English preacher of the nineteenth century, once remarked that a sermon "is not a sermon until it has been preached ten times." Benjamin Franklin, a great admirer of the eighteenth-century evangelist George Whitefield, said that the sermons Whitefield had "often preached" were invariably improved in "every accent, every emphasis, every modulation" by the "infrequent repetition." Dwight L. Moody preached many of his sermons more than

95

a hundred times. "If I find a sword effective, why shouldn't I use it?"

Billy Graham has found that it does not work quite that way with his preaching. It is true he preaches some of his sermons repeatedly. But only after he has "reimmersed" himself in the subject and "rekindled" his urge to speak on it. "The first time I preach a sermon, it is out of my heart and I often am on fire with it. Sometimes, when I try to preach that same sermon again, I've got everything: all the ideas, all the illustrations, all the Scripture passages—everything except the fire. I can preach the same sermon the same way, but if God's hand is lifted, it is sounding brass and tinkling cymbal."

It is, I suppose, because he does not repeat a sermon until he feels he has recaptured its fire that his "repeats"—even the "repeats" of illustrations and ideas—seldom, in the usual sense, sound repetitious.

Perhaps if he had had more training in the techniques of preparing sermons, a Billy Graham sermon would have more of those characteristics which, by literary and structural standards, would mark it as "a finished product." In the well-rounded, well-put sense, there is little style to his preaching, very few phrases which, by the way they are turned, merit being called striking, very few of those carefully contrived epigrams—often alliterative—so dear to the hearts of some preachers. Perhaps he could if he tried. I have not found any evidence that he tries. Perhaps if he did try his preaching would lose some of its authority in the process.

This does not mean that Billy Graham's sermons do not reveal preparation, but only that the kind of preparation they reveal is obviously aimed at some other effect than literary excellence or intellectual titillation. His sermons are what one would expect from his kind of preparation, and the authority with which he preaches them derives, in fact, from the fact that he prepares them that way.

Whatever the process lacks in hours spent in general reading and research, construction and phrasemaking, there is no lack of hours spent in their devotional preparation. His sermons, in fact, are a devotional production: born of and saturated in Scripture reading and prayer. Most of his sermon ideas come in the morning hour—or hours—he spends in private devotions. There he will be reading a Bible passage— one he has read, no doubt, many times, and perhaps preached on before—when, he says, "a wholly new line of thought will suddenly open up—like a curtain raised on a view I had never seen before."

Once after reading and rereading, during Holy Week, the various accounts of the Crucifixion, he wrote to Ruth Graham: "This morning I think I could preach several weeks on the subject. There seems to be no limit to the height or depth of the atonement. It is like so much of the Scriptures—yet, I think, much more so: a diamond with a thousand facets, each sending out a brilliant ray, yet different from all the rest. And when I preach about it my forty minutes pass so quickly. . . ."

When, in his Bible reading, such a "curtain" is raised he will read the same passage in all the translations he has available: the King James, the American Revised, the Revised Standard and, if it is from the New Testament, the Phillips and the Williams translations. He will turn to Cruden's Concordance and Nave's *Topical Bible,* this last, regarded by some as outmoded, one of his indispensable aids, and run down and read related passages. By the time, hours later, he reaches for the dictaphone—his rough notes and several open Bibles in front of him—to get down a draft outline, he is, as he says, "immersed in the subject and saturated in Scripture."

His sermon outlines that I have seen have had an average of fifteen to twenty Scripture references some of which, of course, he does not use. One of them had thirty-nine.

"What other authoritative source book is there for the preacher," he says, "than the Bible? You can quote Doctor Somebody or Professor So-and-So—and many preachers do.

But good and interesting as they may be, helpful as they sometimes are, such quotations can't be a substitute for Scripture. It's not man's word people are hungry to hear preached, it's God's Word."

He never starts to dictate an outline until, first, he has "threshed it out with God." In fact his sermons are as saturated with prayer as with Scripture. Often, dictating an outline to his secretary—generally pacing the floor—he will suddenly switch, without stopping his pacing, from dictating to praying and then, just as suddenly, resume the dictation. He says, "Either a sermon is of the Holy Spirit or it isn't. If it isn't, I want to know it and I won't want to preach it. Praying about it is the only way I know to find out."

Finding out is not always easy. He writes in his diary of "agonizing" over a sermon. "All day long," he wrote to Ruth Graham, "I have been praying as to what my message should be tonight. In my devotions, I have finally decided that I am to speak on faith." Before the opening of one mission he wrote: "I seriously doubt if I have ever preached with more fear and trembling, with such a sense of inadequacy and unpreparedness."

Sometimes after he has preached he questions whether his prayers in preparing the sermon were answered as he thought:

"I don't think in the past year I have had a greater struggle preaching than tonight. I wanted the floor to open up and let me fall through. Only a few people came forward to receive Christ at the end of the service. I have come back to the room deeply disturbed, discouraged. I sometimes wonder why I am ever in the ministry."

His usual testimony, however, is very different. "The Lord thrilled my heart in the preparation of the message." "It was thrilling as I worked, for it seemed the Spirit of God swept over me time after time, giving me assurance." "As I dictated I felt the presence of God there in the room with me."

His most frequent comments have triumph and thanksgiving

98

in them: "I felt the presence and the power of God." "The Lord had laid it on my heart to speak on I Peter 2:1–5. I could sense that the Holy Spirit was working mightily." "Last night, in spite of great physical weakness and this severe cold, I had great liberty. To God Be the Glory." "I sensed this was going to be a glorious night. I felt good in my soul. As I stood in the pulpit I felt more power than any night before, and all through the sermon I was quietly thanking God for the liberty He gave."

There was once, in the United States, a considerable company of so-called "preachers" who claimed that the only preparation required for their kind of "faith preaching" was for them to open their mouths, which thereupon God filled with the right words. Although Billy Graham does not belong to that "school," I am sure he believes it can happen—provided the preacher, before opening his mouth to the Lord, had, for a considerable period before, opened his heart and mind. And if in his case the Lord is not often called on to provide ready-made sermons on the spot, Billy Graham is sure that, not infrequently, He does intervene and change, sometimes near the last minute, his preaching plans.

"Time after time," he says, "the Lord has made it clear that the sermon I was preparing for a particular night was not the sermon I ought to preach; that another message was in order. He knows the need of that particular audience better than I do. So I don't argue. I change."

It is in keeping with this readiness, on short notice but on good authority, to make a quick shift, that Billy Graham when he addresses civic clubs or other special groups dislikes to be assigned a specific subject. He prefers to keep his "freedom to change at the last minute." So far, he says, "the Lord has never let me down."

There is, I think, less danger that the Lord will let him down than that—by doing too much and studying too little— he may spread himself too thin and thus let the Lord down.

That is one of Billy Graham's great concerns and accounts for his plan for longer periods of "recharging" between major preaching missions.

Meanwhile, it is evident that in his preaching, Billy Graham, in every particular, has come a long way from Palatka—save only in the essentials of the faith which and by which he preaches.

"There's nothing about my preaching that can't be improved on," he says, "save the Gospel I try to preach."

"Personally," said a minister whose church had reluctantly gone along in support of a Billy Graham Crusade, "I don't care too much for Billy Graham or for what he preaches or for the way he preaches it. But I'm inclined to think the Almighty does."

6: Out of the South

IT IS POSSIBLE that Billy Graham might have become the kind of evangelist he is even though he had not been born, raised, and had his early education in the South. But it is not very likely. It is also possible he might have become what he is even though, for his later education and the starting of his career, he had not gone North. But that is not very likely either. And it is just as unlikely he would be what he is if somewhere— South or North—he had not met Ruth McCue Bell and married her.

The South into which, in Charlotte, North Carolina, on November 9, 1917, William Franklin Graham, Jr., was born was probably no more religious—per capita—than other parts of the country. Worldliness and the sins accruing therefrom were at least as widespread as anywhere else and the incidence of worse sins—some of them indigenously Southern—was at least normal. Southerners, so inclined, went about their sinning with no less ardor and, perhaps, more flair than their wayfaring kindred elsewhere.

It was not, however, the worldly South but, separated from it by a great gulf, the South of undiluted orthodoxy into which Billy Graham was born. That South, after its manner and with

101

its alleged limitations, was definitely more religious than the U.S. average.

In that South, evangelism—the tent-meeting, repentance-provoking, conversion-producing kind of evangelism—had lost little of its eighteenth- and nineteenth-century vigor and the peripatetic, fire-breathing, love-offering evangelist little of his one-time repute. This was the one area of twentieth-century America where Jonathan Edwards and George Whitefield would probably have felt religiously at home, and where, without much change in the theology of their eighteenth-century preaching or in the way they preached it, they could have been sure of a large, responsive following.

I am inclined to think that Wesley and Moody would have been less at home there—unless to stir the consciences of the presumed-elect as in their day in England and Scotland they stirred them. Wesley and Moody preached a New Testament God of love who drew men to Him, whereas the God of the revivalist South was, oftener, the Old Testament God of judgment who drove them by fear. There were inescapable social implications to the doctrine of personal salvation which Wesley and Moody preached. Their Kingdom of Heaven was, often, uncomfortably this-worldly, not merely an Apocalyptic escape. The prophetic succession in which they stood was not so much that of Ezekiel and Daniel, given to trances and pronouncing doom, as of Amos declaring, "Let judgment roll down as waters, and righteousness as a mighty stream" and Micah, "What doth the Lord require of thee, but to do justly, and to love mercy, and to walk humbly with thy God?"

But whatever, in the estimate of some, may be said to be lacking, the fact is that the religion of the fundamentalist South was and is essentially what most of evangelical Protestantism once was and, by the unrepealed assertions of its basic creeds, still professes to be. Today, many of those essentials, instead of being repealed, are being returned to. It is possible that one day our one-time modernists will, as a consequence of that

102

return, have achieved sufficient Christian grace to admit their debt to the so-called fundamentalist South for having kept these essentials alive and vital until, in God's good time, a neo or some other orthodoxy came along to make them, once more, intellectually acceptable. It is even possible that Reinhold Niebuhr, in the upper intellectual reaches, and Billy Graham, among the rest of us, will in historical retrospect, be bracketed as evangelists of the same revival.

At any rate, in the South into which Billy Graham was born, religion, when it took, took harder than anywhere else in the country. Once taken, it was a matter of more unrelieved, not to say of more deadly, earnestness. First claim on almost every youth of more than ordinary promise was God's. It was as unlikely that such a youth could avoid considering, with parental blessing, a career as preacher, evangelist, or missionary as that, elsewhere, consideration of any such career would be anything but avoided—that, too, with parental blessing. One day in the Graham home, a visiting preacher sent twelve-year-old Billy on his way with the remark: "Run along, little fellow, you'll never be a preacher." I am sure Billy's parents were as chagrined and disturbed by that as parents in the average, casual church family would have been amused that anyone had given such an idea a thought and pleased that it was not meant to be taken seriously.

Billy Graham's father, William Franklin Graham, Sr., six feet two, like his son, only lankier, was born and raised on his father's prosperous dairy farm on the outskirts of Charlotte. He still lives there; the dairy farm is still prosperous, but it is no longer outskirts. All but 75 of the family acres, once numbering 400, have been sold for real estate development. With his younger son, Melvin, he still runs the dairy. How well "Frank" Graham has prospered, he is too Scotch to let his family have an inkling, partly, no doubt, from fear lest if they did, his Scotch frugality could no longer be so faithfully indulged.

Frank Graham's religious raising was Methodist, and in a Methodist revival in his youth he was "soundly converted."

"Frank," said a friend the next day, "your face looks as though you'd been converted."

"That's what's happened," said Frank Graham.

"Do you suppose," said his friend, "you could help me get what you've got?"

He could, and there, on a Charlotte street corner, he did.

"I'd rather have Frank Graham praying for me," a prominent preacher said recently, "than almost anyone else I know."

Both Billy Graham's grandfathers fought for the Confederacy in the Civil War. One of them, Benjamin Coffey, lost his right eye and his right leg at the battle of Gettysburg. Once in the summer of 1955 after lunching with President Eisenhower at Gettysburg the President asked Billy Graham if he had ever visited the battlefield. When he said no, the President forthwith took him on a personally conducted tour in the course of which, explaining the battle's strategy, he asked if Billy Graham remembered his grandfather's regiment. When he gave it, the President took him to the approximate spot where his grandfather had fought and fallen.

Billy Graham's mother was Morrow Coffey—named Morrow as her father had planned to name the prospective minister-son which she proved not to be. She was Presbyterian, well grounded at an early age in the Shorter Catechism, given to memorizing Scripture passages, and, from her own girlhood experiences, a believer in a God who "gives direct answers to prayer." She was never, in the usual and prescribed sense, "converted," a fact which—despite her faith and works—is, I suspect, a cause for regret, perhaps even a little uneasiness, among the converted Grahams.

It should be said that because of Billy Graham's early Presbyterian inculcations from his mother, also because of his wife's unassuming Presbyterianism, he has remained at least as much a Presbyterian as he has become a Baptist. Today in fact he is invited to more Presbyterian functions than Baptist. He has addressed the General Assembly of the Presbyterian Church, U.S. (Southern), the General Assembly of the Church of Scotland, and in 1956 before the General Assembly of the Presbyterian Church, U.S.A. (Northern), gave the opening address at the two hundred and fiftieth anniversary of the founding of the Presbyterian Church in this country.

To return to his parents, it should be said that it was not entirely evangelical considerations which first drew Frank Graham and Morrow Coffey together. From his side there was the fact that she—as a family friend described her—was "a choice parcel of Southern femininity" and, from her side, there was the fact that he "drove around in one of the best buggies in the section."

Billy Graham is the oldest of four children: two boys and two girls. The Graham home was a place in which—from the standpoint of both industry and religion—little was left to chance. Billy began to help with the milking when he was eight. In grammar and high school his day began at 3 A.M.—with up to twenty-five cows to milk before school. After school he often plowed until dark. It is understandable why, on the one hand, he was known as one of the fastest milkers in Mecklenberg County and, on the other hand, why, with such a farm program, his schoolwork was considerably below average. When in high school he made the baseball team and began, nights, to "go tooling around Charlotte" in the family car he fell so far below average that there was some doubt he could graduate with his class—which, however, he did.

The family belonged to the Associate Reformed Presbyterian Church—which, among other Conservative practices, was a psalm-singing church. "I was well into my teens," says Billy Graham, "before I had heard a hymn sung in church." The finer points of Christian nurture were left to his mother. Already, at ten, she had helped him memorize—and sought, no doubt, to help him understand—the questions and answers of

105

the Shorter Catechism from Number 1: "What is the chief end of Man?" through Number 107: "What doth the conclusion of the Lord's Prayer teach us?" It is, I think, a reasonable assumption that some measure of Billy Graham's authoritative no "ifs," "buts," or "maybes" kind of preaching derives from the authoritative answers, totally devoid of qualification, which the Shorter Catechism provides for each of its 107 crucial questions.

Billy's mother also encouraged him to take part—beginning with a "sentence prayer" rehearsed in advance—in the family's daily devotions and to memorize Scripture verses. His first was Proverbs 3:6: "In all thy ways acknowledge Him and He shall direct thy paths."

Other aspects of his Christian nurture and discipline were dealt with less gently by his father. Once, for fidgeting during the undoubtedly overlong sermon, Frank Graham solemnly took off his broad leather belt and, without leaving the church, gave Billy a well-remembered whacking. When one day Billy turned up at the dairy barn with a cud of chewing tobacco in his cheek, his father—although he chewed tobacco himself—gave him another notable whipping, and summarily fired the hired man, an old family retainer and friend, who gave Billy "the stuff."

Frank Graham's disciplines were not only punitive but sometimes precautionary. Thus, when the sale of beer was legalized in North Carolina, he went to town and bought two bottles. Back at the farm, he opened them and forced Billy and one of his sisters to "guzzle." The results were all that could be expected. Billy Graham has not touched liquor since.

The religion of Billy Graham's parents is such that they have taken his phenomenal ministry very much in their stride—as though this was the precise answer they had expected all along to their prayers for a preacher-son.

"Billy," says his father, "is doing just what he's supposed to be doing, and if he weren't the Lord would soon clip his

106

wings. The Lord just put His hand on him for this kind of work. You take Melvin, Billy's younger brother. He's a powerful good dairy farmer. He's also doing what the Lord intended him to do. He's just the same kind of Christian boy as his brother."

His mother says, "So far as I can see, Billy really has this one big God-given talent and no more. I just couldn't imagine him sitting still in one place as the pastor of one local congregation. No, God has set the road for Billy and that's where he's going."

"I want to thank God," said Billy Graham in one of his recent radio sermons, "for a Christian father and mother who faithfully, both by precept and example, brought me up to reverence and worship God. I only hope that I may have as effective an influence on my children as my parents had on me."

Meanwhile, by the time he graduated from Sharon High School in Charlotte in 1936, Billy was dutifully if not notably religious, regular in his attendance on and observance of "the appointed means of grace." He was more than ordinarily good-looking, was popular with the girls, had a car to get around in, and, despite his farm duties, got around in it and was a considerably above-average baseball player.

This was the summer of Billy's conversion under the revival ministry of Mordecai Ham. Despite the certainty of that experience—the story of which is told in an earlier chapter—it appears that baseball was still the nearest thing he had to a purpose in life. He had felt that way since grammar school—a feeling that was fanned into a considerable flame when Babe Ruth, on a visit to Charlotte, shook Billy's hand and assured the boy who wanted to be a first baseman that he certainly had the build for it. Once when, in an unexpected display of talent, he won a school oratorical contest, the school principal told him, with his hopeful parents beaming, "Billy, you've got it in you to be a great orator." To which Billy's deflating answer was: "Thanks. I'd rather be a great first baseman."

He could have played first base for Sharon's semipro team that first summer out of high school. His fielding was good. He batted around .275. There was an offer of $10 to $15 a game. But the local team's finances were shaky; games were too few and far between. So, not anxious to continue the 3 A.M. milking routine, Billy—along with Grady and T. W. Wilson, his closest friends—took the two-hour indoctrination lecture and the two-day trial run that turned him, for the summer, into a Fuller Brush man. He went, however, considerably beyond the requirements of that indoctrination—starting every day's round with prayer and praying as he went from customer to customer. He implemented his praying by working early and late, soon outdistancing the Wilson brothers, and winding up the summer outselling every other salesman in the Carolinas, including the district manager.

"I believed in the product," he says, "and sincerity is the biggest part of selling anything—including the Christian Plan of Salvation."

Billy Graham's conversion having "taken" as conclusively as it did and his parents, in the wake of that experience, having had their prayerful hope for a preacher-son rekindled, it was almost inevitable that that fall after high school he would enroll in a Bible school. Although there are many such schools in the North, their influence in the South has been much more pervasive. Some are hardly known beyond their immediate locality; few have anything much in the way of general academic standing; most of them exist—as faith ventures—on a hand-to-mouth basis.

But they have been and are a potent influence. It is due in considerable degree to them that the beliefs and practices of Southern fundamentalism have so largely escaped the ravages of modern science, historical research, Biblical criticism, and have been passed on so generally unsullied from one believing generation to the next.

I have told in another chapter how Billy Graham enrolled

108

in such a school—Bob Jones College—"just in case," as his parents put it, he might be "called" to the ministry. I have also told there how he moved on from Bob Jones to the Florida Bible Institute near Tampa, Florida, how he was "called" to preach and how he started preaching. When, after three and a half years, Billy Graham in 1940 graduated from the Florida Bible Institute he won a certificate as a Bible-trained student.

He then became a Southern Baptist and, as a consequence of considerable revivalist success as the "Boy Preacher," won ordination as a Bible-believing minister at the hands of a theologically if not academically meticulous Association of Florida Baptists.

When he got back to Charlotte, invitations from a number of communities to conduct revivals were waiting for him. One of them, to York, Pennsylvania, he accepted and there, in the summer of 1940, he conducted, with moderate success, his first revival on his own and his first meeting in the North.

At twenty-one, with the Boy Preacher angle good for a few years more, he could undoubtedly have moved on from there into what must have looked, from where he stood, like "big-time" evangelism. It is possible—since, we are told, with God all things are possible—that he might have gone on from such beginnings into what he has become. But it is far more probable that, instead, he would by now be shaping up as another in the evangelistic succession of Mordecai Hams who still pitch their tents, launch their attacks on sin and their saving call to sinners first in the cities, then in the tank towns, finally in the hill country of the fundamentalist South. That is a long and honorable succession, but not, on any world scale, revival-inducing.

At any rate, with the help of his parents, he resisted the lure. A greater urge was for more education or, rather, for education in something more than the Bible. That fall, after prayerful consideration and with his father spying out the land to make sure this gave promise of an answer to their

109

prayers, he enrolled at Wheaton College, a coeducational school located twenty-five miles west of Chicago in Wheaton, Illinois.

"It was no accident my boy chose Wheaton," says his mother. "He was prayed into that place."

There can be few schools, I think, better qualified to justify such praying. Wheaton was founded by pioneers who, like so many, had come by oxcart, covered wagon, and boat from New England: pious people who with their plows had broken the plains and with their savings and their faith had planted Christian colleges wherever they went and as soon as they pushed the frontier far enough back to plant their crops. Many of these colleges, often against odds which, on any other than a religious level, would have been impossible, have survived. Some of them have prospered. Many of them have kept alive and vital the religious purposes for which most independent U.S. colleges were founded but which some of the more famous among them, for all save ceremonial purposes, have abandoned in favor of aims more reflective of our more secularized society and presumably more appealing to secular-minded donors.

Wheaton College was founded in 1853 by Wesleyan Methodists. In that heyday of denominationalism it was and has remained interdenominational, although today its orthodoxy is probably more Presbyterian than Methodist. It was a venture of faith in the beginning: its first building a one-story limestone schoolhouse. It has remained a venture of faith—with, today, a thirty-five-acre campus, an endowment of nearly $8,000,000 and a student body of 1,600.

Its academic rating is in the top bracket among U.S. institutions of higher education.

Most notable, however, of Wheaton's characteristics is that —faculty, students, and alumni—it still takes seriously the motto carved over the main entrance to Blanchard Hall: "For Christ and His Kingdom."

Each semester at Wheaton starts with a week's evangelistic
110

services. Each day classes start with prayer. There is a daily devotional chapel hour for all students. There are numerous voluntary prayer groups during the week. Campus revivals are not uncommon. The highest honor any student can achieve is election as president of the Christian Council, an honor which, in his senior year, came to Billy Graham.

Of its present president, Dr. V. Raymond Edman—whose visits to Wheaton-enlisted Christian missionaries have taken him eleven times around the world—Billy Graham has said, "I do not know any man who more nearly lives Christ than this man. He literally walks with the Lord."

These notable characteristics have produced notable consequences, not only the usual run of college presidents, preachers, writers, business and professional men and women, but in addition, more than 1,000 foreign missionaries serving today in 88 countries.

They were Wheaton graduates—the first I ever met—whom I visited in the interior of Liberia where they were building and are now successfully operating the first radio station in that part of West Africa and perhaps the first religious radio station on the Continent. There were five families of them—musicians, technicians, language experts—wholly supported by "prayer groups," most of them organized in various parts of the U.S. by other Wheaton graduates. Their kind, I have found since, are not exceptional, but expected at Wheaton.

What response is called forth by the Wheaton combination of high and rigid academic standards and an unapologetic, unremitting emphasis on religion is indicated by the fact that, for the 500 places in the entering freshman class in 1954, there were nearly 5,000 applicants.

Billy Graham's nearly four years at the Florida Bible Institute netted him one year's credits at Wheaton, and he entered as a sophomore. He chose to major—he is not sure why unless from a desire for a closer-up of the animal he was setting out to improve—in anthropology. Academically, however, his rec-

111

ord at Wheaton was short of outstanding save in Bible, where, thanks to the Bible Institute, he was well out in front.

Billy Graham arrived at Wheaton short on cash—his father believing that his son should earn the greater part of his way. But he was soon a marked man on the campus, partly because he was tall, blond, and handsome, with a "come-hither" Southern drawl, partly also because—spick, span, and flashy in other habits of dress—invariably that first year he wore brown, high-top shoes, the kind that reach well above the anklebone. To earn his living expenses he drove a truck, did work for the building and grounds department of the college, and pickup jobs around town. Before long he was able to buy the truck and set himself up in an after-hours hauling business. This, as will appear, was lucky—doubtless, in fact, providential for him.

In one respect—of first importance in the Wheaton catalogue of talents—Billy was in something of a class by himself: namely, as a preacher. Word of his preaching gifts and of the use he had been making of them on the revival circuit had reached the campus from other evangelists and also, no doubt, had been spread by Southern friends who had preceded him to Wheaton. Billy himself seldom turned down a chance to talk about or practice preaching.

His practicing was done in the third-floor room of the house where he lived. He practiced whenever he had time—which was often in the middle of the night. He also did his sermon preparations at unorthodox hours and sometimes by unorthodox methods. His roommate in his senior year—Jimmie Johnson—recalls being routed out of bed by Billy:

"Jimmie, I've got to preach tomorrow night. You've got to help me get an outline."

Jimmie—in this, perhaps, more mouse than man—would crawl out, snap on the light, get out his Bible, and help Billy with the outline.

"Then, the next night," says Jimmie Johnson, "I would go

and hear him preach that outline and he'd do such a tremendous job I'd sit there and take notes on my own sermon."

Billy, in fact, uniformly did such a good preaching job that before long his pulpit fees were sufficient to cover his expenses and enable him to close out the trucking business. In his junior year, so considerable had his preaching reputation become, he was asked to take over as pastor of the Wheaton Student Church—a post which had been held by Dr. Edman until his election to the college presidency.

But more happened to Billy Graham at Wheaton than his development in facility as a preacher. New windows of both mind and spirit were opened for him. Although orthodox in theology and steeped in the Scriptures, Wheaton was a new world intellectually, a world not wholly bounded by the Bible. He came for the first time into serious contact with areas of knowledge which were not necessarily suspect because they were not invariably Biblical. These discoveries, it is true, did not turn him toward scholarship. But they did begin to turn him away from that kind of strait-jacketing religion which for lack of intellectual exposure might have become in him, as it has in others, religious bigotry.

There were other religious consequences. Billy Graham's beliefs were not watered down. Wheaton was not a place where that was likely to happen to such beliefs as his. But Wheaton was a place of wider contact; where narrowness was not rated first among Christian virtues, if virtue at all; where the concept was held, without heresy, that God, in His infinite wisdom, might find ways to make use of others whose theological cast and mold were not, in every large and small particular, precisely like one's own. After Wheaton, Billy Graham's preaching had no less authority—doubtless more. But its tone and content were somewhat less in the tradition of Jonathan Edwards' "Sinners in the Hands of an Angry God" and somewhat more in the tradition of John Wesley, who seldom had anything to

113

say about Hell's fires, never used fear in his altar calls, and for whom God's foremost attribute was love; and also in the tradition of Dwight L. Moody, whose early preaching portrayed "a vengeful deity," but whose later, more fruitful emphasis was "wholly upon a God of love."

The other part of what, of great moment, happened to Billy Graham at Wheaton is more personal. Shortly after his arrival someone—who doubtless had been spying out the land as it had been spied out for him at the Florida Bible Institute—reported that "the most beautiful girl" on the campus was also "the most devout"; that her daily devotional routine was to rise at five o'clock and spend two hours, before breakfast or classes, in Scripture reading and prayer.

That the first part of the report, at least, was not much exaggerated Billy found out, for himself a few days later when— having backed his truck up to the sidewalk of a house on Main Street—grimy and sweating, he was wrestling a large overstuffed chair up the front steps to the porch. She stood there beside the walk as he wrestled, waiting to go to her room: "So cool and comfortable in a dainty white dress it was exasperating; but a vision if I ever saw one."

That the latter part of the report was also true he found out afterward. An entry in his diary—written years later, after they had returned from a Wheaton College banquet in Chicago where Billy Graham spoke—reads: "Ruth and I dressed in our best. She looked so beautiful in the same dress she had worn in London at some of the functions there. She looks twenty-five instead of thirty-five. What a wonderful girl. The Lord certainly was looking out for me back there at Wheaton. I remember that autumn day when I was introduced to her. The light in her face! I had been told she was a woman who got up at five every morning to pray. She still gets up ahead of any of the rest of us to spend time alone with God."

Part of her praying, there at Wheaton, was pretty specific:

114

"Dear God," I prayed, all unafraid,
  (As girls are wont to be)
"I do not want a handsome man—
  But let him be like Thee.

"I do not need one big and strong,
  Nor one so very tall,
  Nor need he be some genius,
  Or wealthy, Lord, at all.

"But let his head be high, dear God,
  And let his eye be clear,
  His shoulders straight, whate'er his state,
  Whate'er his earthy sphere.

"And let his face have character,
  A ruggedness of soul
  And let his whole life show, dear God,
  A singleness of goal.

"And when he comes, *as he will come*,
  With quiet eyes aglow—
  I'll understand that he's the man
  I prayed for long ago."

  "Do you wonder," she says, "that I believe in answered prayer?"

7: The Ruth Graham story

IN HIS FAMED COLUMN in the *Christian Century*, "Simeon Stylites" recently wrote about the "New Look in Preachers' Wives." So far as I know, Simeon had not met Ruth Graham. But she has the New Look he was writing about. She is a pert five feet five; brown eyes, black hair modishly tended, facial lines which, someone has said, are "a joy to news photographers." Her clothes are smart—even those she makes herself. She wears the appurtenances of the conservatively well-dressed woman.

If, as an astonished newspaper reporter remarked, "she is not quite but almost beautiful," she is, at least, notably different from those who aim to make a religious virtue of no make-up, outmoded hair-dos, and clothes lacking in style or color on the assumption, apparently, that drabness is next to godliness and that piety gains in authenticity by being unattractively packaged.

Ruth Graham not only does not countenance such assumptions; she disproves them. Her beauty and her religion are both the real thing and she puts neither under a bushel, but, unostentatiously, on a candlestick where, as naturally in Holyrood

Palace as in her own home, they shine "unto all that are in the house."

Before they went to Great Britain for the Greater London Crusade in 1954, Billy Graham, out of deference to what he believed to be the demands of British conservatism and to the considerable disappointment of the reporters, did not take along his usual—and preferred—assortment of bright neckties, socks, and sport coats. Noticing on the boat that Ruth, in the matter of make-up, seemed to be preparing no such concessions, he one day brought up the subject.

"In England," he said, "I guess you won't want to wear lipstick as you do at home. Church people, over there, might not understand."

"Don't you think," said Ruth, "that that may be something on which the Lord expects us to help their understanding?"

A few weeks later a well-known actress, Joan Winmill, came forward at Harringay to make a "decision for Christ." By chance her counsellor, in the Inquiry Room, was Ruth Graham.

"I didn't know then that she was Mrs. Billy Graham," Miss Winmill has said. "But the first thought that came to my mind when I saw her was: how much sooner people like me might have been attracted to Christianity, if we had met a few such attractive Christians."

Ruth Graham says, "We were brought up on the mission field. But Mother always hoped we wouldn't look like the pickings from a missionary barrel. Thanks to her magic touch, I don't think we ever did.

"It doesn't seem to me to be a credit to Christ to be drab. I think it's a Christian's duty to look as nice as possible. Besides, not caring about one's appearance goes against a woman's nature. That's not going to make anybody a better Christian, either. And it's not fair to the people who have to look at you."

Ruth Graham was raised in a home as steeped in religion

118

as Billy's: a place where possession of the faith once delivered to the saints was sure and the practice of its precepts unremitting.

Her parents, Dr. and Mrs. L. Nelson Bell, were medical missionaries of the Presbyterian Church in the U.S. (the Southern branch of Presbyterianism) in China. Their station was Tsing Kiang Pu, a Kiangsu Province city 300 miles north of Shanghai. There, after his arrival in 1916, Dr. Bell directed the building and was subsequently in charge of a 380-bed mission hospital. When Japanese and Communist invasions finally drove them from China in 1941, the Bells settled in Montreat, North Carolina, and Dr. Bell established a successful surgical practice in nearby Asheville.

Montreat is a beautiful mountain community famed for the salubrious quality of its spiritual as well as its physical climate. One side of towering Black Mountain is a citadel for Southern Baptists. The other side—reputedly a shade less rigorous in theology and discipline, a shade more worldly in its pursuits, slightly more expensive in its appointments—is a citadel for Southern Presbyterians. Many of its permanent residents are retired Presbyterian ministers, retired or furloughed missionaries. All summer long it serves as the exceedingly pleasant, dedication-inducing meeting place for one religious conference after another; sometimes for several simultaneously. The best of Presbyterian preachers the world over—and of others of untainted doctrine—occupy the pulpit in its huge and always crowded Presbyterian Church. The center of its winter life is Montreat College—a strong church institution with some 200 students.

Not only in Montreat, but throughout the reaches of Southern Presbyterianism generally, Dr. Bell, since his return from China, has become a figure of no mean proportions. A man of fine mind, wide reading, great energy, and unyielding convictions, he does not easily take "no" for an answer. On matters of doctrine, I am sure he never does. The defeat by the South-

119

ern Presbyterian Church in 1955 of the long-developing plan for union with the Presbyterian Church in the U.S.A. (the Northern Church) was due, in important part, to him and to the campaign of writing and speaking by which he supported his belief that such union would result in an engulfing of the "essentials" in a sea of Northern Presbyterian modernism.

As a Southern Baptist—a little suspect among some of his brethren for living on the Southern Presbyterian slope of Black Mountain—Billy Graham was not involved in this Presbyterian controversy. As to his own viewpoint in such matters, one of his favorite quotations is John Wesley's statement: "I am ready to go with any man who loves Christ and preaches salvation to men."

His debt to Dr. Bell is a large one: for his sound sense in business matters, his judgment of men, his forthright criticism —untinged with bigotry—of sermon subjects and contents and, most of all, for the way—professionally as well as privately— he contagiously lives what he believes.

"Of all the men I have known," says Billy Graham, "only my own father and Dean Minder at the Florida Bible Institute have influenced my life as deeply as Dr. Bell."

Ruth McCue Bell was born in the mission compound at Tsing Kiang Pu in June, 1920. She learned to speak Chinese before she spoke English. Her first schooling was from her mother; for junior high school she was sent to a school for missionary children in Korea. At the first Christmas away from home, desperately homesick, she informed her parents that she had prayed about it and that God had told her, in reply, that going home for Christmas was His will for her. Her mother's answer, more practical but no less devout, was: "Dear Ruth: You say God is leading you to come home. We say that as long as we are responsible for you, He is going to lead *us* as to what to do for you. Neither your father nor I feel He is leading us to bring you back to China for Christmas. . . ."

Like Billy Graham's mother, Ruth—in the specific time-

and-place or blinding-flash sense—was never converted. She grew. That, of course, does not meet the strictest prescriptions of fundamentalism. Salvation preferably involves rebirth. Rebirth, according to strict fundamentalism, requires a definite "crossing over"—not necessarily, but preferably, accompanied by a strong emotional upsurge—at a rememberable time and place.

In his preaching youth, Billy Graham would probably have been disturbed by the fact that, in this doctrinal particular, Ruth apparently had not qualified. But in this matter, as in some others, his is less a strait-jacket theology than it once was. Conversion, he says, is a many-sided experience. It comes to different people in different ways. Determining those who—whether by "crisis conversion" or by growth—have qualified for salvation is not man's job, but God's.

Ruth herself may regret having missed so rewarding an experience. But her religion being the lively, day-to-day reality that it is, I am sure the idea of being disturbed—as though there were some uncertainty as to her eternal fate—has never entered her head.

Neither, incidentally, does the fact—of concern to some of Billy's well-wishing Southern Baptist colleagues—that she has never been baptized by immersion. When they were first married, Billy himself tried to persuade her, using the best Southern Baptist arguments he could uncover. She, with Southern Presbyterian answers equally well rooted in the Scriptures, refused to be persuaded. She never has been. Though the subject has long since ceased to be an issue, there is a standing offer of $100 from Billy Graham to any Baptist who can persuade Ruth—"as a precautionary measure," says Grady Wilson—to agree to immersion. "No hundred dollars of Billy's," says Grady, himself an immersion-believing Southern Baptist, "was ever so likely to stay unspent."

By the time, at seventeen, she left China for college in the United States, Ruth's mind as to her own future was made up.

Preferably married, but married or single, she would return to China as a missionary. Her chosen field: Tibet.

"As a young girl, out there in China," she says, "I committed my life to the Lord. And I got exactly the opposite of what I'd expected. I thought the Lord wanted me in Tibet, isolated and obscure, and I was happy at the prospect. Instead, what I've got are publicity and the spotlight. Maybe you won't believe it, but in some ways that's harder."

What the Bells—in their remote post in China—were unable to give their three daughters in the way of on-the-scene advice as to men they might marry, they made up for—"more than made up for"—by prayer. And the girls, in their choosing, took into account not only the man, but also God.

Ruth's first date with Billy was to a Sunday afternoon concert of sacred music in the Wheaton College chapel—and after that a long walk home. "I knew then," she says, "that here is a man who knows where he is going: he is going ahead with God. I knew he had one purpose: to please God, regardless." That night she prayed, "Oh Lord, if you'll give me the privilege of sharing my life with this man, I could have no greater joy."

Someone at this point injected a word of warning which for anyone with less firmness of conviction than Ruth Bell might have been upsetting. The warning was that this handsome young North Carolinian was, in the matter of his affections, more than a little changeable. This warning seemed Scripturally reinforced when, on the same day she received it, Ruth Bell in her Bible reading came to the verse in the twenty-fourth chapter of Proverbs: "Meddle not with them that are given to change." The pause which this may have given Ruth Bell was not protracted.

There were, however, two further obstacles. One was Tibet. Her older sister Rosa, also a student at Wheaton, helped her with that one.

"If," Ruth said to Rosa, "God got me here to Wheaton in spite of the war, and if He's provided the money and if He's helped me through my courses—then hasn't He been leading me straight back to the mission field?"

"But did you ever think," said Rosa, "He might have led you here to meet Billy? Maybe God does want you over there in Tibet as an old maid missionary, but I doubt it. I think He wants you right here in this country—as Billy Graham's wife."

The other problem was Billy. "I was as sure as she was," he says. "But she knew what a suitor ought to be and do and I didn't." To her sister Rosa, Ruth said, "He's being cautious. Now you know that's no way to court a girl." That, Rosa suggested, could be quickly remedied: let Ruth have a date or two with someone else. She did, and it worked. Either, said Billy when they next met, she could date him and no one else or she could date the lot sweeping the campus with a grandiose wave of his arm—and forget about him.

They graduated from Wheaton in June, 1943, were married in Montreat in August, and spent their seven-day-seventy-dollar honeymoon at Blowing Rock, North Carolina.

Several years later Ruth was in Boston for the concluding meeting, of what, up to then, was Billy Graham's most successful Crusade. That night 16,000 people jammed Boston Garden; 5,000 stood outside; 1,500 made decisions for Christ. During the service Ruth was introduced and given a standing ovation. Later, unwarned by Billy, she was taken to the room reserved for the team and there introduced to the girl to whom he was unofficially engaged at the Florida Bible Institute and who, with what seemed near-disastrous consequences, had jilted him for a young man "of greater promise."

"I've wanted to meet you for a long time," said Ruth. "I've thanked the Lord so often for answering my prayer about a husband. Now I can thank you for having made it possible for Him to answer that prayer with Bill."

Billy Graham says, "When people used to ask me what Heaven was like, I tried to describe it as it is pictured in the

Book of Revelation. Now I think I know what Heaven is like. It is like being married to Ruth."

"Nonsense," is Ruth's comment on someone's remark that "half Billy is Ruth." But no one close to him doubts the weight and significance of her contribution. "She is a brain," one team member said to me, "maybe more a brain than Billy. She knows the Bible as well as he does. As for theology—she was majoring in it while Billy majored in anthropology. If it weren't for her religion, she might be an arrogant intellectual. But that 'if' makes all the difference."

It is Ruth's touch of worldliness that helps keep the piety in him from turning into piosity; her common-sense and house-hold-fashioned wit that help him, when in the clouds, not to get lost there; her unawed attitude that is a safeguard, for him, against idiosyncrasies, pontifications and, most of all, the sin of pride.

Once attending church soon after they were first married—and very short of funds—Billy put what he thought was a dollar bill in the collection plate and then saw to his consternation that it was a ten. Ruth told him later there was nothing he could do about it.

"And in the eyes of the Lord," she said, "you'll not get credit for ten dollars either, since one dollar was all you planned to give."

Often in his letters he writes, "If you were only here so I could talk over my sermon with you"—or, "I'm puzzled what to preach about. What a help it would be if you were here." When she is, he always asks, "How did the sermon go?" Once after he had preached on the Christian home her answer was:

"It was a good sermon except the timing."

"What do you mean, the timing?"

"You spent eleven minutes on a wife's duty to her husband and only seven on a husband's duty to his wife."

In the Graham home in Montreat one discovers that, in addition to personal attractiveness of a high order, Ruth Graham's

124

gaiety is also a part of her "New Look" among the deeply devout. Perhaps there is gaiety in her religion because her religion is so real she can be natural. Perhaps it is because her good sense—fortified by a knowledge of the Scriptures—rejects the idea of God finding joy in long faces. Maybe it is partly because she feels that anything so important on the terrestrial level as a sense of humor must have some above-ordinary celestial standing.

At any rate, religion at the Grahams' is not worn on the sleeve like a mourning band. It is devoid of dourness or exhibitionist solemnity. Its reverence appears to be rooted in the Gospel "Good News," rather than the obituary pages. There is a lighter touch about it.

"One of the peculiar things about living in a preacher's family," she says, "is the way strangers expect to see halos shining from all our heads. I say strangers; our friends know better. Our friends are fully aware that, for all our striving to make God the center of our home, life in the Billy Graham household is not a matter of uninterrupted sweetness and light. . . ."

Neither is it a matter of uninterrupted agreement.

"At the beginning of our marriage," Ruth says, "some very wise person told me that when two people agree on everything, one of them is unnecessary. But you've got to keep your sense of humor handy when you disagree. If you do, if you don't take things too seriously, then disagreeing can even be a lot of fun."

Since 1946, the Graham home has been a comfortable, definitely modest house—before improvements and additions it cost $4,500—built in a style one presumes to be the North Carolina version of a Swiss chalet and located behind a too-thin screen of shrubs, on one of the main roads into the Montreat conference grounds. As Billy Graham's fame increased it became a mecca for visitors from near and far who —asking no leave and begging no pardon—wandered in and out to see Billy or Ruth or the children—preferably all of them

125

together—peeking into the windows, wandering around the terrace, trying the chairs, taking snapshots. All summer long this steady stream was swelled to a flood by daily visitations from that least inhibited of all Americans: the bus-traveling tourist.

Several years ago, Billy Graham had invested his savings in a down payment on 200 acres of unlikely mountaintop above Montreat. There, during 1955, Ruth directed the building of a new home into which the family moved in the spring of 1956. It is less modest than the first—but still modest, with a view across the Blue Ridge Mountains that is beyond price. A hole has been scooped out of a cliffside and a brook dammed to make a swimming pond for the children. Chief among its advantages: it is reached by a one-lane road too narrow and twisting for busses and for any but the hardiest drivers. It is also—though this can hardly be counted a deterrent—marked "Private." When, after his 1956 mission to India, Billy Graham returned to Montreat he not only found this new home ready but also that its cost had been largely met by the gifts of personal friends.

As for the job of being a homemaker—there are four Graham children—it sounds as though she really means it when Ruth Graham says, "To me it's the nicest, most rewarding job in the world, second in importance to none, not even preaching. Maybe it is preaching."

She tells of a woman converted in a Dwight L. Moody revival who came to that evangelist filled with purpose and zeal:

"God," she said, "has called me to preach the Gospel."

"He sure has," said Mr. Moody. "He's even got a congregation waiting for you: your husband and six children."

The devotional aura which, for Ruth Graham, covers homemaking does not quite stretch to include dishwashing: "I don't like dishwashing. There's no future in it, nothing creative."

She has tried several spiritual devices. One was an embossed motto someone gave her in high school: "Praise and Pray and

126

Peg Away." She hung that near the sink without appreciable consequences. She had considerably better results—in fact, she says, it almost, but not quite, did the trick—with a sentence said to have been similarly posted by a Scottish pastor's wife: "Divine services will be conducted here three times daily."

"I even," she says, "made my dissatisfaction with the dishes a definite prayer concern and still I couldn't dig up much enthusiasm.

"But, as so often happens, my prayers were answered in an unusual way. I took sick at Christmastime. It was Bill, then, who had to take over and do the dishes. What did Billy give me for Christmas? An electric dishwasher."

In their early married life she was not, it is said, much of a cook—her only dependable specialty being, naturally, Chinese dishes which—when they could find the ingredients—she prepared and Billy—partly, no doubt, from being love-struck—professed to enjoy. The notable upgrading and Americanization of her culinary qualifications were helped by the colored cook in the Montreat home of her parents—a task somewhat eased by the fact that food, for Billy Graham, might as well always be steak.

She manages the fiscal affairs of the household—with, her friends report, more generosity than precision. "When," she says, "I hear that nice Mr. Hickey from the bank say over the phone, 'Ruth, this is Billy Hickey. Uh—how are you?' I know it's not my health he's concerned about." She sews like a professional and still makes most of the clothes for the children and—plain or fancy—many of her own. In the spring of 1954, after a reception in the Grahams' honor at Claridge's in London she wrote home: "You should have heard all the titles and seen all the jewels and decorations—and me in a homemade number with zipper trouble!"

Of the four Graham children, Virginia was born in 1945, Ann in 1948, Ruth in 1950, and William Franklin, Jr., in 1952. Prior to the birth of their son, Ruth and Billy had about

127

made up their minds that theirs was destined to be a family of four daughters—which prospect they were more readily reconciled to by the account in the Book of Acts of the household of another, earlier Christian evangelist, Philip by name, who "had four daughters, virgins, which did prophesy."

For Ruth Graham, herself, and for the training of her children, religion is a round-the-clock concern. Less than that, she says, is not enough and quotes Jehovah's stirring admonition in Deuteronomy 6:6–9: "And these words, which I command thee this day, shall be in thine heart: and thou shalt teach them diligently unto thy children and shalt talk of them when thou sittest in thine house, and when thou walkest by the way and when thou liest down and when thou risest up. And thou shalt bind them for a sign upon thine hand, and they shall be as frontlets before thine eyes. And thou shalt write them upon the posts of thy house and on thy gates."

"With four children and the animals," Ruth says, "with guests coming and going, with travel, Bill's work plus the usual household emergencies, a regularly scheduled time for my own private devotions is difficult. So I've found two substitutes:

"One is day-long Bible reading, which seems as natural to the kids as my preparing meals. The Bible stays open in the kitchen all day. Whenever there is a spare minute, I just grab that minute and spend it with the Bible.

"When Bill is away, I'm likely to have the Book open to Proverbs. If I've a problem I almost always get help there. In fact, Proverbs has got more practical child help in it than ten books on child psychology. And its thirty-one chapters fit the thirty-one days of the month like a glove."

She once set down a list—drawn partly from Proverbs—of some of those things "A Mother Must . . . :

"Walk with God. . . . Put happiness in the home before neatness. . . . Not be the victim of her own disposition. . . . Make her tongue the law of kindness. . . . In discipline, be firm but patient. . . . Teach that right means behaving as well

128

as believing. . . . Not only teach but live. . . . Not only speak, but listen. . . . Realize that to lead her child to Christ is her greatest privilege. . . ."

The second part of Ruth's day-round devotions is prayer. "Since I so often don't find any set-aside time, I've tried to learn what Paul meant when he wrote 'Pray without ceasing.' I heard of a lady once who had six children and a very small home. She had no place for privacy. Whenever life got too hectic and she needed God's help she just pulled her apron over her head and the children knew she was praying and quieted down.

"I've never done that, but it's a fine idea. But when I'm dusting, making beds, cooking, sewing, whatever, I think of Christ as being there. I talk to Him as I would to a visible friend. This is part and parcel of our daily lives so that keeping close to God becomes part and parcel of the daily lives of the children."

The Bible—which Ruth reads to them unfailingly every day with longer readings on Sunday—is also part and parcel of the children's lives. From Scotland where, in the spring of 1955, Ruth and Virginia (Gi-Gi) had joined Billy Graham for the last two weeks of the All-Scotland Crusade, she wrote one Sunday afternoon to her parents:

"Gi-Gi and I had about two hours in the Old Testament. I was giving her a running summary of each book and how the whole Old Testament points toward the coming of Christ. But we got bogged down in Exodus and the plagues which she found too interesting to skip over. It was terrific and good for both of us."

About the religious growth of her children Ruth is as natural as about her own.

"It seems to Bill and me," she says, "that the word 'enjoyable' is important in religion. We think that word would somehow be missing if we tried to go too fast with their spiritual growth, with their halo-growing, as it were. We believe that spiritual growth can't be forced without raising a brood of little hypocrites. We prepare the soil and plant the seed and water and weed and tend the plant faithfully but it is 'God that giveth the increase.' We're willing to take our time and let growth come from the inside, through Christ; not merely from the outside through our puny efforts."

Once, after they had gone to church in a strange city, I asked Gi-Gi how she liked the sermon.

"I didn't like it," she said. "You know, all he talked about was the newspapers. I don't believe he even mentioned Jesus."

Someone said to Ann, seven, as her father was getting ready to leave for Scotland, "Isn't it too bad your daddy can't stay at home with you?" "But think," she said, "of all the people who would go to Hell."

Ruth Graham tries to join her husband for part of every Crusade. After the two weeks in Scotland in the spring of 1955, she went on for the great meetings at Wembley Stadium in London. She was with her husband when he preached in the Royal Chapel at Windsor Castle and afterward lunched with Queen Elizabeth and the Duke of Edinburgh. Of their visit, a few days earlier, to the Queen Mother and Princess Margaret she wrote to her parents:

"Last Tuesday we went to Clarence House. I had been told I would visit with the ladies-in-waiting while Bill visited with the Queen Mother, then I would be introduced and we would leave. Fearing some overeager friends had tried to sort of push me in and having had so many people push into our home just to say they had met Bill, I had no desire to do the same. But then I was told the Queen Mother looked forward to seeing us both.

"That's how it happened that our little tan Ford drove up to the gate at 11:45. Two men secretaries met us at the door. We shook hands with them. The doorman held out his hand (for Bill's hat) and Bill shook that, too—to the doorman's evident surprise. We were led into a wide hall where we were joined by the ladies-in-waiting. We all went to a side room

130

where we talked about golf and the Cockell-Marciano fight. Then suddenly the door opened: 'Her Majesty the Queen Mother will receive Dr. and Mrs. Graham.'

"It was something of a shock for I had expected to sit and be properly briefed by the 'in-waitings' before being introduced. But you don't keep royalty waiting, so in we went. Now, Mrs. Jarvis had taught me to curtsy. But the Queen Mother came toward us with her hand outstretched and I didn't know whether to curtsy first and shake hands or shake hands first and then curtsy. I don't know which I did. Bill—the merciless wretch—said it looked as though I'd tripped over the rug. . . .

"Anyway, the Queen Mother was the dearest, most charming person and so was Princess Margaret—a lovely, tiny thing, dressed in a bright pink taffeta dress with a little white cashmere sweater about her shoulders, patent-leather pumps and bag. . . ."

No member of the Graham team, not even Billy Graham, is more single-mindedly concerned for the success of each Crusade than Ruth Graham or more deeply stirred by what transpires. After the concluding meeting in Glasgow—more than 100,000 people in Hampden Park—she wrote: "Tonight so many prayers have been so gloriously answered. Even 100,000 voices raised in singing 'To God Be the Glory' seemed inadequate. Just wait till we get to Heaven!"

From Wembley she wrote: "The great patient crowds sitting quietly in the rain and the cold wind. So many needy hearts, both high and humble. When the invitation was given there was the sound as of sudden heavy raindrops on a roof. But it was only the footfalls of hundreds going forward; there was nothing but those footsteps and the choir singing 'Just As I Am, without One Plea.' . . . The rain fell in sheets across the field lights shining down on thousands of glistening umbrellas. Still they came, 3,400 in all. Many of the counsellors were converts from Harringay last year."

131

"They were all charming people," Ruth wrote, of the guests at a Paris luncheon given for her. "They were all interested in the coming meeting. The opinion was, 'We're all for it. But we've got our fingers crossed.' Or, 'After all, this is Paris.' . . . Or, 'Frenchmen are too skeptical and individualistic ever to go forward in groups. Maybe your husband had better not make his usual appeal.' . . . And more of the same.

"No one seemed to take into account the power of God or the hunger of the human heart. And I needn't sound so smug. Frankly I wondered, too. . . .

"Finally, we went out to the meeting. . . . The setting was confused and uninspiring. But it was the background for one of the most amazing demonstrations of the power of God I have ever seen. . . .

"One young Army officer told me later: 'I prayed that at least one person would go forward to keep Mr. Graham from being embarrassed. . . . But God did the impossible . . . over 600 came. And every night since they've been coming: bearded students, workingmen, glamorous young Parisians, servicemen, countesses, actresses, old and young—all of them walking at a slow deliberate pace as though they wanted everyone to see how sure they were of what they were doing. . . .'"

Ruth Graham does not often make speeches. But when at a dinner in Glasgow at the conclusion of the All-Scotland Crusade, a Crusade official paid tribute to her and to "the price" she had to pay for being an evangelist's wife, she broke her rule and made a response.

"I want you to know that I would rather be an evangelist's wife than anything else in all the world. And I also want you to know—maybe you've guessed it—that, as for being this particular evangelist's wife, I'd rather have Billy Graham, part time, than anybody else in all the world, full time."

8: "... And some, evangelists"

WHEN, IN SEPTEMBER, 1949, Billy Graham arrived in Los Angeles for the opening of a "Christ for Greater Los Angeles Crusade," he had with him only enough revival sermons to last two weeks, plus some sketchy notes which he planned to turn into sermons for the last of the scheduled three-week run. That was his entire supply. Up to then, it had been adequate.

The Los Angeles Crusade lasted not three weeks, but eight. Its 6,000-capacity tent ("The largest revival tent in the world") had to be enlarged to make room for 9,000 and was still too small. Billy Graham spoke to 350,000 people. More than 3,000 made decisions for Christ.

"No one since Billy Sunday," said *Time* magazine, has wielded "the revival sickle" with such success as "this thirty-one-year-old, blond, trumpet-lunged North Carolinian."

"Old-style religion," said an Associated Press dispatch, "is sweeping Los Angeles. . . . This blasé city has seen multitudes of meetings of the supercolossal type, but it is safe to say that this evangelistic meeting is one of the greatest the city ever has witnessed."

By the end of the Los Angeles Crusade, not only had five

133

weeks of new sermons been added to Billy Graham's evangelistic repertory. New authority had been added to his preaching; new significance had been added to its results; and a new prospect had been opened for his future.

Until Los Angeles he had been another evangelist: more youthful, more colorful, more successful, perhaps, than most, but nonetheless not notably different from scores of others before him who, with varying but hardly ever more than local consequences, had pitched their tents and thundered doom and salvation—city by city and town by town—along the country's sawdust-strewn revival circuits.

What happened at Los Angeles is another circumstance in this account which takes one beyond the area where journalists are accustomed to operate. But it is difficult, even for a journalist, to escape the conclusion that at Los Angeles a power greater than Billy Graham began to take Billy Graham more directly in hand and—as such a greater power did with Joshua—to "magnify" him. From having been a revival preacher, he seems to have become, increasingly thereafter, the voice and—increasingly also—the instrument of revival.

Today Billy Graham's associates speak of his career as in two major parts: before Los Angeles and since Los Angeles. But what happened in the period—1943 to 1949—before Los Angeles is an important chapter in the Billy Graham story because it is a part of his past which, for his present worldwide ministry, has proved to be essential prologue. In that period he became —by choice and more, he would say, "by Providential circumstance"—an evangelist and achieved, as though on a trial run, his first, not inconsiderable triumphs in evangelism.

On the matter of a diversity of gifts among the Lord's workmen and of a division of labor in the Lord's vineyard, Billy Graham quotes the familiar words from St. Paul's letter to the Ephesians: ". . . And gave them gifts. . . . And He gave some, apostles; and some, prophets; and some, evangelists; and some, pastors; and some, teachers."

134

Of the last two Billy Graham has had what I think might be called a smattering of firsthand experience. For sixteen months, after his graduation from Wheaton, he was pastor of the Baptist church in Western Springs, Illinois. For three and a half years—late 1947 into 1951—he was part-time president in Minneapolis, Minnesota, of the Northwestern Bible School, an independent Bible and liberal arts college of considerable fundamentalist repute. It could hardly be said that the former experience gave him very deep grounding in the toils, tribulations, and rewards of a pastor or that the latter accomplished any very deep indoctrination in the art and practice of teaching.

This was only partly because, in both instances, the time was short. A more important reason was that Billy Graham could not escape the conviction, and did not seriously try to, that the part of St. Paul's allotment which directly referred to him was: ". . . and some, evangelists. . . ."

If St. Paul—an evangelist himself—had in mind any special spiritual gifts as the qualifying marks of an evangelist, he did not specify them. But I am sure he was aware—since he possessed such a large measure of it himself—that one quality, not necessarily spiritual, was almost indispensable and almost always present. There necessarily has to be in the evangelist more than the share accorded ordinary mortals of restlessness, an above-normal urge to be on the move.

It is true that in the writings of St. Paul there is, so far as I can find, no indication that his "journeyings often" were, for him, anything more than unrelieved hardship from which, after each new journey, he was lucky to have escaped with his life. In the second chapter of his second letter to the Corinthians he sets forth the dire chronicle: "In perils of rivers, in perils of robbers, in perils in the city, in perils in the wilderness, in perils in the sea, in perils among false brethren, in labor and travail, in watchings often, in hunger and thirst, in fastings often, in cold and nakedness. . . ."

It seems to me possible to take that chronicle—of which I

135

have quoted only part—at full face value and still feel sure that there must have been a pleasanter, that there may even have been a lighter, side to the story of his traveling. In fact, reading the record of his journeyings—on which he had embarked even before his conversion—it seems a likely conclusion that, though he learned "in whatever state" he found himself, "therewith to be content," the one state in which it would have been most difficult for him to have been content would have been one which involved no journeying, a state of staying put.

John Wesley made no such sorry bones about it. It was, I think, not wholly due to his organizational genius but, in part, to the uncurbed restlessness of his own temperament that led him to establish, for his Methodist societies, an "itinerant ministry." In fifty years—mostly by horseback—his evangelistic itinerating took him up, down, and across England 250,-000 miles. Fifty times, in those days of sail, he crossed St. George's Channel to Ireland. His *Journal* is not only a record of things spiritual, but also the travel log of a man who has been called "The Happy Traveler." To him, unlike St. Paul, it was by no means all travail.

"I am content," he wrote, "with whatever entertainment I meet with and my companions are always in good humor. This must be the spirit of all who take journeys with me. If a dinner ill-dressed or a hired bed, or a poor room, or a shower of rain, or a dusty road would put them out of humor, it lays a burden upon me greater than all the rest put together."

No difficulty in going seems to have alarmed Wesley so much as the prospect of not going. "Our servant," he wrote, "came up and said, 'Sir, there is no traveling today. Such a quantity of snow has fallen in the night that the roads are quite filled up.' I told him, 'At least we can walk twenty miles with our horses in our hands.' So, in the name of God, we set out. . . ."

When past seventy, unable any longer to travel by horseback, Wesley did not give up traveling but continued—until well into his eighties—to go by carriage: chiefly driven, no doubt, by zeal and concern for his new-founded societies, but also, I am sure, impelled by that restlessness which most evangelists seem congenitally to possess and which, for the demands of their special mission, is probably indispensable.

Minor though it doubtless is, Billy Graham in this respect also stands in the evangelist succession. His traveling involves acute attacks of homesickness, much weariness, an occasional cold brought on by lack of proper sleep and exercise, indigestion brought on by lack of proper food and, in addition, all manner of less, but cumulatively not insignificant, discomforts, inconveniences, confusions, and irritations.

These Billy Graham complains about less, perhaps, than some of us might, but nonetheless in healthy human fashion. But I am inclined to think they are the complaints of one who, in spite of it all, is more than reconciled to—is, in fact, basically happy about—his peripatetic lot, his "journeyings often." If there were no prospect of yet another journey just ahead, I am sure he would take much less delight than he does in each journey just completed. And I am also inclined to think that this restlessness made it likelier that when the Lord called Billy Graham into evangelism, it was not necessary to repeat the call.

The church he held at Western Springs, not far from Wheaton, paid its minister $45 weekly. It had, as edifice, only a basement, no parsonage, and on the Sunday morning of Billy Graham's first appearance, a congregation of 35. If his sixteen months there did not suffice to remedy all these deficiencies, they were sufficient to stir among the people such unaccustomed zeal and fervor as to make their remedying— given a bit more time—inevitable. The building fund he started grew into what is now an attractive church. The Sunday morning congregation now averages in the several hundreds. The

137

preacher has an assistant as well as a parsonage and what passes, among preachers, as a living wage.

Billy Graham, even while pastor, was more evangelist. He preached every Sunday morning, and every Sunday evening as though each service were a revival. In a sense, each service was. He never failed to give a call for "decisions for Christ"; almost always there was someone or several who came forward. He worked out for the church a three-point program based on Bible reading, prayer, and personal evangelism. Evangelism, as he defined and preached it, included not only the evangelization of Western Springs, but of the world "in this generation." Today, as a result, this church supports twenty missionaries in various parts of the world.

Meanwhile, an opportunity to extend his ministry beyond Western Springs was in the making at the hands of a fellow minister, also a Wheaton College graduate, Torrey Johnson by name. Several years older than Billy, Torrey Johnson was a man of great energy, fervor, and imagination who had gone to Chicago on leaving Wheaton, organized his own church—the Midwest Bible Church—and made it a thriving center of evangelism. In addition to directing the activities of his own highly active institution, he had a regular, late Sunday night evangelistic radio program, organized and led Youth for Christ Rallies, and was a professor of Greek in Chicago's Northern Baptist Seminary.

While Billy Graham was at Wheaton, Torrey Johnson heard of his campus fame as a preacher; once heard him preach, and decided forthwith that here was a prospective evangelist of more than ordinary stature. When Billy Graham went to Western Springs, the two men—kindred evangelical spirits with matching zeal and convictions—met several times. It was Torrey Johnson who persuaded Billy Graham not to go on, as he had considered doing, to a theological school—a decision which Billy Graham occasionally regrets. "Get in there and

138

preach," Torrey told Billy. "That's the theological school you need."

One day, early in 1945, Torrey Johnson telephoned Billy Graham from Chicago. "No phone call will ever have a greater influence on my life," he says, "than that one had."

"Billy," said Torrey, "you know I've got a regular Sunday evening radio program. I find I just don't have time to do that program right. I want you and your church to take it over."

"Why he chose me, just one year out of college, I'll probably never know," says Billy Graham, "but I knew it was the chance of a lifetime—our little church on the air, 50,000 watts strong, spreading the Gospel."

There was one considerable hitch. The membership of his church numbered 85. The total weekly church budget— met with some difficulty—was only $125. Weekly cost to the church of the radio program would be $150. Billy Graham called his congregation into a prayer meeting to consider the matter. That evening's prayers were answered with weekly pledges totaling $85—little more than half the required amount.

"Such an opportunity may never come our way again," said Billy Graham. "Let's sign up and trust God for the rest."

His congregation, breathless but believing, agreed.

This was the beginning (Sunday evenings 10:30–11:15 over Chicago station WENR) of *Songs in the Night*—an informal, family-circle kind of "Gospel sing," with Billy Graham—between singing, Bible reading, and prayer—interspersing several three- to five-minute religious "chats," Bible-based and evangelistically beamed. Evidently many Gospel-and-song-minded people of the Chicago area were waiting for just such a program at such an hour. It caught on immediately. Contributions came in sufficient for its financing. First paid soloist was George Beverly Shea—then on Chicago's WBMI as announcer and singer, now "America's beloved Gospel singer" of the Graham team.

139

As unfailingly as always, Billy Graham concluded every program with a call for "decisions for Christ." Soon there were reports of such decisions, increasing each week. Soon, also, Billy Graham's name was widely known beyond Western Springs and invitations to speak, to preach, to assist in revival services—sometimes as many as twenty in a day—began to pour in on him.

Songs in the Night is still on the air; still using the same program format used by Billy Graham; still originating from the same church, "the friendly church in the pleasant community of Western Springs, Illinois."

Then, late in 1944, Billy Graham was laid low with an attack of mumps so severe it took months to recuperate and led to his discharge from the Army chaplaincy for which he had been accepted. For the last several weeks of his recuperation—on the strength of a gift from an anonymous donor who specified only that the money be spent "in the sun"—he went with Ruth to Florida. They were hardly settled in their hotel before the phone rang. It was Torrey Johnson, stopping—"not by chance," says Billy Graham; "the Lord was in it"—at the same hotel.

During the following days the two men met, talked, and prayed together often and Torrey Johnson shared with Billy Graham his dream of an international, interdenominational evangelistic movement among young people. Such a movement was already stirring in Youth for Christ which was then working largely among servicemen and of which Torrey Johnson had become the recognized national leader.

Youth for Christ was—and still is—"an evangelistic movement specializing in mass evangelism, particularly among youth." Its chief feature was the Saturday night Youth for Christ Rally. Its methods, along with the tried-and-true techniques of old-time revivalism, included all manner of attention-getting-and-holding attractions: ventriloquists, magicians, close-harmony quartets. On the night in the week when—so almost everyone told Johnson—"you'll never get the kids to turn out," these rallies got them: packing large halls, even filling Chicago's Soldier Field.

Now, Johnson told Billy Graham, the time had come for the "Big Push"—a rapid expansion both in the United States and abroad. On the last day of their vacation together, Johnson asked Billy Graham to be part of that worldwide push, to become YFC's first "field representative." His salary of $75 a week plus expenses was already pledged by two Johnson supporters in Chicago.

"Give up the pastorate?" Ruth asked when Billy told her.

"That's right," he said. "And take up what the Lord's really called me to do: evangelism."

A month later, early in 1945, Torrey Johnson and Billy Graham walked into a barren two-room office in downtown Chicago, got down on their knees, and asked God's blessing on their plans and dreams for reaching young people around the world for Christ.

"There was only one thing left to settle," says Ruth Graham. "Me. What was I going to do? It wasn't practical to start hiking over the country with him. For the first time we decided to call Montreat home." She moved in temporarily with her parents. Moving itself was no chore: "We didn't own a stick of furniture."

Billy Graham's first Youth for Christ Rally was in Chicago. They had rented Orchestra Hall and he was scheduled to preach for twenty minutes. It was, for him at that stage, an awesome occasion—his first large audience.

"The prospect of talking to 3,000 people," he says, "filled me with terror. The old fright and embarrassment which, when I was at school in Florida, had sent me out to the swamp to preach to the birds and stumps returned in full force. I shook in my boots."

But when, after he had preached, he gave the invitation,

141

40 young people—an unprecedented number—came forward to make decisions for Christ.

During the next twelve months, Billy Graham traveled nearly 200,000 miles by plane. He spoke in 47 states to Youth for Christ Rallies of up to 20,000, mostly young people. More than 7,000, under his ministry, made "decisions for Christ."

He also added, en route, the second member of what is now the Billy Graham team. It was at a YFC Rally in Asheville, North Carolina. At the last minute the regular song leader had failed to appear. Someone suggested that in the audience that night was a young man with some experience as a song leader.

"This meeting," said Billy Graham, "is too important to take a chance on an amateur."

There was, finally, no choice and the amateur—as reluctant to try as the preacher was to have him—took over. After he had conducted a song or two, Billy Graham whispered to the chairman, "He's great stuff. What did you say is his name?"

"Cliff Barrows," said the chairman.

It was not long thereafter before Cliff Barrows—in the succession of John and Charles Wesley, Moody and Sankey, Sunday and Rhodeheaver—took over the music for all Billy Graham's meetings. Today, he is probably closer to Billy Graham than any other member of the team, his counsel continually sought on many matters besides music. "He comes near to being the indispensable man," says Billy Graham.

During this three-year period with Youth for Christ, Billy Graham traveled 750,000 miles—including four trips to Europe. He ran afoul, in his evangelistic crusading, of all manner of opposition—most of it opposition from within the churches, chiefly among ministers. Some were against Youth for Christ because William Randolph Hearst's newspapers seemed to be for it; some because it had a theology not of "solid meat," but of "milky abstractions"; others because its leaders were too evangelistically minded and still others because the techniques they used were "learned from business and particularly from commercial radio."

Whatever the reason—and there were others of about the same order of profundity—there was back of each of them a discernible measure of ministerial discomfiture that this corps of young upstarts—"Christian gypsies," they were sometimes called—could move in, stir, and enlist great numbers of young people unreached by the church, and—most discomfiting of all —do this with a Gospel message which many churchmen were sure was the least promising of all means whereby such a science-minded, socially sophisticated generation of young people could possibly be reached. Even the *Christian Century,* at the end of an almost wholly adverse article, "What about 'Youth for Christ'?" felt impelled to say:

"Yet the fact that it has gone so far as it has is proof that something close to spiritual famine exists among large sections of our population, including the rising generation, who are more hungry for faith than their elders. The churches are not feeding these starving people and they cannot be indifferent to the challenge which this attempt to use the new channels of communication for preaching the Gospel offers them. They should do likewise, and better."

But the fact that he met with so much church hostility did not shake Billy Graham's belief that successful evangelism must be church-centered and that any evangelistic enterprise with which he was associated would be. On one Youth for Christ trip to England in 1946, he arrived in Birmingham to find that the city council had withdrawn permission for him to use the city auditorium for the rallies. Inquiry revealed that this action was the result of opposition to the meetings from local ministers. From a supporter among the clergy Billy Graham got a list of the preachers most strongly opposed to him. One by one he called on them—"Not," he said, "to argue, only to explain and, if you don't mind, to pray." One by one they were won over and the city council rescinded its action.

143

"I wasn't interested," one of these ministers subsequently wrote. "We had plenty of soul-winners right here in Birmingham, without taking on any of America's surplus saints. But Billy called on me. He wasn't bitter, just wondering. I ended up wanting to hug the twenty-seven-year-old boy. I had failed. I called my church officers and we disrupted all our plans for the nine days of his visit.

"Before it was over, Birmingham had seen a touch of God's blessing. This fine, lithe, burning torch of a man made me love him and his Lord. . . ."

During these years of his increasing evangelistic effectiveness and repute, one man had kept a righteously covetous eye on Billy Graham. He was Dr. W. B. Riley, an aging but still fiery evangelist who, as a preacher of more than ordinary intellectual achievements, had founded in Minneapolis in 1902 —first as an adjunct of the First Baptist Church of which he was pastor—the Northwestern Bible School. This school—much like the Bible schools of the South—was a means for the propagation, unsullied, of the Bible-centered evangelical faith. By 1925, in its own building, enrollment in its Bible courses was 300. In 1935, a theological seminary was added; in 1944 a liberal arts college, and in 1948 the school moved into a new million-dollar plant in Minneapolis.

The more Dr. Riley saw and heard of Billy Graham the surer he became that here was the man to succeed him as president of the institution. To this Billy Graham—when he first heard of it—gave an unequivocal "no" for answer. But his—or, for that matter, any man's—"no" meant very little to Dr. Riley. He made an alternative offer—strongly bolstered with Biblical quotations indicating, as Dr. Riley saw it, that this was not only his plan, but God's will. The alternative was that Billy Graham should serve the school as president four days a week, three days a week with Youth for Christ. He asked: Would Billy let him know in time to announce the joyful news at the 1947 commencement?

144

"I have sought to discern the will of God," said Billy Graham in reply. "If God has blessed me with a particular field it has been that of an evangelist. I told the Lord two years ago that I did not care to be a great preacher, but that I did want to be a great soul-winner. . . . How to reconcile work at Northwestern with the tremendous evangelistic opportunities open to me is difficult. . . . May I have until July 21 . . . ?" In July he wrote: "I have been waiting for Heaven's signal. I have not received it. . . ."

In August, Dr. Riley—on, as he believed, his deathbed—besought Billy Graham to visit him. There, in a firm voice, the old man read to the younger the story of the prophet Samuel's choosing, from among the sons of Jesse, of one to be king over Israel and how he chose the youngest, David, and how Jehovah said, "Arise, anoint him; for this is he."

"Beloved," said Dr. Riley, "as Samuel appointed David King of Israel, so I appoint you head of these schools. I'll meet you at the judgment seat of Christ with them."

Pressure pitched on such a level Billy Graham did not know how to resist without feeling that, by doing so, he might be resisting the Almighty. Thus, for six months after Dr. Riley's death, Billy Graham served as interim president; then, for six months, as acting president and, finally, in 1948 he agreed to accept the post of president—on condition that he could continue much of his evangelistic work. It was a remarkable setup, admirably suited to the credit of no one and, perhaps, to a minimum of benefit to the Lord: Billy Graham continuing to live in Montreat, president of a school in Minneapolis, traveling the revival road much of the time.

In June, 1951—the school having grown substantially in enrollment, funds, and reputation during his three and a half divided years—he resigned as president. "I have been trying to do the work of two men. It isn't working. I must choose one or the other. The leading of the Lord seems clear and I must

145

follow it." This time there was no one to arrange the Lord's contrary intervention.

At Northwestern Billy Graham, among other things, learned about the educator-category mentioned by St. Paul as, at the church in Western Springs, he had already learned about the pastor-category. Facility at neither was the Lord's "gift" to him. Occupationally, this left only evangelism.

One further Northwestern discovery was a young Southern Baptist minister, administrative assistant to Dr. Riley and teacher of theology and Hebrew. When Billy Graham in 1950 was about to set out from Minneapolis for an evangelistic campaign in New England, Jerry Beavan said to him one day, "I'd give my right arm to go with you. I think I could help out with the press."

"Okay," said Billy Graham, "you're going along." He has been going along, "helping out with the press," ever since.

Today the promotional setup of every Billy Graham Crusade is Jerry Beavan's responsibility. I have heard him called a "genius." I have seen at close hand enough of the way he operates, months ahead of a Crusade, with half-committed ministers and reluctant laymen, to believe that—from the enthusiasm he engenders and the effort he enlists—there is a good deal of truth in that description.

"Sure, we've got to have organization," he says, "and for that we're sometimes criticized. But, organizationally, we aren't even in the same league with some of the denominations to which some of our critics belong. You can't get anywhere with any kind of business these days without organization. I happen to believe that, for Christ's business, we need the best."

A prize-fight promoter with above-average box-office know-how once said to Jerry Beaven, "Boy, how I'd like to have 20 per cent of your Billy Graham."

The promoter may or may not have understood Jerry's reply: "If you or I had 20 per cent of Billy Graham we might be broke but we'd still be two of the world's richest people."

146

Thus, in early September, 1949, Billy Graham came to Los Angeles. There were, by then, three other members of the Graham team: Grady Wilson, Billy Graham's boyhood friend, associate evangelist; Cliff Barrows, director of music; George Beverly Shea, soloist.

"We weren't sure," says Grady Wilson, "but that in Los Angeles we'd tackled something too big for us. Perhaps our faith wasn't geared up to it. Only a short time before we had been in Baltimore. Our meetings there were held in the Lyric Theater. That, for us, was a great act of faith, for the Lyric had 2,800 seats. Our prayer was that it would be filled, but until the very last meeting of our series it never was. In that Los Angeles tent there were 6,000 seats; it was breathtaking."

For the first two weeks and into the third, the Los Angeles meeting ran the usual revival course: good crowds, but no overflow; some scores of decisions; offerings sufficient to meet expenses. Midway through the third and presumably last week, the size of the crowds for no discernible reason jumped from a well-filled to a packed-out tent, with hundreds standing. By Friday night—with a record-breaking attendance—the question was: End, as scheduled, on Sunday or continue another week? On that question, for the next two nights, there was a lot of late praying.

Billy Graham—following a practice which, when Christians expected more of God, was a commonplace among them— asked the Lord for a sign: some visible, unmistakable evidence before the Sunday night meeting that continuing was His will; lacking which that night would be the last.

I am sure that those who expect nothing from God, and most of those who do not expect much, will put it down as sheer coincidence that that Sunday night, when Billy Graham arrived at the Crusade tent at Washington and Hill streets in downtown Los Angeles, there was waiting for him the largest contingent of reporters, feature writers, and newspaper photog-

147

raphers he had ever faced. That morning, from his fabled retreat at San Simeon, the aging William Randolph Hearst had sent a two-word telegram to the editors of the Hearst press: "Puff Graham."

This may have been sheer coincidence. And the fact that Mr. Hearst was involved in it will be proof enough to some that the Lord was not. The important point is that, to Billy Graham, it was not coincidence, but an answer to prayer. If he had concluded otherwise—that it was not prayer, but coincidence—then the Los Angeles meeting would have ended that night and Billy Graham would have gone his evangelizing way, diminishing as he went; not immediately aware any more, perhaps, than Samson was that "the Lord was departed from him."

But, says Billy Graham, the prayers that were being answered that Sunday night in Los Angeles began weeks before: "Los Angeles had more of everything. It had more publicity, more people, more decisions for Christ. But back of all these there was one indispensable thing that Los Angeles had more of: more people doing more praying."

That—whatever weight one may wish to give it—seems to have been true. It was in Los Angeles, for the first time, that organized prayer support was set up weeks in advance of a Billy Graham Crusade—set up under the auspices of an organization called "Christ for Greater Los Angeles." By the time the Crusade began more than 1,000 prayer groups had been formed in and around Los Angeles. For several weeks they had been meeting regularly to pray for the Crusade's success. These continued throughout the Crusade and they were supplemented by special prayer meetings in scores of churches. There were also many "prayer chains" in which volunteers recruited by Grady Wilson at the Crusade meetings divided the day and night into half-hour periods so that, twenty-four hours around the clock, the Crusade was continually being prayed for.

This, too, may belong in the department of coincidence but it is remarkable to note three of the persons who were converted in the first five days that followed that "final" Sunday night.

One of them was Stuart Hamblen, Southern California's best-known radio personality. To his radio audience and then at a Crusade meeting he said, "If anyone had told me I'd ever stand where I am standing tonight, I'd have said he was a candidate for the sanity commission. I don't know any fancy religious words. I've done practically everything everyone else has done. I've been a sinner. I also know that a few nights ago, I accepted Christ as my Savior."

Along "The Strip" in Hollywood, the odds were 10 to 1 it wouldn't last. It has.

Like many of those converted in Billy Graham's Crusades, Hamblen carries a pocket New Testament and, when there are a few odd minutes, reads it. He was reading it one day in the railroad station of a Canadian city. A soldier, sitting next to him, opened up a conversation.

"I've never had much to do with religion."

"You've missed something," said Hamblen.

"Well," said the soldier, "I just can't see myself following someone like Jesus Christ who's been dead 2,000 years."

"You say Jesus Christ is dead," said Hamblen. "That's strange. I was talking to Him, right here, not twenty minutes ago."

That week in Los Angeles also saw the conversion of Louis Zamperini, Olympic miler and one of the country's foremost war heroes. Today, from having been an aimless, drink-hounded ne'er-do-well, he runs a Christian camp for boys. Most startling of all, perhaps, was the conversion of Jim Vaus, henchman of and wiretapper for the notorious gangster, Mickey Cohen. Vaus today is in full-time religious work, as a lay evangelist.

During the five weeks into which that first week-long extension grew, the Los Angeles Crusade continued to gather momentum. It was front-page news in Los Angeles; it became a feature story nationally. More than 700 of the city's 1,000 Protestant churches—many of which had been cold to lukewarm toward Billy Graham—were, at the end, at least nominally supporting him.

"This city," said the minister of one of these churches, "with its 1,000 ministers preaching every Sunday, was going lazily along with the man on the street unimpressed. Then came Billy Graham. In eight weeks, he had more people thinking and talking about the claims of Christ than had all the city's pulpiteers in a year's time. When the Crusade closed, we faced a community that was at least willing to talk about the claims of Christ. My church got a dozen members, but it got more than members. It got new inspiration, zeal, and a spiritual uplift that can never be described."

"We had gone to Los Angeles unheralded," says Billy Graham. "When we left we knew that the Spirit of God had moved on that California city as never before. We believed also that there He gave proof that He would bless and use our ministry 'exceeding abundantly, above all that we ask or think.' "

Billy Graham: his most recent portrait. (Fabian Bachrach)

A characteristic speaking stance, with Billy Graham declaring, as he repeatedly does, "The Bible says . . ." (Jay B. Leviton from Black Star)

In Toronto's Coliseum, the first few of nearly 700 people who that night made "Decisions for Christ" come forward in response to Billy Graham's appeal. (© 1955 Time Inc. Courtesy Life Magazine)

Ruth and Billy Graham, in the fall of 1955, look over the construction of the new mountainside home into which they have now moved, above Montreat, North Carolina. (©1955 Time Inc. Courtesy Life Magazine)

Billy Graham's ardor for golf — his favorite relaxation — is not appreciably dimmed by the fact that he seldom shoots below 90. (Jay B. Leviton from Black Star)

During his 1954 Greater London Crusade, Billy Graham spoke to one of the largest crowds ever assembled in Trafalgar Square. "Britain," he said, "is at the beginning of what could be the greatest spiritual awakening of all time." (Combine Photos)

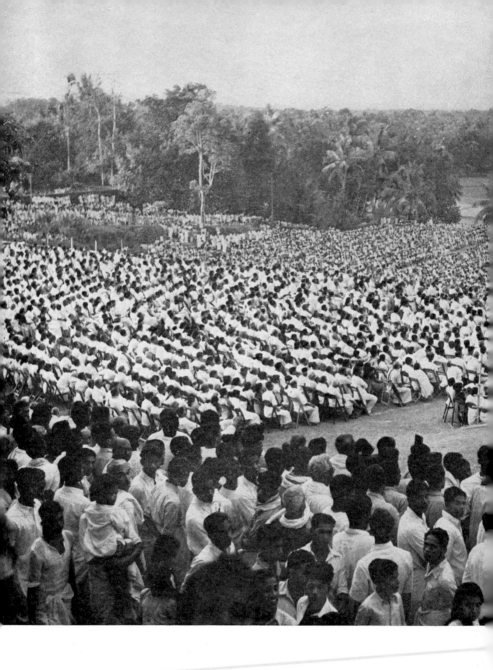

During his 1956 tour in India, Billy Graham, in city after city, drew larger crowds than had gathered a few weeks previously to hear Russia's emissaries Khrushchev and Bulganin. Here, in

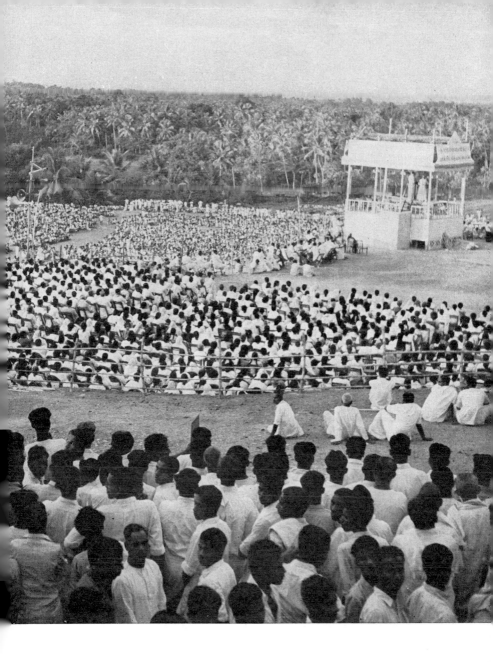

*an improvised stadium in a small south Indian city, more than
100,000 people, many of whom have traveled great distances
on foot, have assembled to hear him.*

Billy Graham, returning from his 1954 Crusade in Europe, is met at docksi in New York City by his family. Left to right: his wife Ruth Graham, An Billy, Ruth, Virginia. (United Press)

9: It takes money

SINCE LOS ANGELES—where Billy Graham's preaching began to be, in the historic revival sense, big-time evangelism —the scope of his ministry has extended until organizationally and financially it is now big-time business. It is a business which involves not only his meticulously organized Crusades but also radio, films, a newspaper column and books.

Some idea of the scope of his ministry can be gathered from this 1955 summary. In that year he held full-length Crusades in Glasgow, Scotland, for six weeks and in Toronto, Canada, for four; one seven-night mission at Wembley Stadium in London; another mission of five nights in Paris; and, in the course of a Continental tour, one-night meetings in twelve cities in seven countries in addition to several appearances before U.S. servicemen. During the year, in these meetings an estimated 4,100,000 persons heard Billy Graham face to face and a much larger, unestimated number listened to him by radio relay. Some 146,000 made "decisions for Christ."

Every Sunday during 1955, as it had been for five years, Billy Graham's radio program *The Hour of Decision* was on the air. Carried over three networks—the American Broadcasting Company, the National Broadcasting Company, and the Mutual Broadcasting System—this program is on 700

151

stations in the United States, 90 in Canada, and 50 abroad.

The average Sunday afternoon listening audience for *The Hour of Decision* is estimated at more than 20,000,000.

In its "film ministry" the Billy Graham organization has produced and distributed five evangelistic films. They are *Mid-century Crusade, Mr. Texas, Oil-Town USA, Souls in Conflict,* and *Fire in the Heather.*

During 1955 those five films were shown in the United States to 150,000 audiences with an estimated total attendance of several million.

In addition to this, Billy Graham's newspaper column, "My "Answer," runs five days a week in some 200 U.S. newspapers with a daily readership of 28,000,000.

His 1954 book *Peace with God* had, by the end of 1955, sold more than 500,000 copies and had been translated into 15 languages. A second book, *The Secret of Happiness,* published in 1955, was rapidly overtaking the first in sales. During 1955 Billy Graham also launched a television program over the facilities of the first commercial TV station in Great Britain.

When questioned, as he often is, about the multiplicity of his activities, Billy Graham, as one would expect, has a Scriptural answer: the statement of St. Paul to the Corinthians that "I am made all things to all men, that I might by all means save some."

Billy Graham says that almost every organization, business, agency, almost every person with something good or not so good to sell uses the miracle of modern machinery and modern communications to sell it: "Why not the churches and religion?

"We have a greater opportunity than Paul ever had. I imagine that if Paul can look down here he is champing at the bit. How he would like to be on television! How he would like to have a radio hour! How he would like to get on a plane and go from Corinth to Rome! How he would like to use some of the facilities we have for saving the lost!"

Altogether the Billy Graham organization is an operation

which runs to considerably more than $2,000,000 a year. When the budget for his "film ministry" and the cost of the individual Crusades—which is always raised and expended locally—is included the total would be more than $3,000,000.

So far as the fiscal side of the Billy Graham setup is concerned, there are two notable facts about it. The first is that fiscally it operates by use of the most modern business methods and, down to the last penny, entirely in the open. The second fact is that these highly efficient business methods are employed with a sense of religious mission not noticeably less than that which characterizes Billy Graham's direct evangelistic preaching.

Earlier in his revival ministry Billy Graham followed the somewhat loose financial practices which have characterized other evangelists and which unhappily in many places have seemed to put the dollar sign on revivalists and their methods. Billy Graham's awareness of this problem came to a focus at the end of the six-week Crusade in Atlanta, Georgia, in 1950. In that Crusade a collection—customarily called a "love offering"—was taken for him and Cliff Barrows. That this method of finance could prove to be a detriment to his ministry was made more apparent by the fact that an Atlanta newspaper published a picture of Billy Graham holding a huge bag which contained this cash collection.

Soon thereafter he took counsel with various people and soon worked out a plan which once and for all totally eliminated the "love offering" method and regularized—more effectively, I think, than any evangelist before him—his own finances and that of his organization.

Today there are two financial aspects to every Billy Graham Crusade. One has to do with the Crusade's local expenses; the other with the finances of Billy Graham and his team. Each Crusade is locally incorporated under the laws of the particular state or country, with a board of directors made up of interested local businessmen, professional men, and clergymen.

The actual money for the Crusade is almost wholly raised by the regular collections made at each Crusade meeting. These collections are not solicited from the platform by a member of the Billy Graham team, but each night by a local businessman or minister. The board of the local corporation prepares a budget for the Crusade; supervises the expenditures; and at the end makes a public accounting published in the local newspapers, giving a detailed and audited financial statement.

Because of the importance of such reckonings in revealing the integrity of the Billy Graham operation, I am including here the audit which was published in the Nashville newspapers at the conclusion of the Billy Graham Crusade early in 1955.

(As published in *The Nashville Tennessean*, Sunday morning, February 27, 1955.)

Report of Audit
BILLY GRAHAM CAMPAIGN FUND

Statement of Receipts and Disbursements . . .
Dec. 30, 1953 to Dec. 15, 1954

OSBORN AND PAGE
CERTIFIED PUBLIC ACCOUNTANTS
2012 BROADWAY
NASHVILLE 4, TENNESSEE

HILARY H. OSBORN, C. P. A.	NASHVILLE, TENNESSEE
FRED G. PAGE, C. P. A.	2012 BROADWAY
ROBERT ADAIR, C. P. A.	
EUGENE R. MULLINS, C. P. A.	KNOXVILLE, TENNESSEE
ALBERT M. MILLER, C. P. A.	FIDELITY BANKERS TRUST BUILDING

The Greater Nashville Evangelistic Crusade, Inc.
Nashville, Tennessee
Gentlemen:

We have examined the accounts of The Greater Nashville Evangelistic Crusade, Inc., Nashville, Tennessee, for the period ended December 15, 1954. The results of our examination are presented in this report which consists of these comments and the following designated exhibits:

154

Exhibit "A"—Statement of Cash Receipts and
Disbursements, December 30, 1953,
Through December 15, 1954.

Exhibit "B"—Condition of Budget, December 30, 1953,
Through December 15, 1954.

Our examination was made in accordance with generally accepted
auditing standards applicable in the circumstances, and accordingly
included such tests of the accounting records and such other auditing
procedures as we considered necessary.

Minutes of directors' meetings were examined in order to ascertain
whether the financial transactions were handled in accordance with the
wishes of the directors and in accordance with the authority delegated
by them.

The Greater Nashville Evangelistic Crusade, Inc., was incorporated
in the State of Tennessee on December 30, 1953. The purpose of the
corporation was to sponsor, promote, and conduct religious, evangelical,
spiritual and evangelistic revivals through preaching and teaching of the
Gospel of Jesus Christ in the Nashville area.

Cash on deposit with Third National Bank, Nashville, Tennessee, in
the amount of $13,431.23, at December 15, 1954, was verified by rec-
onciling the books with the amount reported to us by the depository.

We mailed requests for confirmation to a representative number of
suppliers of materials and services to determine if there were any outstanding liabilities. At the date of this report only minor amounts had
been reported. After payment of all liabilities, the amount of which
appears to be nominal, the remaining balance is to be transferred to the
Billy Graham Evangelistic Association for the Hour of Decision.

In our opinion, the Statement of Cash Receipts and Disbursements,
and Condition of Budget, fairly reflect the financial transactions of The
Greater Nashville Evangelistic Crusade, Inc., Nashville, Tennessee, for
the period from inception, December 30, 1953, through December 15,
1954, in conformity with generally accepted accounting principles.

Respectfully submitted
Signed:

Osborn and Page
Certified Public Accountants

January twenty-five
1955

GREATER NASHVILLE EVANGELISTIC CRUSADE

with Billy Graham

February 19, 1955

To the People of Greater Nashville
Dear Friends:

The Treasurer and Finance Committee of Greater Nashville Evangelistic Crusade, Inc., wish to present to you a full accounting of all funds committed to them.

A letter from Osborn and Page, who offered their accounting services free, indicates the scope of their certified audit.

We would like to call to your attention in brief form a few of the highlights.

Total budgeted amount agreed on by your local committee for local expenses including the $20,000 for lighting Vanderbilt Stadium: $80,721.00. Total expenditures for local expenses were: $75,324.75.

Receipts for local expenses consisted of:

Advanced Gifts	$31,268.48
Collections at Meetings	57,374.62
Profit on Song Books	946.63

Collections for local expenses were stopped a full week before the Crusade ended.

The difference between receipts and expenditures will be forwarded to the Hour of Decision with the condition that any additional contingencies arising be drawn from such surplus.

Hour of Decision Sunday offerings of cash were counted and deposited here and a check sent to Minneapolis. Envelope offerings were sent direct to Minneapolis.

Total Hour of Decision offerings, cash and envelopes, were $80,-497.64. $38,000 was set aside for the European Crusade.

The Special offering for Rev. J. D. Blinco was counted and a check deposited to his account in the amount of $5,943.75.

Spiritual accounting of the Crusade rests with our God, and for the success of the Crusade, to Him be the Glory.

> *Ben Whitmore,* Treasurer
> *Ernest J. Moench,*
> Chairman Finance Committee

THE GREATER NASHVILLE EVANGELISTIC CRUSADE, INC.

Nashville, Tennessee
Exhibit "A"
Statement of Cash Receipts and Disbursements
December 30, 1953, Through December 15, 1954

RECEIPTS—

Collections at Meetings $57,374.62

Gifts	31,268.48	
Sales of Song Books	5,446.63	
Refunds and Sales of Materials	1,112.22	
Income from Showing of Film	1,083.37	
Third National Bank—Note	995.00	
Banquets	396.50	
Redeposit of Petty Cash Fund	100.00	

Total Receipts for The Greater Nashville
Evangelistic Crusade, Inc. $97,776.82

Collections Handled for Others:
Hour of Decision $22,509.98
Rev. J. D. Blinco (of England)   5,943.75   28,453.73

TOTAL RECEIPTS $126,230.55

DISBURSEMENTS

Budget Expenses (Exhibit "B")   75,324.75
Add—Amount of Receipts
Credited to Budget Expenses:
Sales of Song Books   5,446.63
Refunds and Sales of Materials   1,112.22
Banquets   396.50
Interest Deduction—Note   (5.00)   82,275.10

Expense of Showing Film   713.56
Billy Graham Evangelistic
Film, Inc.   369.81   1,083.37

Third National Bank—Note   1,000.00
To Set Up Petty Cash Fund   100.00
Less—Taxes Withheld from Salaries   (112.88)

Total Disbursements for The
Greater Nashville Evangelistic
Crusade, Inc.   84,345.59

Remittance of Collections
Handled for Others:
Billy Graham Evangelistic As-
sociation—Hour of Decision   22,509.98
Rev. J. D. Blinco (of England)   5,943.75   28,453.73

TOTAL DISBURSEMENTS $112,799.32

Bank Balance, December 15, 1954 $13,431.23

THE GREATER NASHVILLE
EVANGELISTIC CRUSADE, INC.

Nashville, Tennessee
Exhibit "B"
Condition of Budget
December 30, 1953, Through December 15, 1954

	Amount Budgeted	Amount Expended
STADIUM AND FIELD HOUSE—		
Lighting	$20,000.00	$20,000.00
Platforms	1,000.00	1,341.22
Other Construction	1,250.00	1,454.07
Tent, Chairs and Lights	1,250.00	1,450.96
Public Address Systems	1,500.00	1,450.00
Insurance	500.00	592.98
Decorating	500.00	.00
Maintenance	1,000.00	3,436.41
Field House	500.00	223.91
Miscellaneous	500.00	851.88
Total	$28,000.00	$30,801.43
ADVERTISING—		
Newspaper	$ 1,000.00	$ 787.96
Radio and Television	1,000.00	1,473.70
Outdoor	4,000.00	3,952.18
Poster	1,000.00	424.75
Miscellaneous	1,000.00	45.67
Total	$ 8,000.00	$ 6,684.26
CRUSADE OFFICE—		
Rental	$ 1,500.00	$ 1,247.66
Salaries	2,000.00	3,082.38
Equipment	250.00	448.82
Supplies	1,250.00	992.25
Telephone and Telegraph	500.00	762.49
Miscellaneous	500.00	511.74
Total	$ 6,000.00	$ 7,045.34
PRINTING, MAILING, ETC.—		
Printing	$ 5,000.00	$ 3,975.45
Postage	1,200.00	2,164.12
Supplies	800.00	354.63
Miscellaneous	500.00	.00
Total	$ 7,500.00	$ 6,494.20

158

COUNSELING AND FOLLOW-UP—
Pre-Campaign:

Salaries of Team	$ 1,655.50	$ 678.00
Materials	471.00	2.45
Salary and Expense of Team Members	1,952.00	3,528.20
Materials Used in Counsel Room	800.00	1,700.01
Follow-Up Through Churches	420.00	.00
Counseling and Follow-Up—Other	1,452.50	.00
Instruction Classes	105.00	9.45
Office Expense	865.00	320.54
Total	$ 7,721.00	$ 6,238.65

THE EVANGELISTIC TEAM—

Salaries*	$12,500.00	$ 7,720.50
Expenses	6,500.00	$ 9,734.52
Total	$19,000.00	$17,455.02

MISCELLANEOUS—

Badges	$ 300.00	$ 206.39
Freight and Express	750.00	298.80
Equipment Rental	250.00	7.00
Organ and Piano	750.00	62.00
Song Books (Net)	500.00	*(946.63)
Nursery	250.00	106.28
Utilities	500.00	.00
Banquets, etc. (Net)	1,000.00	743.62
Unforeseen Contingencies	200.00	128.39
Total	$ 4,500.00	$ 605.85
Grand Total	$80,721.00	$75,324.75

*Sales	$5,446.63	
Cost	4,500.00	
Profit	$ 946.63	

EXECUTIVE COMMITTEE

REV. JAMES M. GREGG
Crusade Chairman

DR. WALTER R. COURTENAY
Co-Chairman

ALBERT P. ROSE
Vice-Chairman

REV. CECIL D. EWELL
Secretary

REV. CLARENCE BOWEN
Asst. Secretary

BEN A. WHITMORE
Treasurer

JOHN O. ELLIS
Asst. Treasurer

REV. W. C. WESTENBERGER

Honorary Chairmen: GOV. FRANK G. CLEMENT . . . MAYOR BEN WEST
. . . HON. J. PERCY PRIEST . . . BISHOP ROY H. SHORT

COMMITTEE CHAIRMEN

DR. W. F. POWELL
Pastor's Advisory

DR. H. THORNTON FOWLER
Co-Chairman

CHARLES M. GRAY
Men's Prayer Meeting

MRS. HARVEY REESE
REV. RALPH SCHURMAN
Cottage Prayer Meeting

JOHN T. BENSON
Music

LEE DAVIS
Ushers

LEWIS E. MOORE
Auditorium

DR. GEORGE H. JONES
Publicity

DR. LEONARD STIGLER
Counseling and Follow-Up

ERNEST J. MOENCH
Finance

MRS. KEITH VON HAGEN
Children

DAVID C. RUTHERFORD
Young People

MRS. TOM STONE
Nursery

GAYLE L. GUPTON
Delegations

*No amount was paid to Billy Graham for Honorarium. This amount represents payment to other members of the team.

THE GREATER NASHVILLE EVANGELISTIC CRUSADE, INC.

In most Crusades the regular collections more than cover the local costs. The board of directors is authorized to dispose of this surplus. Most often it is contributed to a local charity, occasionally to the work of the Billy Graham Evangelistic Association.

It is through the Billy Graham Evangelistic Association, Inc., that the second aspect of the Billy Graham operation is regularized: namely, the financing of Billy Graham and his team. This association, which has its headquarters in Minneapolis, Minnesota, is a result of the launching in 1950 of *The Hour of Decision.* The story of how that radio program—which almost overnight made him a national figure and resulted in the expansion to its present large-scale proportions of the Billy Graham operation—got on the air merits being told here in some detail because it is, I think, a dramatic revelation of the quality of Billy Graham's faith and how that faith, implemented by prayer, figures in his decisions.

This story reaches its amazing climax in the lobby of the Multnomah Hotel in Portland, Oregon, a few minutes before midnight, August 16, 1950. But it began two months before in a roadside diner near Ocean City, New Jersey.

That day, Billy Graham, attending a conference in Ocean City, had driven into the country with a fellow preacher. They stopped at this diner for lunch. As they walked to a table, a stranger rushed up to Billy Graham, tears in his eyes, and said, "This can only be God's doing."

This was his story. A preacher in Philadelphia, with considerable local radio experience and some wider contacts in the field, he was an admirer of the young and then much less renowned evangelist. During the previous night he had wakened with what he described, in Quaker terminology, as a "concern" to put Billy Graham's message on a radio network. Since he believed Billy Graham was in Europe, he dismissed the idea. The next morning, however, the same concern returned—this time with such urgency that he finally decided to drive to the shore "to shake it off or figure it out." To him, this meeting in the diner where he, too, had stopped for lunch, was not "chance" but "a Providential directive."

Billy Graham was sympathetic to the man, but totally unconvinced—"be it said to my shame"—of the Providential origin of his idea. He had never, he said, given any thought to a national radio program. He explained that he had no funds or organization, not even any network contacts. The preacher, undaunted, promised that he would be heard from again. Billy Graham quickly forgot the incident.

But two weeks later at a Bible conference in northern Michigan he was unexpectedly called on by two advertising executives. One of these was Walter Bennett, head of the Walter F.

Bennett Advertising Agency in Chicago. The other was his Philadelphia associate, Fred Dienert. Both these men were active churchmen. Bennett, a Lutheran, had been active for years in the promotion of other famous religious broadcasts. Dienert happened to be a member of the church in Philadelphia served by the minister who met Billy Graham in Ocean City.

Although they had never before met Billy Graham, they explained to him at their meeting in northern Michigan that they had heard of his interest in a radio program: "We have come to see what we can do about it."

Billy Graham assured them there was nothing they could do. His schedule was already overcrowded. He simply was not interested.

Within a week they reappeared, this time at Billy Graham's home in Montreat, North Carolina. They had enlisted the interest of a broadcasting company; a thirteen-week schedule at a good Sunday afternoon hour was available; the cost: $92,000. "That," says Billy Graham, "was the kind of money I knew nothing about"—and the discussion abruptly concluded.

In Portland, Oregon, that July, Billy Graham began what, up to then, was his most successful Crusade, with 18,000 people, night after night, crowding the specially built "tabernacle." But hardly a day passed when, to his increasing irritation, he did not hear, by telephone or telegram, from Bennett and Dienert who had made themselves the self-appointed promoters of a Billy Graham radio program. One weekend they appeared in person.

The program, they said, could be launched for an initial $25,000. Thereafter, the cost—something more than $7,000 a week—would be met by voluntary contributions from the radio audience. What they got from Billy Graham was another curt "no"—"the whole thing, beginning with the $25,000 I didn't have or know where to get, was altogether fantastic."

162

When, ten days later, they returned, he refused to see them. They waited a week. Then, having booked air passage home, they left a parting message for Billy Graham with the promise that they would drop the whole idea and pressure him no more. As a "goodbye courtesy," he invited them to his room.

Then, recalling the incident in the diner, Billy Graham began to wonder whether "perhaps this was the Lord's doing; perhaps He did want me on the air." When, therefore, Bennett and Dienert arrived at his room, he told them that, on the human level, his decision was unchanged. But the final decision, he said, should be "not mine, but the Lord's." The three knelt and Billy Graham prayed—"The kind of prayer I have never prayed before or since."

He said in his prayer that he would accept it as proof that a radio program was "the Lord's plan" for him, if, by midnight that night, there could be placed in his hands the sum of $25,000.

Up to then, the largest single contribution Billy Graham had ever received for his work was less than $500. Sure that he had asked the impossible, the two visitors bade him goodbye and left for the airport.

Before his sermon that night Billy Graham told his overflow audience of the radio offer; of his repeated refusal to consider seriously a venture so far beyond his means; of his desire to settle the matter in accord with God's will. He did not mention his prayer or the sum required. "We won't be seeking you out," he said. "But if you think this is God's plan, you can seek us out."

At the end of the service, after he had spoken to those who had made "decisions for Christ," he went to the room reserved for members of his team. Grady Wilson, his associate evangelist, stood in the door. A long line was queued up in front of him. An old shoebox which Wilson held was filling with cash and with pledges scribbled on business cards, newspapers, sheets torn from songbooks, odd scraps of paper. An Idaho lumberman left a pledge for $2,500. A schoolteacher and his wife from down the Oregon coast pledged $1,000: "The contents of our saving account, but we can think of no better investment." A high-school boy pledged a month's earnings from his newspaper route.

The total was just over $23,500.

Waiting nearby were Bennett and Dienert. They had gone to the airport, boarded their plane, and then suddenly decided they would wait one more day.

"This is a miracle," they said to Billy Graham. "You're as good as on the air."

"No," he said, "it's not a miracle. The Devil could send us $23,500. It's all or nothing."

"We'll guarantee that last $1,500 ourselves."

"No, that's not the answer we prayed for."

It was almost midnight when, considerably let down, they reached the hotel. Grady Wilson asked at the desk for mail. There were three letters for Billy Graham. One of them was from another city, from a person unknown to Billy Graham expressing the conviction that his sermons should be regularly heard on radio. To start a Billy Graham radio fund, a check was enclosed for $1,000. Each of the other two letters, in hotel envelopes, contained checks for $250.

"Now," said Billy Graham, "I'll grant it's a miracle." In his room that midnight, there was another prayer meeting.

"Since then on several occasions," says Billy Graham, "our bank balance has been down to a few hundred dollars. But, in more than five years we've never asked for a loan and every bill has been paid on time.

"The Lord who heard us that night in Portland is still giving proof that He does answer prayer."

A large share of credit for the promotion of his radio and newspaper ministry and for the worldwide circulation of his books, as well as for his wisdom in other business matters, must go to Walter Bennett and his associate Fred Dienert in the Walter F. Bennett Advertising Agency. It is not likely that many businessmen have given themselves to any cause with greater energy, imagination, and devotion than these two men have shown in extending the message of Billy Graham.

That night in Portland, Billy Graham had no idea what to do with the for him—large sum of cash which had been collected. Overnight it was kept guarded in his hotel room by an unsleeping Grady Wilson. The next morning Wilson took it in a huge bundle to a local bank. The problem of what to do with it thereafter was still unresolved. To undertake the resolving of it, Billy Graham that day sent a hurry-up call to his friend George Wilson—no relation to Grady Wilson—who was business manager of the Northwestern Bible School in Minneapolis, where Billy Graham had served as interim president.

Out of the $25,000 contributed for the launching of *The Hour of Decision* came the Billy Graham Evangelistic Association, Inc., which Wilson—who goes about his job with a notable combination of business shrewdness and religious zeal— still directs. He himself is secretary-treasurer of the Association's board of directors. The other members are Billy Graham as president, Grady Wilson as vice-president, Cliff Barrows and Ruth Graham. The accounts of the Association are audited by a local firm of certified public accountants.

Billy Graham's salary is $15,000 a year. It is paid by the Association. So are the salaries of the other members of the Billy Graham team, as well as all of the 125 Association employees in Minneapolis. Billy Graham's only additional income is from the proceeds of the sale of his books. That income is being set aside as a trust fund for the education of his children.

The funds which were handled through the Billy Graham Evangelistic Association for the financing of the Billy Graham operation amounted in 1955 to over $2,000,000. It is a mark of the efficiency of the organziation that in the expenditure of this sum, including the amounts spent for promotional mailings,

165

only 2¾ per cent went for overhead. The major item of expenditure is of course the radio program, *The Hour of Decision*, which runs to approximately $30,000 a week. The second major expenditure, in addition to salaries, is the subsidy paid out for the deficit of the film ministry.

All of the funds of the Billy Graham Evangelistic Association come, of course, from the voluntary contributions of supporters of the Billy Graham ministry. On each of the Sunday afternoon radio programs an appeal is made, not in so many words asking for financial contributions but, more subtly, asking for support. Listeners desiring "to support this ministry" are asked to write to Billy Graham, Minneapolis, Minnesota. Most persons who respond to this invitation know what is expected of them and send contributions.

Since its organization the Billy Graham Evangelistic Association has received one contribution of $50,000 from a foundation and one check of $5,000 from an individual. Those are the largest gifts ever received. Most contributions are so modest that the average runs to a little more than $5 each. The mailing list of contributors, built up over the five years since the Billy Graham Evangelistic Association was formed, numbers now nearly 1,000,000. This list is kept meticulously current. In addition to formalized letters from Billy Graham thanking these individuals for their specific contributions, all of the nearly 1,000,000 persons on this list receive from the Association a regular promotional mailing once every two or three months. Many persons contribute repeatedly: some of them once a month, some twice a month, some of them having averaged from once to twice to four times a month—for sums varying each time from $2 to $5—for the last four years.

The Billy Graham Evangelistic Association started in 1950 in a three-room office with one employee. Today it occupies part of three floors of a modern four-story building with 125 employees. In addition to the Minneapolis office, a headquarters is maintained for the team of Washington, D.C., where also are located the offices of the Billy Graham Evangelistic Films.

In the offices in Minneapolis George Wilson has installed business machinery and methods which would do credit to the most up-to-date mail-order establishment. There is, however, a religious plus about the operation of this office which, so far as my experience goes, puts it, businesswise, in a class by itself. Every morning, for example, the 125 employees gather in a cleared space between the files for a twenty-minute devotional service conducted, when he is there, by George Wilson.

Many hundreds of the letters received every week by the Billy Graham Evangelistic Association contain no contribution. They are written by persons seeking spiritual guidance. These letters from all kinds and conditions of people and with all kinds of problems are promptly and carefully answered, with no accompanying financial solicitation.

The seven women who read this "problem mail" begin their day's proceedings—before they have read a letter—with a special "season of prayer" in which, as one of them explained it to me, "We ask God to give us understanding and wisdom in classifying this mail and suggesting how it can be answered."

Most of the problem mail falls into definite categories, of which there are about forty. The substance of a reply for the problem in each of these categories has been prepared, given a number, and can be run off by pressing a button. In addition to this formal reply, there is, in most instances, a personalized introduction and conclusion written for each letter by an associate of George Wilson, also a minister.

Occasionally letters come for which no prepared reply seems adequate, of which unclassified category the following is a sample:

"My wife and I will doubtless go to Heaven. We have been married, and peacefully, for many years. We are nearly sixty and are almost typical. We sort of mind our own affairs, never cause anyone any trouble. My problem—I just can't imagine

167

spending an eternity with my wife. One hundred thousand years or so, yes. But eternity—well I just don't see how I can stand it. Isn't there some way I could avoid going to Heaven and at the same time not go to Hell?"

Even the operators of the business machines—some of them Billy Graham converts—likewise begin their day's work with the prayer that "God will help us this day to do good and accurate work in using this machine in His service."

Not long ago, several efficiency engineers called on George Wilson and after he had taken them through the plant, expressed their amazement that he could have set up and continued to run with such efficiency so highly technical an operation without any previous technical training.

"In our business," they said, "we have books that have to be mastered before we can be masters of these machines."

To which Wilson replied, "Believe it or not, we have a book too—the Good Book." As one of the experts subsequently remarked, "Ordinarily we would have laughed that off—but not after having seen his operation."

I spent a number of days in the offices of the Billy Graham Evangelistic Association in Minneapolis. I got, I think, a thorough and complete account of its operations, of the monetary intake and outgo. But I came away with the feeling that, efficiently as the business is handled, its real audit is shown in no ordinary balance sheet.

One afternoon, pointing to a series of filing cabinets, George Wilson said, "Here is where we keep our real accounting. These cabinets are a file of the 146,000 persons who under Billy Graham's ministry made 'decisions for Christ' in 1955. It is the record kept in this room which makes every one of us feel so sure that whatever our specific job may be, the work we are doing is the Lord's work."

10: London: revival drama

MANY THOUGHTFUL OBSERVERS agree that not since the Dwight L. Moody revival in the late nineteenth century, perhaps not since John Wesley, has Great Britain been more widely or deeply stirred, religiously, than during Billy Graham's Greater London Crusade in the spring of 1954.

"Three months," wrote one British editor, "have transformed the atmosphere of Britain.

"The Archbishop of Canterbury became enthusiastic; the Prime Minister sent for Dr. Graham; the First Sea Lord got up in public and went to the Inquiry Room. So likewise did many thousands from all walks of life—many being persons of leading rank or high in the learned professions and big business.

"The effect seems to be a calm, a confidence, an escape from the house built on shifting sands to that built on rock. This remarkable occurrence is of first historic importance."

It was also an event of first importance for the ministry of Billy Graham. It added maturity to him—both in and out of the pulpit. It modulated somewhat the phrasing of his messages —without modifying their essential content. It gave him international stature. Moreover, in Great Britain, for the first time, his preaching stirred an entire nation.

If, in fact, the ministry of Billy Graham kindles in the Western world the fires of an authentic religious revival, it will almost certainly be found that the place where that kindling began was London, in the spring of 1954.

A later chapter in this book will recount some of the consequences of the Greater London Crusade and attempt to appraise their significance. This chapter is the story of that Crusade itself. It is a story told, for the most part, in the stirring and highly human letters of Mrs. Billy Graham to her parents. First, however, it will be helpful, I think, to sketch in the background.

In advance of his going, London was held to be, and undoubtedly was, the most difficult city Billy Graham had ever faced. In the beginning, to judge from the secular press, it was outwardly the most hostile.

British church life was at a low ebb, probably lower than at any time in this century. There were few, if any, signs in Britain of the religious upsurge which was swelling church membership in the United States and filling its churches. Church membership—60 per cent of the U.S. population— was only 5 to 15 per cent in Britain. As against 34 per cent of the U.S. population which regularly attend church, the percentage of churchgoers in England was only 10 per cent.

The prevailing British church atmosphere, even in many churches of evangelical tradition, was, to put it moderately, cool to "revivalism"—and much more so to the American brand of it. The attitude in more than Anglican circles was that of the vestryman who voted against the participation of his church in the Crusade: "I don't like all this preaching about conversion. It isn't Church of England."

The Crusade was sponsored by more than 1,000 Greater London churches of all denominations, two-thirds of them Church of England. But many sponsoring ministers went along reluctantly at first, hoping—probably praying—that, though no great good could be expected, no great harm would come.

170

Six nights a week for twelve weeks, from March through May, Billy Graham preached in Harringay Arena—a 12,000-capacity, barnlike sports palace which, so his associates were warned, few sports events ever filled and no man in Britain, save possibly Churchill, could hope to fill for so long as two nights in a row.

For 72 nights—except for three when there were serious storms—Billy Graham's preaching filled it. Repeatedly two, sometimes three, evening services were necessary to handle the overflow. On a network of land wires, the Harringay services were sent to capacity audiences in halls and churches in 400 communities throughout England, Scotland, and Wales. On the last day of the Crusade, in the afternoon, 65,000 people filled White City, an outdoor stadium; in the evening 120,000 filled Wembley Stadium.

In all, nearly 2,000,000 persons heard Billy Graham. There were 40,000 decisions for Christ.

In all this, no one, save Billy Graham himself, was more deeply concerned or more actively engaged than Ruth Bell Graham, his wife. Her days in London were filled with engagements all single-mindedly aimed to help her husband's ministry. Every night at Harringay she worked as one of the 600 trained counsellors meeting with those who made their public decision and came for guidance to the Inquiry Room.

But Ruth Graham found time to write her parents in North Carolina intimate, colorful, deeply moving letters of what was happening and her part in it. Those letters tell better, even, than statistics or editorial comment, the amazing story of the Greater London Crusade.

They begin late in February, when Billy and Ruth Graham and several associates, arriving in England, were greeted in the press with an outpouring of scorn and open hostility. Billy was headlined as a "Hot Gospeller"; his Crusade, a "Gospel Circus"; his organization, "£100,000 of Hot Gospel"; his beliefs as "Fifty Years Out of Date." When, at London's Waterloo

Station, he was met by the biggest crowd since the arrival in 1924 of Mary Pickford and Douglas Fairbanks, one headline was: "Film Stars—So Why Not Billy?" Now comes an "expert" from "God's Own Country," wrote a *Daily Mirror* columnist, "to tell us what to think and what to believe."

Ruth Graham wrote:

"Dear folks:

"This is all fantastic. Last Tuesday, somewhere between the Isle of Wight and Southampton, a tug full of pressmen pulled alongside the liner: 25 reporters, 11 photographers. I knew they were after Bill's scalp and there was nothing we could do but pray for wisdom and be as courteous and gracious as we could. Several followed me. Their first observation was: 'I see you still wear make-up.' 'Is it true,' one asked, 'that your husband carries around his own special jug of water for baptism?'

"Bill wore a gray flannel sport coat and tie with small gray and black checks. So one headlines: 'No clerical collar, but my! what a lovely tie.' Another told me, 'Mrs. Graham, I am disappointed in your husband.'

" 'Is that right?' (I can't imagine anyone being disappointed in Bill.)

" 'Yes, we expected bright, hand-painted ties, flashy socks, and a sort of mass hysteria, but he is quite an ordinary chap.'

"Ashore, Bill had to be interviewed by television, so I had to stand beside him. The first question was: 'Who invited you over here anyway?' Then such killers as, 'Do you think you can save Britain?' 'Don't you think you're more needed in your own country?' 'What do you plan to do about Russia?' Bill's answers were wise, really terrific. God sure helps that man!

"There was one movie star aboard who should have had the press. I think one reporter interviewed her. It was ludicrous. The greatest reception England has given anyone at Southampton—and to a preacher!

"But we could see God beginning to cause the wrath of man

172

to praise Him. As we went through customs, the customs man said, 'Welcome to England and good luck, sir. We need you.' A dock worker came up and said, 'God bless you, sir. I am praying for you.' At the station, a little soldier recognized Bill and came over saying he was a Christian and that a group from the Royal Army Medical Corps was coming to Harringay: 'God bless you, sir. We are praying for you.' As we boarded our third-class compartment, the conductor said to Bill, 'I'm not much on religion, but could do with some.'

"It was about an hour to London. We had Bible and prayers. The train pulled in at Waterloo station at 1:19 and we stepped out into a perfect mob. Cheers rose, then a few familiar faces grew out of the blur. The press of the crowd was really terrific. But everyone had a wonderful smile and the air was filled with: 'God bless you,' 'Welcome to England.' Suddenly the crowd began singing: 'And Can It Be That I Shall Gain an Interest in My Savior's Crown?' By getting on something high I could see Bill's slow progress through the throng of singing, cheering, laughing folks."

(Total cost of the London campaign was about $400,000. More than one half was paid by the Billy Graham Evangelistic Association of Minneapolis, including the salaries of Billy Graham and his associates. Each of the team members, including Billy Graham, took a 50 per cent salary cut while in Britain.

Chairman of the London campaign committee was Major-General Wilson Haffendon; foremost among his early supporters was Dr. H. R. Gough, Anglican Bishop of Barking. "The man I most feel sorry for in this Billy Graham business," wrote Hanon Swaffer, columnist for the Socialist *Daily Herald,* "is the Bishop of Barking, who, after an honoured life, has become the American evangelist's best-known British sponsor.")

"Dearest folks:
"Some cute stories came out of that welcome at the station.

Bill was being interviewed by a reporter from the *Herald*. He asked if Bill didn't feel that the crowd at Waterloo were fanatics, to which Bill replied: 'Not unless you consider some of your leading clergymen, leading generals, members of Parliament, and the good Christian people who have been praying for these meetings—not unless you consider them fanatics.'

"That afternoon I had three interviews. One wanted a story from my angle: 'Is your husband difficult to live with?' 'Do you have to handle him with kid gloves?' 'Do you ever feel a twinge of jealousy over the attentions your husband receives?'

"At six o'clock we had a team meeting in the lounge. There was a straight-from-the-shoulder talk from Bill on how we must conduct ourselves as Americans in England. General Wilson Haffendon spoke. When the Bishop of Barking came in we had just requested a prayer for him as the *Herald* had been most unkind. Hanon Swaffer had been unkindest of all. The general said, 'Now don't you bother to pray for the Bishop. He is where Christ put him. You get busy and pray for Hanon Swaffer.' And the Bishop agreed heartily and stood saying, 'Don't you worry about me, Billy. If for a few days the newspapers have made me appear a fool for Christ's sake, I shall be only too happy to appear a fool with you.'

"Did I tell you that last night in one cold, unheated building 800 people prayed all night long on their knees for this meeting?

"Lucy Gough and I went to shop for some long evening gloves since on Thursday Lord and Lady Luke are to entertain us at Claridge's with a terrifying list of lords and ladies. It was this evening that Bill burst in having just returned from meeting Lord and Lady Luke and scared stiff over the guest list and the idea of having to address them."

"Dearest folks:

"Where was I? I think Bill had just come back from meeting Lord and Lady Luke. We dressed and were ready at 7:45. It

174

was stated on the engraved invitations: 'Full Dress and Decorations.' That meant medals. Claridge's is sort of a Waldorf-Astoria in London. Only more so.

"The guests were already assembling so we quickly checked our wraps and were taken into a lovely room where we were stopped by a man in bright red cutaway coat and knee-britches. He asked our name and then announced in a loud, deliberate voice: 'Dr. and Mrs. Billy Graham.' We stood in line with Lord and Lady Luke and one by one the guests arrived, were announced by the man in red, shook hands with us, and then went through and were served cocktails, I think you would call them. Even the evangelical bishops over here take wine and sherry. Bill and I were so full of orange juice I thought we would never want to see any again.

"The guests were a charming and impressive group: ninety in all. I couldn't help wondering what would be the outcome. If even a few of them could be won for Christ, they could win so many others. Bill gave a special message on why our two great nations that have stood together in every other way must stand together spiritually, and closed with a brief word of testimony.

"The Bishop of Worcester told me there is not a denomination in England which has not had some great leader who was a product of Dwight L. Moody's meetings and not a city that has not had a civic leader who came to Christ under his ministry. We pray it may be so again. All London is watching, talking, waiting. Something is going to happen.

"Friday noon Bill spoke at a luncheon of nearly 1,000 ministers. Friday night he was guest at a dinner at the House of Commons. Around 300 attended. Saturday the team had a luncheon with all the committee. All our old friends were there with some very important people, but mostly dear, sweet, godly folks who longed to see a great spiritual awakening come to Britain and were willing to climb out on a limb inviting Bill over 'sight unseen.' "

(At Harringay, on Monday evening, March 1, Billy Graham preached the first sermon of the Crusade. Nearly 200 newspapermen, many still gunning for Billy, were present. "All the tricks of the modern demagogue," wrote one. Someone remarked, "Only the people seem to be for Billy.")

"Dearest folks:

"Last night it was cold and snowing. Jerry called from Harringay about six saying only a couple of thousand had arrived. Bill looked stunned. Poor man: a splitting headache, and I knew it was nerves. We got there and practically no one was going in. They all seemed to be rushing by to the dog races just behind Harringay. Then at the door: 'The Arena is jammed!' What a sight! And what a thrill to hear them sing: 'All Hail the Power of Jesus' Name!' How they can sing! Bill brought a message on 'Does God Matter?'

"Two hundred and twenty-one came forward. God is doing abundantly, way and beyond all we asked."

"Dear folks:

"Briefly to bring you up to date. Saturday night by six the Arena was about half filled with people who had no reservations. As the 7:30 service was completely booked by coach parties, they called Bill to hurry over and closed the doors at 6:30 and had a wonderful service. Then, at 7:15, they dismissed that crowd and let in the reserved crowd outside. Policemen said between 30,000 and 35,000 were waiting. There were 11,000 from Wales alone.

"The house mikes were turned off and the entire congregation sang, 'Guide Me O Thou Great Jehovah'—thrilling, majestic, imploring. Later the dear folks from Wales sang, 'I Will Sing of My Redeemer' to their old Welsh tune. They break into parts and sing in strong tenors as if their hearts would break. And you're quite sure yours will.

"After the second service, they were dismissed and hundreds
176

more who had waited patiently outside were let in. Bill preached a third sermon."

"Dearest family:

"Thursday Bill spoke at the London School of Economics. Brother, they gave him a bad time, I guess. When he was introduced, the professor said, 'This is the first time a minister has been on that platform. We don't allow them here. This school was founded on secularism.' (Deafening applause.) Bill joked along with them, then got dead serious and told them what Christ had meant to him, what Christ had done for him. They could take it or leave it.

"They were listening closely when suddenly a student crashed through an upstairs window and stood there scratching himself like an ape. Bill joined in the laughter, then remarked, 'He reminds me of my ancestors.' Everyone laughed. 'Of course,' Bill continued, 'all my ancestors came from Britain.' That brought down the house. Then Bill gave it to them with both barrels. After he left they started calling the office wanting to debate with Bill, complained he had crammed religion down their throats. Bill isn't here to argue or debate.

"A schoolteacher has sent us a sheaf of prayers her little nine- and ten-year-olds had written in Bill's behalf and asked her to send to him. They are the sweetest things, all very formal. One I will never forget ended: 'And dear God, do for Dr. Billy Graham all that you possibly can.' "

(From London and elsewhere throughout Great Britain, where church membership and attendance had reached an all-time low, reports now began to come to the Campaign Committee of a marked increase of worshipers, of unprecedented numbers applying for church membership, of volunteers for Christian work. "It is not too much to say," said the London *Times,* "that Mr. Graham and his associates, like the evangelical Protestants here, have been surprised at the scale of the Crusade's success so far.")

"Dearest family:

"Did I tell you about one young woman converted at Harringay? She got off the bus next day looking for a Church of England clergyman and found one at St. Paul's Church. She told him what had happened and asked him how she could get to the mission field the quickest. Then she told him what had happened at work that morning when she walked in. The people with whom she worked looked at her curiously and one finally asked, 'Good Lord, what has happened to you?' 'That's exactly what has happened to me,' she replied. 'The good Lord has come into my heart.'

"One night I was introduced to a rather rugged-looking white-haired man who, when he found I was Mrs. Graham, took my hand in a most un-English way and kissed it. He was a pit miner up from Newcastle. He had spent his entire year's vacation pay in London attending the meetings.

"I know I have made some bad faux pas. But the worst I have discovered: I was talking to the Bishop of Worcester and asked if he had attended any of Mr. Moody's meetings. He looked a bit strange and said, 'No, I was not quite old enough.' I have learned since what I should have known long ago, that Mr. Moody preached here eighty years ago."

"Dearest family:

"Harringay was packed again. I sat beside Sandra, the little Russian girl. She has a Bible now, but I had to help her find her way. She is growing beautifully.

"Saturday afternoon there was another tea for young women converts. It was wonderful. There was a terrific testimony by a drama student who was converted last week. She has a marvelous personality and a sense of humor. She kept putting off Christ for fear He might interfere with her good times. And

178

her idea of a rip-roaring good time was an all-night party. In fact, she had one scheduled herself for last week. It was a 'Heaven or Hell' party. You went dressed as a citizen of one or the other place. She had kept coming to Harringay and kept fighting off conviction. She knew for one thing if she received Christ she would have to call off that party, and that she could not do.

"But finally the conviction got so heavy she knew it was 'now or never' and she gave in and yielded her heart and life to Christ. Her eyes fairly danced as she told of the peace and joy that have been hers since. Of course word got round the drama school of her conversion, due to the canceled 'Heaven and Hell' affair, and she is carrying on as a jolly good witness.

"One wonderful thing is the way Christians are bringing non-Christians. One man has started 'Operation Andrew' in his community. They have brought, so far, close to 300 unconverted friends to the services, of which 76 have been gloriously converted.

"You all keep praying we will reach the right people, say the right things, accept the right invitations and so on. I am not interested in social engagements for the sake of social engagements. But if only we could win some of those wonderful people for Christ. As I have said before, I am the world's worst soul-winner."

"Dearest folks:
"I am still laughing and there is some man in London with a mighty red face. This is how it all happened. On Sunday, after lunching, I headed for Hyde Park Corner. There was a huge crowd and about eight or so people holding forth. Well, great drops of rain began to fall. I had left my umbrella, so started for shelter. As I headed for the hotel someone fell in beside me. It was a young man with a cigarette.

" 'Pardon,' he said, 'where are you going?' (Woe is me, I thought, what's up now?)

" 'Back to my hotel.'

" 'An American?'

" 'That's right'—and all the time we were dodging traffic and the drops were coming thick and fast.

" 'Have time for a cup of coffee?' he asked.

" 'No thanks, I'd better get back.'

" 'How about tomorrow night? Are you busy?'

" 'Yes,' I replied, 'I'm going out to Harringay. Couldn't you come?'

" 'Perhaps I could. How about Tuesday night?'

" 'I'll be going out to Harringay Tuesday night, too.' (I was enjoying it by now.)

" 'Tuesday night, too! Well, will you be going to Harringay every night this week?' he asked, incredulous.

" 'Every night,' I assured him.

" 'You wouldn't be connected with Billy Graham, would you?'

" 'His wife,' I replied and burst out laughing. 'But I do hope you will come'—as I turned down Oxford Street.

" 'I might,' he croaked, and disappeared."

(How the tone of the press had begun to change toward Billy and the Crusade is clear from the account of William Hickey, columnist for the *Daily Express,* of a night at Harringay:

"We parked the car in front of the rows of coaches that had come from the South, the West, and the North. We passed the queues and went in. They were singing hymns. The force of it hit you. I don't know quite where. But I felt different.

"Billy Graham is not a particularly good preacher. But it doesn't matter. The choir leader and his wretched trombone didn't matter a tinker's cuss. What did matter was that thousands of British people were there who were feeling the need of God. A button in the human mind had been pressed and a fantastic reaction had taken place, a reaction that made those releases of atomic energy small-time stuff.

" 'Shall we pray?' said Graham. Every head was bowed. Every eye closed. 'I am going to ask you to come and stand quietly here, to surrender yourself to Christ.' And then the wooden boards of the hall started to creak under the footfalls. I shall never forget that creaking as long as I live.

"Some hurried. Some walked slowly with measured tread. The choir was singing softly, the same verse over and over again. A man and woman walked forward hand in hand. A man followed them in tears, his head bowed. They all went forward singing—just as they did in Nero's arenas, with a smile of unearthly happiness on their lips.

" 'This is God's doing,' said Graham. 'There is no other answer.'

"He never spoke more truly.")

"Dearest family:

"While I was winding up your letter, I heard band music. They were playing 'Whosoever Will, May Come.' It could be none other than the Salvation Army which I cannot resist. So on went my coat and off in search. They were conducting a meeting across Oxford Street. The last hymn they played was 'What a Friend We Have in Jesus.'

"Suddenly I looked up and there on the opposite corner stood the Negro strip-teaser who is staying at our hotel. She is a striking-looking girl who came over on the boat. She is rather aloof and I can imagine why. With a hotel full of us preachers and what have you she probably feels: 'Ye Jews have no dealings with us Samaritans.' I can't help liking her. I watched her closely. She never moved. She drank it in. Then they closed and she never moved. She watched them out of sight. I started back slowly, hoping perhaps she would catch up and I could just pass the time of day. But she kept behind me and I could hear her singing in a throaty voice, 'What a

181

Friend We Have in Jesus.' It must have stirred memories in her heart. We never know when we are witnessing for Christ just who is listening.

"Last night a counsellor told me of a man he had talked to. He came from down on the south coast. His wife, for months, had been praying for his salvation, unknown to him. He was unmoved. They came to Harringay. He was unmoved. Undaunted, she continued praying. One night as they tucked their little girl in bed, she said, 'Mummy, I'd like to have Jesus come into my heart.' Even this did not touch him.

"Then one day he was down on the beach walking by himself when he was suddenly overpowered with a sense of sinfulness and guilt. When he got home he told his wife, 'I wish I could go to Harringay again, but I haven't the money.' His wife said, 'I have been saving for an Easter outfit.' They found there was just enough for two round-trip tickets. So they came and he got converted. She didn't get her Easter outfit, but, as the counsellor said, 'he got a robe of righteousness.'

"And then there was this surgeon here in London, a woman and quite successful. She was given three tickets, so took two patients to Harringay. Both were converted and the surgeon says they haven't been back since for professional services. 'Which proves,' said the Englishman who gave the tickets, 'that what some folks need is doctrine instead of doctoring.'

"As I walked into Harringay, I was stopped by a very attractive young couple. A really pretty girl and a laughing, handsome husband with a blond little girl. 'Don't you remember us?' they asked. Then I did. They were the couple who had come forward Monday afternoon, the Spitfire pilot and his wife on the verge of breaking up. So happy I could hardly believe they were the same couple. 'You've made my wife so happy,' said the pilot. I felt like saying, 'It is you, sir, who have made her happy.' Really, his hard face was absolutely transformed. But it wasn't he or the general or me, but the Lord—that's what's so thrilling."

182

"Dearest family:

"Sunday noon Billy, Jerry, and I left for Cambridge, a gorgeous drive. The main service, held after the churches were out Sunday evening, was in Great St. Mary's Church. There were two overflow services. Billy stopped at each and greeted the packed crowds and then spoke at Great St. Mary's and his message was relayed to the other two. The church was jammed, sitting in the aisles, on the steps. Undergraduates only—and how they listened.

"The invitation was clear-cut. Then he asked all those who wished to do so to leave quietly while those who wished to receive Christ as both Savior and Lord to remain. I raised my head. It looked as if the church was still full. I couldn't believe my eyes. Bill couldn't either, evidently. He explained again, quite simply and clearly. He made it as hard as he dared. Then to make sure he asked again for those who wished for the first time to receive Christ in their lives to come to the front for booklets and prayer. They all got up to go, jamming the aisles till they had again to be seated. The Christian undergraduates stepped in among them to get names and addresses. All was deathly quiet in that old church, with a wooden crucifix looking down from the wall and stone slabs marking the graves.

"God is working in incredible ways."

(To the *Daily Mirror* columnist who had greeted him as an unwelcome American "export" Billy Graham wrote, asking for the privilege of meeting him. The columnist, Cassandra, replied: "Will you," he said, "meet someone fairly hell-bent and not averse to a little quiet wickedness? Why should we not meet in a pub called 'The Baptist's Head'? You could drink what you choose while I sin quietly with a little beer."

After their meeting Cassandra wrote: "He came into The Baptist's Head absolutely at home—a teetotaler and an abstainer able to make himself completely at ease in the spit and sawdust department, a difficult thing to do.

183

"Billy Graham looks ill. He has lost fourteen pounds in this nonstop merciless campaign. But this fact he can carry back to North Carolina with him. It is that in this country, battered and squeezed as no victorious nation has ever been before and disillusioned almost beyond belief, he has been welcomed with an exuberance that almost makes us blush behind our precious Anglo-Saxon reserve.

"I never thought that friendliness had such a sharp cutting edge. I never thought that simplicity could cudgel us sinners so damned hard. We live and learn."

On a rainy Saturday afternoon, May 22, Billy Graham preached the Crusade's concluding sermons to two outdoor audiences. The first filled White City Stadium with 70,000 people. At the second, 120,000—more than were ever drawn there by the 1948 Olympics—filled Wembley Stadium. When, with the Archbishop of Canterbury at his side, Billy Graham gave the invitation, more than 2,000 walked across the turf to stand, in the downpour before the improvised altar, to register their "decision for Christ.")

"Dearest family:

"Well, it's all over, yet in one way it has only begun. But first let me back up to where I left off. The service at Harringay on Friday night would have been sad if we had let ourselves realize it would be the last. It was absolutely jammed. Bill had to pick his way through a narrow aisle to the pulpit. How they sang!

"The Bishop of C—— was back on the platform. (He's the sweet old man who refused to pray before and then changed his mind.) Cassandra was there—and I don't know who all. The Inquiry Room was packed and they just kept coming and coming.

"The wing commander came by just to say goodbye again and how their lives had been changed. Remember, he is the Spitfire pilot who came forward with his wife the day Bill spoke

184

on the home. They have come back night after night. He looks like a new man now.

"Right there is an example of what makes the hardness of this work worthwhile. You meet a young couple, ready to break up, making one last desperate effort to solve their problems. You watch them come to Christ. You see the change that takes place. A Christian home is started. So you see, if White Stadium had been empty, if the church had continued to stand apart, if the press had sent Bill off as skeptically as they greeted him, it still would have been worth it all. That is only one example. Only eternity will disclose them all.

"If only you could have seen the sea of busses going to Wembley. I was put in the Royal Box, of all places, but on the way I was stopped and introduced to the Archbishop of Canterbury and Mrs. Fisher, also to the Lord Mayor of London and his wife.

"The enormous stadium is spread out before us like a great, unbelievably big oval packed with flecks of color which are people. People at the end of the stadium were all standing. Scores had camped at Wembley overnight. I can't begin to explain it: the coldness of the weather, the immensity of the stadium, the thousands upon thousands of people, the quietness of it all, the sense of God's presence. The sermon was simplicity itself. At the invitation hundreds upon hundreds streamed forward. Then the Archbishop prayed—simply, clearly, movingly, and pronounced the sweetest blessing I have ever heard.

"And the reporters! They are friendlier, but just bewildered. 'Whatever it is that Billy Graham has got,' wrote one of them, 'he's got more of it than anyone else.' The people were so sweet singing 'To God the Glory' and calling out 'God bless you,' 'Come back soon' as the bus with all the team on it pulled slowly off. We would have felt sad, but there was too much happiness and gratitude in our hearts for everything."

185

(On board the departing bus was a friend of the Grahams', an American newspaperman. "As the team's private bus inched through the milling crowd," he wrote, "Billy Graham stood in the aisle and said, 'I want all of us to bow our heads right now and give thanks to God for all He has done and is doing. This is His doing and let none fail to give Him credit.'

"Only moments before, the young man had stood before 120,000 people with the Word of God in his hand, in his head and in his heart. He now stood with bowed head, just another sinner saved by grace.

"A few seconds after the end of the prayer, Bev Shea began to sing softly, 'Praise God from Whom All Blessings Flow.' Others took up the words and the song grew in volume as the bus passed along through the quiet streets."

That night the London *Evening News* published a special "Billy Graham Edition," with front and back pages wholly devoted to the evangelist and the Crusade. Across two front-page columns, the lead story began with the Gospel of Luke: "What went ye out into the wilderness for to see? A reed shaken with the wind? A prophet? Yea, I say unto you, and much more than a prophet.")

11: Europe and Asia:
The universal hunger

THAT, in many countries vastly different from his own in religion, race, and culture, he meets with an unprecedented outpouring of interest and response is for Billy Graham personally a source of continuing astonishment. On the level of things spiritual—where he does most of his reflecting—he is not astonished. On that level he would only be astonished if what happens failed to happen.

"There are all kinds of hunger in our world," he says. "But the most nearly universal of them all is spiritual hunger. For this there is one universal answer: the Good News of the Gospel of Jesus Christ. Even though I did not believe that by faith—as I do—I would be forced to believe it by what, in so many nations, among so many people, I have seen.

"There is a sentence in a song we sing in our Crusade: 'For He has broken every barrier down.' He does. If He failed to do that I would never preach another sermon. But He doesn't fail."

In the summer of 1955—following the Crusade in Glasgow and the mammoth meetings in London's Wembley Stadium—Billy Graham undertook what, up to then, was described by some observers as his most "hazardous venture": a four-week mission to the continent of Europe. He preached in twelve cities in seven countries. In every meeting—save his appearances before U.S. servicemen in Germany—he spoke through an interpreter. Exclusive of radio audiences, he was heard by more than 500,000 people.

"Many were the predictions," said the *Christian Century,* "that once Mr. Graham left the area in which English is spoken and the Protestant evangelical tradition is still predominant, his appeal would fall flat. If the numbers of those who wanted to hear him are any indication, the precise opposite turned out to be the case."

In Paris—where he spoke on five successive nights—French Protestantism had never before undertaken a project so ambitious. The huge Vélodrome d'Hiver, where the meetings were held, was, I am sure, one of the unlikeliest and least worshipful auditoriums in which the Gospel was ever preached. The most prominent features of the décor—rimming the balconies—were the cognac advertisements.

En route to the first night's meeting, Billy Graham—uncertain what or how large the crowd would be and whether it would respond—remarked that "if we have as many as 5,000 people tonight and 100 decisions I'll think the meeting was all that we have prayed for." The audience was nearly 10,000. There were more than 600 "decisions"—the largest number ever recorded in a Crusade meeting of that size.

At the conclusion of five such meetings, the Paris newspaper *Le Monde* commented: "Is not the availability of such crowds symptomatic in itself? It would be unjust for us to indulge in irony on the American style of such a religious manifestation. . . . Better bow before the spiritual dynamism of this man, whose formula and phrases are perhaps infantile, but who touches his public. . . . His technique may offend European intellectuals, but the fact remains that he is successful. The French Protestants who, despite some reservations, did not

188

hesitate to ask him to come to our country made no mistake."

One of the French Protestants who had reservations—so many, prior to the meetings, that he washed his hands of the whole affair—was Dr. Marc Boegner, for many years French Protestantism's foremost leader, formerly a president of the World Council of Churches. Weeks later, at a meeting attended by more than 1,000 Parisians who had made "decisions," Dr. Boegner—from a seat in the rear of the hall—got up to "testify" as to several people he had previously known and whose lives had been "transformed" at the Vélodrome d'Hiver:

"I didn't take any part in the campaign," he said, "and I'm sorry I didn't. I have been shown very clearly that the decisions were real and I believe they will be lasting. I want to state in public that if Dr. Billy Graham returns to Paris for a campaign, I will be privileged and happy to support the meetings in any way possible."

It was the same in every city. In Geneva, according to the Associated Press, the crowd filled the stadium and "spilled out over the grassy hills." In Zurich: "More than 60,000 persons assembled in two stadiums, 200 yards apart" to hear him. There were 30,000 in Frankfurt. From Mannheim Ruth Graham wrote: "There must have been 50,000 present—every seat filled and thousands sitting and standing on the turf. There is such hunger here in Germany. They come forward so quickly and quietly. This time there was no sound at all, for the turf deadened the footfalls. Twilight was beginning to settle as they came: husky young men in leather shorts, soldiers, an old woman in a shawl, a man with a hard face. They stood quietly, hands folded in front of them as they are taught to do when praying. And the man with the hard face wiped his eyes with his handkerchief. There were over 1,500. If only we knew the story of each. Someday we will."

Six months later, Billy Graham put his faith to an even severer test and saw it validated by an even greater success. Early in 1956 he made an extensive tour of India, including,

189

also, one-meeting stops in Manila, Bangkok, Hong Kong, Formosa, Tokyo, and Seoul. The story of this mission—particularly of the mission to India—is without precedent, not only in the ministry of Billy Graham, but, more importantly, in the history of religious contacts between the East and the West.

Not since the war has any emissary from the West—diplomat, statesman, or head of government—received in Asia, from people of all classes and beliefs, a spontaneous reception so great or so enthusiastic as that accorded him. No message from the West has been heard with greater eagerness and understanding than his simple, spiritual appeal. His tour, at first dubiously received by some free-world diplomats, proved to be for both America and the free world a spectacular victory.

In India, Billy Graham's arrival followed, by only six weeks, the propaganda journey of Nikita Khrushchev and Nikolai Bulganin, chiefs of the Soviet Russian government and spokesmen for world communism. Preaching hate for the democratic West, the crowds that greeted them were hailed as a Communist "triumph" and aroused concern in every free-world government.

But the "triumph" of the Russians was officially promoted by the Indian government and by the dominant Congress party. Wherever they went, India's revered Prime Minister, Jawaharlal Nehru, traveled with them. In every city, to insure vast crowds, schools, government offices, many businesses were closed.

In striking contrast, Billy Graham's visit had only the backing of India's Protestant churches. In a population of 380,-000,000, the total membership of those churches is less than 5,000,000. Most of that membership is drawn from India's villages and from the lowest, poorest classes. Yet the crowds—Christians and non-Christians—which came to hear Billy Graham equaled, in some instances greatly surpassed, those that gathered to hear Khrushchev and Bulganin.

Of 2,500,000 people in the city of Bombay, where Billy

Graham landed, there are said to be only 16,000 Christians. Yet, for his public meeting there, nearly 30,000 reserved-seat tickets had been given out, on application, before his arrival. Communist-led political rioting, which was under way when he arrived, forced the cancellation of that meeting. Since bloody street fighting was still in progress it was expected that not more than a half-dozen reporters would appear at his press confer ence. There were more than forty—a near-record, reportedly larger than the number who met with Krushchev and Bulganin. Almost all were Indian and non-Christian.

"I have come to India," he told them, "with an attitude of learning, for we have much to learn from you. India is a deeply religious country. Some seem to believe that Christianity is a Western religion. That is wrong. Christ was born in the East. There were Christian churches in India before America was discovered. I have not come here to get into political entangle-ments. Our message is simply the Kingdom of God."

"Welcome, Billy," was the headline in the Bombay *Free Press*. Instead of preaching ill will, "Dr. Billy Graham," said an editorial in the Bombay *Evening News*, "is on a mission to bring man and God closer together."

Billy Graham wrote in his diary:

"The most amazing and startling part of that press confer-ence was that none of the questions had to do with communism, Americanism, John Foster Dulles, economic aid to India—any of the things you would think they were most interested in. Every question was of a theological or spiritual nature. They wanted to know about conversion, the Bible, the new birth, how the teachings of Jesus apply in everyday life. They weren't so much interested in what I believed as in what the Bible had to say. I felt almost as though I should have given an invitation. But if the Lord ever allowed me to preach the Gospel it was right there to those reporters."

His first public meeting was in the south India city of Madras. "Seldom in his crowd-filled career," reported *Time* magazine, "had he met with such enthusiasm. Madras was clogged with out-of-towners seeking rooms; one group of 100 rode the train four days and nights and one man walked 400 miles to hear him. Caste was ignored in the stampede to see Billy."

In his diary he wrote:

"Every church compound is filled. Hundreds will be sleeping on the sidewalks. There is a spirit of expectancy. Christians have started round-the-clock prayer meetings: more than 5,000 people praying every hour of the night tonight. This is God at work. . . ."

At seven o'clock the next morning he spoke to a meeting limited, by ticket, to Christian pastors and workers. When he arrived, "people were pouring in from everywhere. Everybody had a Bible and a notebook. More than 7,500 came—the largest ministers' meeting, of course, I ever addressed. I began to speak just as the sun came up in a gold and purple sky. When I stood up I knew God was with me. I could feel the concentrated prayers of thousands of people all over the world. . . .

"Immediately after the service, the ministers crowded around the platform, wanting either to touch me or get an autograph or just look a little closer into my face. I almost felt as Peter did when 'all the people' crowded round him after he had healed the lame man: 'Men of Israel, why marvel ye at this? or why look ye so earnestly on us as though by our own power or holiness we had made this man to walk?' I was humbled by it all and felt myself unworthy even to loosen the sandals of many of these simple, but great men of God. . . ."

At a similar sunrise service the next morning the attendance was more than 10,000.

For their single appearance in that city, the Russians, Krushchev and Bulganin, drew 22,000 people to the Madras stadium. Billy Graham, his sermons translated by two interpreters into Tamil and Telugu, spoke on three successive nights in the same stadium. His audience, on the first night, numbered

192

32,000, on the second 37,000, on the third more than 40,000. He wrote:

"I noticed immediately the quietness of the crowd: practically no talking, no moving about. Hundreds had been there since two o'clock, sitting in the boiling sun. When we arrived, thousands of them had been there, singing as they waited, for two to three hours.

"What a sea of people: thousands squatting on grass mats in front of me; other thousands standing behind me and then, on the houses all around, people crowding the roofs. . . ."

Prior to this mission, Billy Graham, during weeks of study, had prepared eight sermons especially adapted to what he believed to be the different and distinctive interests and needs of the Indian people. On that first night in Madras he started with the first of these special sermons. He never finished it.

This is his account of what happened:

"I had not been preaching five minutes before it came to me, as clearly as though I had been audibly interrupted, that this vast gathering of people had not come to hear the Gospel adapted to India. They had come solely to hear the Gospel: the Good News in which, as much in our day as in St. Paul's, as much in India as in the United States, England, Scotland, or France, 'there is neither Greek nor Jew, circumcision nor uncircumcision, Barbarian, Scythian, bond nor free, but Christ. . . .'

"And there, as I was preaching, I was given a new text and a new sermon. Thereafter, wherever I went, I preached that sermon from that text."

The text was John 3:16:

"For God so loved the world, that He gave His Only Begotten Son, that whosoever believeth in Him should not perish, but have everlasting life."

"I had been told," he wrote, "that the Hindu is different, that the Indian is different, that they would not respond to the same message, the same invitation we have preached in

193

America, Britain, and Europe. But what I gave was the same, simple Gospel message and then I gave the same invitation. I tried to lay down all the conditions of accepting and following Christ. Between four and five thousand came—nearly all adults. They came more quietly, more earnestly, more thoughtfully, it seemed to me, than any who ever responded in any of our meetings anywhere. All you could hear was the tramp, tramp, tramp of bare and sandaled feet.

"Yes, the same God Who was with us at Wembley and Harringay and Kelvin Hall is with us here in India."

In the agitation to swing India toward communism, there are, Billy Graham was told, two kinds of Communists. The first —"the Unconscious Communists"—are recruited "among the masses of the poor who have no idea what it's all about except that they have been promised more land and rice."

Traveling in south India, he met some of these. This is his story of the encounter:

"In one section we passed a number of Communist parades: flags waving, shouting their slogans and songs, giving the familiar clenched-fist salute. We got out and marched along three or four hundred yards with one group. I would wave at them and smile and they would smile back—all very friendly. In another group I got out again and asked Bishop Jacob to translate for me. I held up my hand and the crowd quieted down.

"Then I began to preach. I told them what Christ meant to me; that He had the only answer to their problems and the world's problems; that I had come to India not to talk politics but only to talk Christ.

"As I spoke about the change that Christ could bring in their lives, they began to drop their clenched fists. They began to lower their hammer-and-sickle banners. They stood quietly, it seemed to me reverently, until I finished.

"Of course they want an answer to their problems of rice, land, schools, health. But it is frightening that so often the

194

Communists make their answer so much more appealing and seemingly more practical than we Christians make Christ's."

Then there is the second kind of Communists—"the Intelligent Communists"—recruited largely from India's college and university students. "If India goes Communist," Billy Graham was told, "it's students will lead the way." Their influence in Madras, an intellectual center, is reportedly great and growing. There, warned of the hostile reception he might receive, Billy Graham spoke—as he did wherever he went—to a student gathering:

"It was seven o'clock—barely sunup! But they were there: lovely girls in their saris, the men in all kinds of assorted apparel. There were more than ten thousand of them!

"I spoke on the subject: 'Who is Christ?' I tried to present the Gospel as clearly and as straight as I knew how. They listened carefully, attentively, quietly. Many hundreds of them, I could see, were taking notes.

"Perhaps it is true that communism is in the ascendant in the colleges of Madras. But this morning it was the Spirit of God that had the ascendancy. When I gave the invitation, hundreds came out of their seats and boldly took their stand for Jesus Christ. What a sight: to see these students marching, not for communism, but for Christ.

"Whether true, I have no way of knowing, but Indians told me that this morning's meeting was the most remarkable student gathering ever held in free India. I could only thank God for the glorious privilege of witnessing for Him to such a company of India's future leaders."

The morning after Billy Graham arrived in Kottayam, a city of only 40,000 but a Christian stronghold near India's southern tip, he was awakened before sunup by the sound of Christian singing. In preparation for his meeting that night, more than 5,000 Christians had assembled—as they did on three successive mornings—for a four o'clock prayer meeting. Many had come on foot and by oxcart from jungle villages scores

195

of miles away. Bearing an invitation to Billy Graham to speak in their village, one group had walked 114 miles.

"How many do you expect tonight?" he asked the Bishop of the Church of South India.

"Tonight there will be 75,000; tomorrow night more than 100,000."

"Where will you put them?"

From a nearby cliff, the Bishop pointed out the meeting place. It was a hillside rising out of the rice paddies. There, for days, a great company of Christian volunteers—working entirely by hand, carrying the dirt in baskets—had been leveling off and filling in until they had built, row on row, a terraced amphitheater. In three nights, Billy Graham preached there to more than a quarter of a million people.

In Delhi there are no more than 10,000 Christians. But his first meeting there drew 20,000. "The biggest indoor congregation," reported the *Times* of India, "ever to assemble in the Capital." That meeting was presided over by an Indian Princess, Rajkumari Amrit Kaur, who in 1930 left her father's palace to become a Christian and is now Minister of Health in the Nehru cabinet.

"Billy Graham," she said, introducing him, "is one of those rare jewels who tread this earth periodically and draw, by their lives and teachings, millions of others closer to God."

Not only in India, but in Bangkok, Manila, Hong Kong, Formosa, Seoul, and Tokyo, Billy Graham—with an appeal aimed solely "to draw others closer to God"—was heard by audiences unequaled by any visitor from the West. "To a mammoth crowd from Manila and outlying provinces," reported the Manila *Chronicle*, he said that "the hope for world peace lies not in what statesmen, politicians, scientists have to say, but in what God says." In Hong Kong, said the *South China Morning Post*, a "huge gathering that filled two football stadia, that came in busses, trams, private cars, taxis, bicycles, and on foot heard his Gospel message." In Tokyo, said

196

the daily *Mainishi*, "the greatest crowd in Japan's religious history, young and old, rich and poor, people from all walks of life, turned out to hear Billy Graham as he delivered the words of God." An editorial in Tokyo's *Nippon Times* declared: "While Japan is not a Christian nation, she can profit greatly from the message which Dr. Billy Graham brings. The truths Dr. Graham speaks are universal. They go beyond national boundaries, racial differences, and even religious divisions. The common denominators of faith, humanity, and peace are with all men who believe in the Divine Being—whatever their individual approach. . . ."

When, en route home, he stopped for a single meeting in Honolulu—to which an unprecedented 20,000 came—the Honolulu *Advertiser* carried a headline across the top of its front page: "You Have a Date at 3 P M. Today—Keep It" and underneath an editorial:

"We people of Hawaii have a date to keep at Honolulu Stadium this afternoon when Billy Graham is going to talk to us about God. No matter what our personal approach to God may be, or whether we believe in God at all, this man Graham has something to say to us that will be to our individual profit. . . . Humbly he presents himself as the bearer of Christ's message. We would be gravely mistaken to turn a deaf ear to Billy Graham this afternoon. The message he carries will bring us closer to God. . . ."

Flying from Hawaii to the U.S. mainland, Billy Graham made the final entry in his diary:

"Eight weeks! One miracle after another! How different, on the surface, people are; yet, in their hearts, how much alike! What human needs I have seen! What a challenge they are to us, so abundantly blessed, to help these Asian peoples help themselves! But there is a deeper need, rooted in the same spiritual hunger, the hunger after God that I have found everywhere. That hunger is the great common denominator among all people.

"Perhaps the Communists can match us in material aid. But for this deeper need they have no answer. There is our greatest opportunity: to go beyond material and military aid, to help, with moral and spiritual leadership, to speed this turn to God.

" 'Not by might, nor by power, but by my Spirit, saith the Lord.' "

12: Religion reaches
the man in the street

THIS IS an account of how, in a Billy Graham Crusade, religion—as something to be talked about, to be faced up to, to be declared—someway breaks out of the cloisters and away from the conventions that usually confine it and permeates—into the unlikeliest highways and byways—an entire community.

Few facts about a Billy Graham Crusade are more startling than this. For a brief period of four or six or eight weeks—too brief a time, some will say, to prove anything—there is a confrontation of a sort which, unhappily, too seldom happens: religion confronting the world on the world's own ground. The least expected people in the most unexpected places discuss religion openly and without embarrassment: in offices, shops, and plants and on the street corners, in luncheon clubs, at bridge parties, even at the nineteenth hole. Young boys go whistling "This Is My Story" along a crowded street and nobody seems surprised. Shopgirls, between sales, hum the same tune and nobody looks askance or asks, self-consciously, "What's that?"

In bookstores, people you would assume were looking for

the latest best-selling novel ask, as naturally as though they were, to buy a copy of the Bible and often go out carrying it under their arm, unwrapped. The hotel porter shows you his "stand-by" list of a dozen or so guests who have asked him to put them down for tickets for "the revival meeting," if any should show up. A taxi driver opens up the conversation: "I'm driving days now, so I can sing nights in the Crusade choir."

And every day, in the newspapers, the Gospel is a front-page story as though, after twenty centuries, it had just been discovered that that Gospel is not only "Good News," but *The* Good News."

I saw this dramatic phenomenon, firsthand and over a period of several weeks, during the All-Scotland Crusade in Glasgow in the spring of 1955. That is the locale in which I am going to describe it. But there is ample evidence that what I saw happen in Glasgow can be seen during every Billy Graham Crusade: religion breaking out of bounds, getting, so to speak, out of hand, surmounting, as though they did not exist, all sorts of man-contrived barriers and divisions.

In every city the extent of the news coverage is, itself, phenomenal. Several London papers ran special "Billy Graham editions." Prior to the Houston, Texas, Crusade, the Houston *Press* ran a seventeen-part biography of Billy Graham. During the Crusade in Nashville, Tennessee, the Nashville *Banner* printed each of Billy Graham's twenty-five sermons in full, beginning the text, each day, as a front-page story and later, "at the request of thousands," making reprints available. "Nashville," said the *Banner*, "has never witnessed anything quite like the Billy Graham Crusade."

"There has been nothing unusual," said an editorial in the Seattle *Post-Intelligencer*, "about the amount of space given Graham's meetings. The greater the spiritual awakening which arises the better and bigger the news."

"Judged by any standards," said the Pittsburgh *Sun-Tele-*

graph, "Billy Graham's campaign is big news. The *Sun-Telegraph* is giving its reports space and position allotted only to major news stories and feels it is justified in doing so. . . . The conclusion is inescapable that Billy Graham is right."

Often, the news headlines and stories have an amazingly straight-out religious slant. Over a full page of Crusade pictures, the Detroit *Times* ran the streamer headline. "Billy Graham: 'Let Jesus in Today.' " Over a similar page, the headline in the Detroit *Free Press* was "O Come All Ye Faithful."

"Wherever Billy Graham goes," said an editorial in the Detroit *News,* "the celestial balance sheet shows a substantial profit."

At the conclusion of the Houston Crusade, John H. Gurwell wrote in the *Press:* "Billy Graham has left a legacy, a picture of God's Kingdom and the beauty of His work, a realization in the minds of his listeners that Christ's heart is open. . . . All you have to do is enter. . . ."

In every city, also, there is testimony of the way in which religion—as a subject of conversation and a matter of personal concern—pervades the life of the community.

Having seen the Crusade in Washington, D.C., a distinguished Church of England clergyman remarked, "A city becomes almost as Christ-conscious as St. Andrews is golf-conscious. What more could be said?"

"Everybody is asking himself," said an editorial in the Columbia, South Carolina, *The State,* during the Crusade in that city, 'Am I a Christian?' That is the biggest compliment ever paid to Billy Graham."

At the end of the Crusade in Detroit, the mayor said, "Billy Graham has left a spiritual impact on this city that will never be erased. We have been made religion conscious."

"The entire atmosphere of Shreveport," said an editorial in the Shreveport, Louisiana, *Journal,* "is charged with devotional upsurge that cannot be explained away as the result of natural causes. It must have shaken the pits of Hell if the Devil was looking in." "This campaign," said Shreveport's mayor, "is the greatest thing that has ever happened to our city."

"This," said an editorial in the London *Evening News* at the end of the meetings in 1955 in Wembley Stadium, "can truly be called the phenomenon of the mid-century."

It is a phenomenon which for the moment at least sometimes makes the usual differences between Christians somewhat less divisive. In one U.S. city a woman, a Roman Catholic, told a member of the Graham team that she had asked her priest what his advice would be as to attending a Crusade meeting. "My advice," he said, "would be not to attend." "I am sorry," she said, "but I think I am going anyway." The priest replied, "So am I."

In another city, Billy Graham played golf one day with a Roman Catholic priest who the night before had attended, in civilian clothes, a Crusade meeting. "While there," he said, "I counted eight other priests—all, like me, in 'civvies.'"

The publicity is also sometimes unexpected. In one city, the newspapers ran the photograph of a locked-up liquor store which had this sign in its window:

"Closed at 10 A.M. Get Owner at Home. I'm Out of Business. Was Converted Last Night."

In another city this advertisement appeared:

"At _____'s

THE WORLD'S GREATEST BARGAIN

and

Sour-Pusses

"The next time you meet an old sour-puss who was born in the objective case and weaned on a pickle and he starts talking about all the money that Billy Graham and his associates are going to get out of this revival, just tell him this:

" 'Say, Mister, did you know that what goes on and in the collection plates at the Graham revival wouldn't be chicken

202

feed in those gyp joints and dives where people waste their money? The whole budget of the revival is less than passes over a crap table in an hour in those Hell dives that don't seem to worry you. And did you know that the crimes of one man, John Dillinger, cost many millions? The G-Men spent a million dollars running him down and ending his bloody career. If Billy Graham did nothing else but convert one potential Dillinger or Frank Costello he would earn every cent that they will take up in a thousand revivals.

" 'Let him make a million if he can—two million or more. He'd spend most of it spreading the Gospel and doing good in the world. And did you ever hear of a preacher leaving a fortune for his heirs to fight over?

" 'Say, Mister, that stuff you're peddling is what the devil germinates and starts and fools swallow!'

"Yes, religion is the biggest bargain in the world. Even greater bargains than _____ Furniture has. . . ."

Through the Red Army paper, *Red Star,* Soviet Russia got this report of the Crusade in Washington, D.C.:

"Americans are in hysterics about Billy Graham—a charlatan and a quack. Meetings have been attended not only by simpletons inexperienced in politics, but also by correspondents, avid for sensations. . . . American Senators and members of the House come with humble looks and blissful smiles. They listen to the howlings of a preacher who goes into rantings. . . ."

To which Billy Graham's reply was: "If this revival could happen in Russia, the world could live in peace. . . ."

But when it is seen close-up and at firsthand, the story of religion invading and investing the secular life of a great city becomes, I think, authentic drama.

In Glasgow, early on the morning of Saturday, March 19, 1955, a crowd of some 3,000 people waited in cold, cavernous St. Enoch's station for the arrival of the overnight express from

London. There were more women in the crowd, perhaps, than men; more under thirty-five than over; a cluster of newspaper reporters and photographers—looking ill-fed and ill-clothed, as British newspapermen generally do and sometimes are; a larger cluster of clergymen: black vests, turn-about collars; and on the train platform a welcoming committee of Glasgow city officials, a couple of members of Parliament, the Moderator of the Church of Scotland, an Episcopalian bishop or two looking a bit awkward in the midst of so much nonconformity.

As the crowd waited, it sang "Faith of Our Fathers," and "The Lord's My Shepherd," which, to the tune Crimond, is the best-loved of all the songs of the Scottish church. When, a little after eight o'clock, the train came and a tall, bare-headed, smiling young American stepped onto the platform, the crowd broke through the lines of police and surrounded him, making, as a trainman remarked, "St. Enoch's rafters ring to some mighty strange music," singing as though they had rehearsed it:

> "This is my story, this is my song,
> Praising my Savior all the day long;
> This is my story, this is my song,
> Praising my Savior all the day long."

That night the Glasgow *Evening Citizen* ran streamer headlines over its front-page story and photograph:

"Thousands Sing Welcome . . . Amazing Scenes . . . Crowd Surges around Billy Graham."

It could happen, I believe, almost anywhere, because almost everywhere in the so-called Christian West multiplied millions of people are stirred by the same dissatisfaction with answers which are wholly secular, with purposes which have material achievement as their alpha and omega, with living as though the need for security, for comfort and convenience were an adequate substitute for the need for God. But Glasgow, as tough a port city as any, was evidently waiting for such a chance as this to make religion—if only momentarily—once again one of its chief concerns.

In the old days when the claims of religion on the Scots—including the Scots of Glasgow—were more pressing than the claims of industry and commerce, the city was given a motto by one of its early bishops. The motto read: "Let Glasgow Flourish by the Preaching of the Word and the Praising of His Name."

As, however, secular concerns increased and those of religion diminished this slogan, so it seemed, became increasingly unfitting until—the hustle and bustle of the market place having taken over—it became outright embarrassing. But it was not abandoned. It was only reduced to advertising-agency dimensions better designed to serve presumably more up-to-date objectives: "Let Glasgow Flourish."

The All-Scotland Crusade recovered and, for the time being at least, restored the original. A Glasgow firm, contributing its services, erected over Kelvin Hall the largest electric sign the city had ever seen and, blazoned in lights, the city saw, for the first time in many decades, the motto as it once was and might be again: "Let Glasgow Flourish by the Preaching of the Word and the Praising of His Name."

There was some argument among Glasgow churchmen, prior to the Crusade, as to how ready their city was for such a return.

"We were soon reproached," said one of those who had doubted, "for our lack of faith. We had shamefully underestimated the hunger of the people for the Word of God."

There were no adequate Crusade headquarters and centrally located office space was not available until, one day, one of Glasgow's leading businessmen—a man with no church connections—provided, rent-free, more-than-adequate space in a downtown office building. A master painter, likewise no churchman, took over the decorating. The managing director of the city's largest office-supply office fitted the quarters with

205

typewriters, mimeograph machines, filing cabinets, desks, tables, chairs. At no cost, the city's two best-located, most costly billboards were made available. Hearing of this, a firm of painters and sign writers volunteered its services to paint the message: "Hear Billy Graham at Kelvin Hall." One of Scotland's leading advertising agencies took on, at less than cost, the job of advance publicity, drawing up its own highly uncommercial, two-point objective:

"1. To fill Kelvin Hall nightly;

"2. To make Glasgow realize that God is doing something great in her midst."

There was initial skepticism, also, about hiring so huge an auditorium as 16,000-capacity Kelvin Hall. Five or six thousand nightly was regarded as a safe estimate of attendance. So "terrible" was this risk regarded that plans were discussed to erect temporary walls and cut down the available capacity to about half. Only the insistence of Billy Graham's associates persuaded the committee to use the entire hall.

The hall, itself, is an uninspiring structure of concrete, steel, and glass, totally unrelieved by any touch of beauty. But, unexpectedly, one of Britain's largest scaffolding firms voluntarily took over a rebuilding job, created an auditorium which— with pulpit and choir area—took on the semblance of a huge sanctuary. Chairs, repainted at city expense, were provided by the Park Department.

For six weeks, six nights a week—in rain, snow, and sleet and, now and then, fine weather—Kelvin Hall was filled with 16,000 people. During the last week, by dint of much crowding, the average was 18,000. Night after night, hundreds stood in the streets outside, joined to the crowd inside by loudspeakers, singing as they sang in Kelvin Hall, bowing as they prayed, listening as Billy Graham preached, responding, scores of them, when the invitation was given to decide for Christ.

There was also some argument as to whether in Scotland, and especially in Glasgow, Billy Graham should start right in and, on the first evening, call for people to come forward to make decisions for Christ.

"Scots," the argument ran, "aren't used to making a public display of their religion. Maybe we had better wait for that until we see how things go."

But Billy Graham did not wait. On the first night—with a capacity crowd inside and a blinding snowstorm outside—he gave the invitation to "get up from your seats and walk down these aisles and confess Christ unashamedly before men." That, also, seems to have been what many, perhaps for a long time, had been waiting for. The first who came were two women—too much in earnest to be held back by their obvious embarrassment; then a mother with three teen-age children; two young couples, holding hands. The total that night was 470—the largest number of first-night decisions in any Billy Graham Crusade up to then. By the end of the six weeks, the number of those who had responded to Billy Graham's appeal in Kelvin Hall was more than 20,000.

That first night was a heavily headlined front-page story in every Glasgow newspaper:

"500 Answer Billy Graham on First Night . . . Crowds Queue in Snow and Sleet . . . A Housewife Waits Four Hours."

"All-Scotland Crusade Under Way. Hundreds Respond to Appeal of Mr. Billy Graham. Sermon of Simple Words."

"The Great Crusade Starts with a Warning: You Must Be on Time Tonight."

The Crusade was a front-page story in Glasgow's papers, not only that first day, but every day for six weeks. "In this time," an editor told me, "I have seen more religion in the headlines and more Scripture in the news than in all my previous thirty years in this business put together."

A correspondent for the Glasgow *Herald* wrote: "Mr. Graham has jolted us out of our customary bashfulness. Men and women who might fairly be called conventional Christians have been compelled to think, really to think, about the Christian faith in its personal and social implications, and they have been talking about these things as they have not done for generations."

As religion thus took over first place in the attention of the city, there were some unexpected consequences. One paper one morning ran a story of how the night before—Kelvin Hall being "packed out"—Billy Graham spoke to 2,000 standing outside in the rain. Underneath that story was another with the headline "Election Meetings Suffer": "The rush to hear Billy Graham at the Kelvin Hall is being partly blamed for the poor attendance at Glasgow's municipal election meetings, said Bailie T. B. Duncan today. The attraction at the Kelvin Hall is diverting many electors from the town council hustings."

Mr. John Henderson, a Scottish member of the House of Commons and a supporter of the Crusade, wrote that, due to the Crusade, "it has been a fairly common experience among members of Parliament to find that in their speeches they have found it easy—almost necessary, in fact—to include and put new emphasis upon matters above and beyond politics: the spiritual and moral aspects of life."

Someone reported a greeting current among shopgirls: "See you at the Kelvin." An enterprising barber put up a sign: "If you're not going to Billy Graham to be saved, come in to Tony's to be shaved."

Not all the reactions were friendly—but even the unfriendly ones indicated, perhaps more so, how far from its conventional confines religion was penetrating. Glasgow's Communist paper, *The Word,* kept up a running attack on both Billy Graham and the Crusade, devoting, in one issue, nearly three full pages to the subject.

One morning the pavement of a downtown street corner had this chalked ditty:

208

"Billy Graham came to town,
Preaching his baloney;
He puts up at the best hotels,
Boy, are his clothes toney."

A few days later when "This Is My Story" had become the most frequently heard tune in Glasgow, this variation appeared:

"This is my story, this is my song,
Preaching baloney all the day long."

Underneath was the familiar line: "Religion is a drug."

This penetration was evident, also, at the other end of the intellectual scale. During the Crusade, Glasgow and Oxford universities met in Glasgow in a debate. It was the first such meeting between the two schools. The subject was: "Should Billy Graham be deported as an Undesirable Alien?"—Oxford taking the affirmative, Glasgow the negative. The student attendance was one of the largest in the history of the Glasgow Union.

Oxford argued—with much stamping and "hear-hearing" from the crowd—that Billy Graham preached "escapism" and offered, from the realities of the world, "a spiritual hide-out." "How does his conversion differ from Hitler's brainwashing?" "Sure, he draws the crowds. But so did Hitler—with the same cheap techniques and perilous authoritarian consequences."

To which Glasgow's lead-off speaker replied:

"Let's imagine, for a moment, that 2,000 years ago two Scribes, proud guardians of a religious status quo that profited them much and others little, met on a street corner in Jerusalem.

" 'This fellow from Nazareth,' said the first Scribe, 'what slick techniques: miracles and all that. . . . He's hoodwinking the people.'

" 'Imagine,' said the other, 'He preaches not in the temple, but in the market place. And He speaks in parables so that the people understand what He says and hear Him gladly. This is getting dangerous.'

"And they began to take counsel together, those Scribes, not how to deport, but how to crucify Him."

There was less shouting, stamping, and "hear-hearing" at this. But when the vote was taken, Glasgow won.

To get an account of the Crusade from an observer of acknowledged intellectual repute and "with no ax to grind," the Glasgow *Evening Citizen* called on Mr. Noel Stevenson, lecturer in social anthropology at Glasgow University and chairman of the British Broadcasting Company's widely followed program *A Matter of Opinion*. Here, in part, is Mr. Stevenson's stirring and remarkable report:

"Last night I heard Billy Graham. The myriad lights in the wide, low Kelvin Hall shone down on thousands of men and women who must have been wondering, as I was myself, just what their motives were for being there. . . .

"I thought of the outburst of a young man in a youth program I chaired some weeks ago. He faced a group of industrialists and religious and civic leaders who wanted to know why modern youth was feckless.

" 'We are a lost generation because you are lost,' he accused. 'How can you guide us when you don't even know where you're going yourselves? You have no aims we can seize upon as really worthwhile.'

" 'No aim worthwhile!' That was the thought that kept running through my mind as I looked about me. . . . The more I thought the more I was convinced that here was the answer. Religion means action as well as belief; beliefs are the tools with which nations are made or broken. Was it because our beliefs are not being put into practice that we were there— seeking a way to do it?

"Across the way from me three young reporters—a girl and two men—gave me some clues. When Billy Graham began his address with an exhortation about original sin and the immortal soul they sat unmoved whispering among themselves. . . . But when he turned to the problems of the Christian way of life, they sat mute with a sudden realization on their faces. They were held spellbound. If their thoughts were like mine it was not emotion that held them—it was the feeling that here was something practical that could be acted upon, not a negative and selfish aim or personal salvation through not doing wrong, but a positive aim of peace in God by doing a thousand small things right . . .

"Then the flow began. A young man broke from the restraining fingers of his friends and joined the widening stream. Near me, most were young or in early middle age. I saw a sprinkling of university students among them and thought again of the young man in the radio program and his cry for leadership. I knew I should have been standing there amongst those youngsters, giving a lead in the public declaration of my faith. Panic held me. . . . As the tail end of the stream flowed past and out of sight I heard, in the depth of my conscience, the first cockcrow."

Few days passed during the entire six weeks without at least one meeting, generally at the noon hour, for workers in the Clydeside shipyards—meetings sometimes addressed by members of the team, sometimes by Billy Graham. At one meeting I attended, 2,000 men stood for three quarters of an hour in the driving rain to hear Billy Graham.

And few days passed which did not witness some daytime gathering of the business, professional, political, and social leaders of the life of Glasgow and of Scotland. Most remarkable of these was a luncheon given by Mr. Hugh Fraser—one of Scotland's foremost businessmen—which called together some 400 people and which, led by the Lord Provost and his wife, was described to me by a newspaper editor as "one of the most inclusive assemblies of the nobility of Scotland and its business and political leaders ever to have met in one

211

place." Billy Graham's message—after preliminary remarks suited to the occasion—was as forthrightly religious as at Kelvin Hall.

The influence of the Crusade penetrated far beyond Glasgow. Noting that Billy Graham's schedule included no visit to Dundee, *The People's Journal* of that city asked in a three-column headline: "Why Not Dundee, Mr. Graham?"

"What's wrong with Dundee—as far as the Billy Graham organization is concerned?

"Are we completely equipped in the religious sense?

"Or are we not worth bothering about?

"The enthusiasm in the city is considerable. But we have had Billy Graham in voice only. There is still time. . . ."

Delegations to Kelvin Hall came from the farthest north to the farthest south in Scotland by many hundreds of chartered busses, by more than fifty special trains, by a score of chartered airplanes. The *Scottish Sunday Post,* most widely circulated newspaper in Scotland, ran a countrywide contest: "Why I Want to Hear Billy Graham." Winners, ten busloads of forty people each, were awarded trips to Glasgow, provided with tickets to Kelvin Hall, fed and lodged and returned to their homes, all at the *Post's* expense.

"Since I was fifteen years old," said one winning letter, "I have been in church only once—to be married. During my Army service padre after padre gave me lecture after lecture to restore my faith, without success. I wonder if this man Graham can do it."

"In May, 1954, I lost my youngest son," said another. "Since he went the joy of living has been taken away. When I heard of Billy Graham I had a great hope that he is the one to help me to face up and restore my faith."

"If," wrote another, "the churches of my city had some of the spirit and power of a Billy Graham Crusade, they would all be better churches and we would all be better people."

Perhaps there is no better evidence of the way in which the

212

All-Scotland Crusade, from having at first been a matter of popular interest became, in the opinion of hard-bitten newspaper editors, a subject of downright personal religious concern than the series of articles run by the *Sunday Post* as the Crusade concluded: "What It Means to Be a Billy Graham Convert." The replies were the kind of testimonies one expects to hear—but, even there, much too seldom—only within the limited precincts of a church.

A Glasgow housewife: "The last five weeks of my life have been the happiest I have ever spent. For over thirty years, I had been an agnostic. I had become increasingly aware as the years passed of the emptiness, bitterness, and hardness such a belief engenders. I went forward at Kelvin Hall, saying, 'I don't believe with my head, but I will have faith and act as though I do.'

"Now, after five weeks, I cannot help but believe as day by day, fresh power, serenity of spirit, and a changed outlook on life testify to the power of Christ.

"To test this new power I gave it something to do I couldn't do for myself—to stop smoking after twenty-five years. It is now five weeks since I've had a cigarette and what a glorious freedom from being a slave.

"The cynics sneer and say we converts will soon return to the spiritual vacuum from which we came—but I know, and thousands like me, that my life is changed irrevocably."

An ex member of the Royal Air Force: "My story begins a year ago when I heard Dr. Graham at Wembley. I was in the RAF and went by coach party to hear Billy. I was deeply moved but did not go forward because I had not the guts to get up in the middle of all the chaps who knew me.

"My story restarts on the first Wednesday night of the Glasgow Crusade. I had no ticket so I went into the overflow to watch the service on TV. As soon as the appeal was made, I went forward. I did not feel emotional or excited. I just real-

213

ized I needed Christ to help me live a life I didn't have enough will power to live myself.

"In my everyday life, I have found comfort, security, happiness I never knew before. I have made new friends. In a Christian church I have found a new home."

Husband and wife: "I write on behalf of my husband and myself. Prior to accepting Billy Graham's call I frankly admit for many years the word happiness was never to be found in our home, owing to continual quarrelling between my husband and myself due to excessive drinking.

"Now our lives are changed in many ways. To attend church was unheard of in our home for years. Now we attend regularly. Happiness prevails in our home. My husband and I thank God for the wonderful change that has taken place in our lives."

A workingman: "I went to Kelvin Hall out of curiosity. Being by nature for over twenty years a man of loose habits, such as gambling and drinking, I felt that no matter what was said it would not affect my way of living.

"Little did I know what a transformation it would mean to me and mine, for I can truthfully say that from the minute I took my seat I was affected in a way I could not understand. Since that night I have felt and acted as a Christian should— not gambling, drinking, vulgar talking, but going on with the Lord.

"I am now a member of the church. My future life will be dedicated to Christian endeavor."

On the last day, save one, of the All-Scotland Crusade, 60,000 people—many hundreds of whom had stood five hours in line—filled Glasgow's famous Ibrox Stadium. On the next afternoon, for the final meeting, a crowd of some 100,000 filled Hampden Park. The press, reporting these concluding meetings, included one apparently minor incident which, I think, significantly sums up how much, in so short a time, religion had become a part of the life of so many people and

214

how far beyond the person of Billy Graham or his organization that concern had penetrated:

"The Billy Graham Crusade is over. What a host of memories it leaves. On Friday night over 30,000 people spilled out of the meeting at Ibrox Stadium and queued 30-deep outside the subway station along Copland Road. For a moment the queue was silent, thoughtful. Then a window in an overlooking tenement was shoved up. Three girls poked their heads out. And until the queue had disappeared they led the thousands in community singing. They sang 'The Lord's Prayer,' 'This Is My Story' and many others. In its own way, surely, a worthy finale to a great campaign."

As with many other aspects of the Billy Graham ministry, it is beyond my journalistic powers to explain how all this happens, how a great city is, for this period, so widely and so deeply permeated with religious concern. One thing I am sure of: it is obviously a phenomenon of far too great proportions to be ascribed to the workings of the Graham publicity "machine" or to the employment of modern methods of advertising and promotion. The best that the most expert of such technicians and techniques ever achieve for any other cause is still far short of this.

I am likewise at a loss to appraise the lasting consequences. That there are lasting consequences and that some of them may be momentous I have no doubt. For example, William H. Stoneman, head of the foreign service of the Chicago *Daily News*, cabled to his paper after the Billy Graham meetings in Paris:

"By this date his efforts to create a great religious awakening in Europe have developed into a potent crusade which, because it is spiritual in nature, is already serving as an antidote to the Communist anti-Christ and the purely materialistic gospel of the Russians.

"Graham also has the unique distinction of being just about

the only living American to whom Europeans seem willing to listen."

It seems also to be the considered judgment of objective observers that no American in this postwar period has made so many friends for America and gone so far toward offsetting the widespread conviction that material rather than spiritual matters are America's sole significant concern as Billy Graham during his amazing tour of Asia in the winter of 1956.

I am sure also that closer at hand the consequences of a Billy Graham Crusade must have some permanence. Glasgow, for example, may now be again very much what Glasgow was before. But something, little or much, of this exposure to and concern for religion must have gone more than skin-deep and —imperceptible though it may be to the casual observer— entered into the life of the city. It seems a reasonable conclusion that the Power which was competent enough to bring it about will be competent to prevent its total dissipation.

When asked about the "lasting" consequences of a Billy Graham Crusade, Ruth Graham sometimes says, "Who can be sure? But just wait till we get to Heaven."

Short of that I do not know any way to determine finally the permanence of what happened—as in scores of other cities— to Glasgow. I am willing to leave it for such a celestial accounting.

13: Does it last?

IN A WESTERN WORLD which, in the sober judgment of some of its best-qualified observers, is weakened by lack of a vital, transforming, durable religious faith, there is one question about the ministry of Billy Graham and his Crusades more important than all others. That question is: Does it last?

In many places in this book from many sources there is evidence which seems to me to point toward an answer to that question.

There is, in addition to the results of my own firsthand inquiries, much other evidence. All of it seems to me to bear out Billy Graham's contention that today's most nearly universal ill is spiritual hunger:

"Millions have tried to nourish themselves on every kind of bread: science, education, better living, more pleasure. Now, unsatisfied, they have begun to ask for the Bread of Life."

His ministry is proof, I think, that this hunger reaches across the usual barriers of geography, language, social and economic position. In whatever country he preaches the record-breaking crowds that hear him seem to listen just as gladly whether he is heard through an interpreter, or, miles away, through telephone relay. To his appeal all kinds and conditions of people respond: the churched and the unchurched, high-placed and low, educated and untutored. Many ministers in many places have had experiences similar to that of the Anglican vicar who told me in some amazement that three of the active converts added to his church during the Greater London Crusade, all three of them converted on the same evening, were a garage mechanic, a member of Parliament, and the daughter of a peer.

After the meeting in Geneva, Switzerland, in June, 1955, Ruth Graham wrote to her parents:

"The meeting was at the Palais des Expositions. Over 18,-000 people were gathered. Over a thousand made decisions. Everywhere people have said, 'It can't happen here.' 'London, yes. But not Glasgow. The Scots are too dour and reserved.' 'Scotland, yes,' they said in Paris. 'But never in Paris. You don't know the French.' In Zurich they said, 'The fun-loving French? Yes, they might respond. But never in Zurich. The German mind, you know.' And here in Geneva again they said, 'Not here. This is the intellectual headquarters, so to speak. They will never go forward.'

"But they did. Quietly and quickly. It isn't a culture or a personality responding to a program or a man, but the soul responding to the God who made it. . . ."

This spiritual hunger which Billy Graham finds wherever he goes reaches, also, into the churches and includes, there, not only church members, but often the clergy. In fact, as I have indicated elsewhere, Billy Graham believes that it is in the churches that today's revival need is greatest and that it is there that a religious revival—if there is to be one—must begin.

Despite the fact that some of the severest and, I think I can safely add, some of the unfairest criticism that has been and continues to be leveled against him comes from churchmen, Billy Graham's loyalty to the church and his zeal for its upbuilding are unwavering. This, of course, sets him aside from some evangelists of the not distant past who, often, have attacked the church with almost as much vehemence as and only a little less venom than sin and the hosts of Hell. Moreover, Billy Graham's concept of the church is, to use the ecclesiastical word for it, ecumenical. It reaches beyond those denominations whose theology most closely approximates his own and includes, with the same devotion and perhaps somewhat more concern, those which seem to have departed from what, to him, is orthodoxy.

At the service of dedication prior to the All-Scotland Crusade, in the Church of Scotland Cathedral in Glasgow speaking to what was described as "one of the most representative congregations of churchmen in Scotland's history," Billy Graham said, "I am here to serve the church, whether it be a humble Brethren assembly or the congregation of this ancient cathedral . . ."

"We were deeply aware," said one of the leading ministers of the Church of Scotland, "of that unity in Christ without which no work can prosper."

Yet Billy Graham is far from sure that the present upsurge in church membership and attendance in the United States means that there has been a like increase in vital religion. In the winter of 1955, on the TV program *Meet the Press,* he said, "We have a hundred million Americans members of some church. If a hundred million Americans were putting into practice the teachings of Christ in the office, the home, and the shop we would not have the moral and social problems we have."

He has also said, "Though the pews are often filled, the people who fill them often go away empty. They have been offered good advice and good argument, everything but the Good News of the Gospel of Jesus Christ. The multitudes may be interested. But they are not fed."

Perhaps the most dramatic meeting of the All-Scotland Crusade in the spring of 1955 was not at Kelvin Hall where the public services were held, but in a downtown church where, at the end of the Crusade, Billy Graham spoke to 1,000 ministers. His message was: "Be sure you have a Gospel to preach; then preach it with authority."

A dissatisfied minister, he told them, went to an actor friend.

" 'Tell me, how is it your audiences respond to your words while my congregations seem deaf to mine?'

" 'There is this difference,' said the actor. 'I speak my fiction as though it were fact; you speak your fact as though it were fiction.'

"Either Jesus Christ is *the* answer to all mankind's needs or He is *no* answer. There is no record of His saying, 'I think so,' 'perhaps,' or 'maybe.' The Bible says, 'He spoke as one having authority.' To Satan tempting Him He said, 'It is written.' For our confused, frustrated, fearful generation, He says, 'This is the Way; walk ye in it.' "

Then to this gathering representing every segment of Scottish Protestantism—from Episcopalians and the Church of Scotland to so-called "splinter groups"—the largest gathering of its kind assembled in Scotland, Billy Graham said:

"Some ministers have said to me, 'Billy, I've never really known Christ'; others, 'My heart has grown cold'; others, 'I have so many doubts I have no authority.'

"I am going to do something I have never done before. I am going to ask you, ministers of the Gospel, to bow your heads, to forget you are ministers, to remember only that you are sinners in need of God's saving and empowering grace. The seat where you sit can be your altar. Will you now pray with me: 'Lord, here am I. I want new power in my life, new power for the church, a new religious day for the people of Scotland.' "

They all prayed. At Billy Graham's invitation for a public sign of rededication it looked as though all the thousand of them raised their hands. And a thousand voices joined as one of them began to sing the familiar, much-loved song: "The

220

Lord's My Shepherd." The entry in my notes reads: "Lifted rafters."

The minister-correspondent for a British church paper wrote: "Nothing, so far as our Scottish churches are concerned, can ever be the same again."

There is evidence—some of which will be set forth in this chapter—that not only in Scotland, but elsewhere and after a longer time, there are many churches where nothing will ever be the same again.

In the early fall of 1955, Billy Graham went to England to conduct a mission at Cambridge University. He landed at Southampton. From the letters he wrote to his wife there are stirring illustrations of how frequently, en route, he met up with people who—nearly eighteen months after the conclusion of the Greater London Crusade—were eager to give their testimony.

"On the boat the next-door steward was 'Match' who, as you remember, was converted, listening to a Harringay relay in Southampton. He is a glowing, radiant Christian and on the morning I gave the sermon at the ship's church service he went up and down the ship telling everyone to turn on their radio because I was speaking. . . ."

"When we got off the boat a number of the customs officials said, 'We're glad you're back,' and a policeman rushed up and grabbed my hand and said, 'I was converted through one of the relays from Harringay.' One of the baggage men asked for my autograph and said that he, too, was converted at Harringay. . . ."

"On Friday I went to our office in London which handles our mail and affairs from that side. One of the beautiful young secretaries came up to me and said, 'Mr. Graham, my husband and I were converted at your Wembley meeting. What a difference it has made in our home.' A little later we were stopped in the street by a man who said, 'Aren't you Billy Graham?'

I said, 'Yes.' He said, 'Hallelujah! Through you, Christ changed my life and the life of my family.' "

From the country home of one of England's most prominent businessmen, Billy Graham wrote of the family chauffeur: "During Harringay, they had brought him to the service and at the end of it had gone back to the car, but he was nowhere to be found. Thirty minutes later he appeared with a big smile on his face and said, 'I was converted tonight.' Since then, they said, his life has been remarkable and thrillingly different. And he told me, 'That was the most important day in the life of my family and of me.' "

Numerically, incidents like these even multiplied as they could be prove, perhaps, very little. What they prove, on a higher level, is something else. If we accept Jesus' assertion that "joy shall be in Heaven over one sinner that repenteth," it seems likely that even from so small a number, Heaven's rejoicing must have been considerable.

To get what might be accepted as a more conclusive answer to the question—Does it last?—I went to England in the spring of 1955 to make a firsthand inquiry. The results of that inquiry are set forth in this and the succeeding chapter of this book. Prior to telling what seems to me to be the dramatic story of what I found, there are, I think, two facts which need emphasizing.

The first is that any altogether accurate accounting of the lasting effects of a Billy Graham Crusade is beyond the power of statisticians, reporters, or even thoughtful churchmen to find out. The best one can do—in the way of quoting the considered opinions of laymen and clergymen and of recording individual case histories—still leaves unprobed large areas of life and many thousands of lives which were touched and, in great or small degree, were changed through the ministry of Billy Graham.

A second fact is that the final answer to the question: Does it last? is not solely Billy Graham's responsibility. Neither is

222

it only, or, for that matter, chiefly Billy Graham's ministry which is measured, pro or con, by the answer. For Billy Graham does not take the converts of his meetings and provide them with warmth, shelter, and nourishment under an organizational wing of his own. Neither does he, like some evangelists, turn them loose to flounder. Each of them, by the most emphatic and precise directions, is sent to a church and, with equal emphasis and precision, a minister, immediately and with all needful data, is sent to each of them.

Some of the converts of every Crusade would not, even under the closest, most effective spiritual tutelage, survive. For a variety of reasons, emotional or otherwise, their "decisions" did not involve them at a deep enough level. But for those—a considerable majority, I think—who, in the beginning, really mean business or, with at least momentary sincerity, think they mean business, the subsequent results are a measure not so much of the ministry of Billy Graham as of the ministry of the churches and the clergy to which these "infants in the faith" are sent.

But even for those who, for lack of sufficient conviction or adequate nurture, do not survive, how can one be sure that some lasting good has not accrued? After attending a Billy Graham meeting during the Toronto Crusade in the fall of 1955, Frank Tumpane, columnist for the Toronto *Telegram*, wrote:

"Many came forward the night I was there. They were sober-faced, not stern-faced. They came quietly and with no hysterics. They simply came forward and stood quietly before the platform upon which Billy Graham stood. Their names were taken and they will be put in touch with one of the Toronto churches which will minister to their spiritual needs.

"How many of them will be backsliders? I don't know. But I think it's better to be a backslider time and time again than never to make an effort to move forward at all. . . ."

When I went to England in the spring of 1955 a year had

elapsed since the three-month Crusade at London's Harringay Arena. That Crusade, as I have pointed out elsewhere, was sponsored by more than 1,000 Greater London churches of all denominations. Hundreds more throughout England and Wales were joined to the Harringay services by telephone relay. Nearly 2,000,000 people heard Billy Graham. There were 38,-000 "decisions for Christ."

In books, pamphlets, and dozens of articles, pro and con, about Billy Graham and the Crusade, in scores of interviews with prominent churchmen of many denominations, ministers of large and small parishes, church editors, executives of religious organizations, laymen, converts of all ages and many backgrounds, I sought the answers to these questions:

What has happened to the Crusade's converts, twelve months after the Crusade? What remains of the dedication and zeal which were stirred among so many preachers and churches? Was it all a passing show, as some allege and a few hope; and if not, what were the lasting benefits?

These, supported by a weighty preponderance of facts and firsthand testimony, are the answers I got:

That in numbers beyond expectation, the Crusade's converts are carrying on; that in dedication and zeal, what began at Harringay, far from waning after a year, is on the increase; that of lasting benefits, "Billy Graham," in the words of Dr. W. E. Sangster, one of Great Britain's most prominent Methodist ministers, "has broken the door of opportunity wide open for a spiritual advance, an opportunity, such as we have not had in this century, to claim the soul of the nation for God."

Dr. Sangster's own church received "decision cards" of more than sixty Harringay converts. At the end of a year, all but six were "carrying on": full-fledged church members, increasingly active in its work. "But something has happened," Dr. Sangster says, "that is more important than statistics: last year's Crusade produced in England a growing appetite for religion."

Officially, the churchman who spoke for 23,000 free

churches in England and Wales was the Reverend F. P. Copland Simmons, a Presbyterian minister, Moderator of the Free Church Federal Council.

"Starting with last year's Crusade and growing ever since," he said, "there is now, in England, a greater urge toward religion than I have seen before in my lifetime."

Throughout England and Wales, Mr. Copland Simmons had addressed that year many interdenominational meetings arranged by the Free Church Council. The theme of the year's meetings, "taking our lead from Billy Graham," was evangelism. "Audiences have been record-breaking: two to three times as large as the year before the Crusade."

In a coastal city during Britain's 1955 general election, he met a campaigning member of Parliament who complained that, on three previous evenings, his largest political audience was under fifty. In the same city, on those nights, Mr. Copland Simmons spoke on evangelism to packed churches.

"Of Billy Graham's great and enduring service to our country there can be no doubt," says the Right Reverend George Bell, the Anglican Bishop of Chichester and a former president of the World Council of Churches. "Spiritually, England was waiting for such a challenge. There are evidences all about, many in my own diocese, that clergy and laymen have been aroused by that challenge and that the message of the church to the nation is being given new force and authority."

One notable evidence from the Bishop's diocese was the week-long Chichester Crusade in February, 1955. Almost a year after Harringay, it was a "Harringay in miniature," the first campaign of its kind in the city's history. A prominent Chichester businessman, converted at Harringay, proposed the idea and got it under way. Laymen raised the funds. Harringay converts organized the supporting prayer groups and provided many of the counsellors. Churches of all denominations cooperated. The Bishop of Chichester endorsed the

225

Crusade and presided at one service. More than 15,000 attended the meetings; there were 592 decisions.

"There are two answers to the question of the Crusade's lasting benefits," said Dr. Townley Lord, who was then president of the Baptist World Alliance. "One is visible. In my own congregation, twenty-three of the twenty-five Crusade converts sent to us have entered wholeheartedly into our work. During this past year, almost wholly as a result of Harringay and its continuing influence, Baptist churches of Great Britain reported an increase of baptisms 25 per cent above the increase of the previous year. That is the largest increase ever recorded, twice the average of preceding years.

"But there is another answer that is not so visible but of great meaning in the future: the atmosphere and attitude of England toward religion have perceptibly changed from prevailing coldness and indifference to increasing warmth and concern."

"Before Harringay," says Sir Frank Medlicott, prominent London lawyer, Conservative member of Parliament and active free-church layman, "if you wanted to avoid embarrassment, you didn't talk about religion save, occasionally, in an abstract way about an abstract God. Now, thanks to Billy Graham and the Crusade, the average layman like me can talk without embarrassment to other laymen about the personal reality of Jesus Christ and know they won't be embarrassed either. An even more remarkable fact is that that is what so many laymen are doing."

A leading layman of the Church of England, one of its lay delegates to the 1954 meeting of the World Council of Churches in Evanston, Illinois, is George Goyder, chairman of British International Paper, Ltd., largest supplier of newsprint to Britain's newspapers. In the spring of 1955, during the evangelist's week of meetings at London's Wembley Stadium, Mr. Goyder invited the editors of Britain's leading newspapers to a luncheon to meet Billy Graham. All but two came. Representing a total daily circulation of more than 45,000,000, it was the most inclusive meeting of British editors in many years. Introducing the guest of honor, Mr. Goyder said, "I love Billy Graham because he is bringing something back into English life we had nearly lost: the freshness of an infectious faith; a frank and open declaration of the Gospel of Jesus Christ given freely to all men regardless of where they stand or what they are—and now there is a new spirit abroad: ordinary men and women inquiring and longing for faith. I believe Billy Graham is here to help England become again what she once was—the nation of a Book, and that Book the Bible."

"There have been more prayer and Scripture reading in England in this year since Harringay," an officer of the British Evangelical Alliance told me, "than in a century or more."

During the twelve months following Harringay, the Scripture Union, an interdenominational organization to promote regular Bible reading, has had—"a direct result of Harringay" —the largest increase in membership in its history. London's bookstores reported an increase in Bible sales breaking all records.

Early in 1954, in London there were 500 prayer groups, organized to pray for the success of the Greater London Crusade. In the spring of 1955, throughout England, there were 2,800 such groups and 100,000 "prayer partners" pledged to pray for the All-Scotland Crusade in Glasgow.

A vicar of the Church of England elbowed his way through the station crowd as Billy Graham, in March, 1955, passed through London en route to Glasgow.

"A year ago," he said, "I wouldn't have believed it. But my church is filled tonight with a Scotland Crusade all-night prayer meeting."

When it was announced, in the spring of 1955, that meetings of the All-Scotland Crusade would be available throughout Great Britain by telephone relay, requests were received for more than 2,000 installations in nearly 600 communities.

Meeting places included churches of all denominations, movie theaters, Army and Air Force mess halls, hospitals, prisons, and, perhaps more remarkable, some of England's most famous cathedrals.

I went to such a relay meeting in a rural community, population 400, about 40 miles from London. Its ancient church was without a regular vicar. Attendance at services occasionally held by a visiting clergyman averaged 15 to 20. Laymen had organized this rally, paid for the installation and announcements, and, each night, conducted the service. There were 500 present.

Throughout Great Britain, attendance at these relay services was nearly 2,000,000. Instruction courses were prepared and sent out for 25,000 counsellors. There were more than 30,000 decisions.

Critics of Billy Graham predicted that in the months after Harringay, its converts, "victims of emotion," would speedily and by a large majority fall away. J. B. Priestley, writing in the spring of 1955 in *The New Statesman and Nation*, was sure that only "a tiny minority are genuinely converted." The net result: "No great harm, no great good, mostly just another show."

A London newspaper columnist, after telephone inquiries to several Anglican vicars, "estimated," early in 1955 that, "of outsiders, that is, genuine converts," not more than 10 per cent will be found still in the church.

In February, 1955, the influential *British Weekly*, nondenominational church paper notably neutralist on Billy Graham, undertook to find a more conclusive answer. It polled a cross section of British clergy of all denominations on "What's Left of Harringay?" At the end of nearly a year it found that, of outsiders, neither church members nor churchgoers, converted at Harringay, 64.03 per cent—after nearly a year—"are still attending church and taking part in church life regularly."

After traveling through the country, in contact with all denominations, Mr. Copland Simmons said that even that remarkable percentage was too low.

"The proportion of authentic, lasting conversions—after this year of testing—is, I believe, greater than from any previous such campaign in England's history."

"We expected some to fall away," said the Right Reverend Hugh E. Clough, the Bishop of Barking. "We never expected they would be so few. We knew some would carry on. We did not believe they would be so many or that they would carry on with such leavening conviction."

The *British Weekly* poll revealed another remarkable fact: that, in scores of churches, the total of the Crusade's converts continued to increase after the Crusade. Many people, exposed to Billy Graham's message but undecided at the time, "moved slowly and thoughtfully to the Christian faith over a period of months."

One minister reported that, of the busload of people which his church recruited and sent to Harringay, none went forward. During succeeding months, however, twelve of them acknowledging their debt to Harringay, applied for church membership. "Our one outsider," another minister wrote, "has now brought two others." "Six, who signed no cards at Harringay," said another, "have now joined the church through Harringay influence."

At All Souls' Church in London, the Reverend John R. W. Stott preaches to one of England's largest Anglican congregations. "Spurred by the Crusade," he says, "conversions in our church have continued. Now, a year after the Crusade, we have eleven weekly classes for new converts. Enrollment in our courses for lay leaders has nearly doubled."

After the Harringay meetings John Betjeman, a well-known Anglo-Catholic writer, described in the London *Spectator* the challenge which Billy Graham had left with Britain's churches:

"I pictured the vast half-empty chapel on some clattering

High Road, the sea of pitch-pine pews, and the few people in them leaning forward in their seats, and shading their eyes as the brave disheartened minister asked for God's blessing on Billy Graham and his team. I foresaw the objectors: the old-fashioned left-wing atheist who sees in it only a plot by American and English businessmen to get the workers to work harder for less money; the smug type, who thinks it all 'dreadfully vulgar and noisy,' the confirmed pessimist who regards it all as a flash in the pan. In the end the truth will triumph. And maybe Billy Graham has lessened the time of waiting."

In May, 1955, Billy Graham returned to London. It was then a full year since Harringay. Great Britain was in the midst of a general election campaign notable for the apathy of voters; the slim attendance at political rallies. For seven nights Billy Graham preached at huge Wembley Stadium. For five nights a cold rain swept his outdoor audience. Yet he spoke, in that week, to more than 400,000 people. There were 23,000 decisions.

From London, U.S. journalist and editor David Lawrence wrote in his syndicated column that Britain's "Number One news" is "not the general election," but Billy Graham's "simple and direct exposition of the doctrines of Christianity": the answers he gives to "people hungry for a deeper understanding of God's influence in their lives."

"Here is a man," said the London *Daily Star,* "who knows the innermost needs of his fellows and can abundantly satisfy it with his old but ever new evangelical answers."

"Never before," said the London *Evening News,* the world's largest evening newspaper, "have so many people come to one place to hear in so short a space of time as a week, the Word of God. It can truly be called the phenomenon of the mid-century—all the more remarkable because fifteen months ago it would have seemed impossible. It may not be too much to hope that it may be the start of a spiritual renaissance."

"I have traveled the world over," said one widely known

religious leader, "but nothing I have seen, nothing I have read save the account in Acts of the revival at Pentecost compares with what I saw at Wembley: 4,000 people streaming across the turf in the pouring rain to declare their decisions for Christ. And we now know an even greater miracle: that with such few exceptions, these thousands mean it."

Led by the great choir, 90,000 people, on the last night at Wembley, sang the song of praise and testimony which is a part of every Crusade meeting: "To God Be the Glory, Great Things He Hath Done."

Billy Graham, waiting to speak, turned to a member of his team: "This must have been what Jesus meant in those last three verses of the ninth chapter of Matthew."

These verses read:

"But when he saw the multitudes, he was moved with compassion on them, because they fainted, and were scattered abroad, as sheep having no shepherd.

"Then saith he unto his disciples, The harvest truly is plenteous, but the laborers are few;

"Pray ye therefore the Lord of the harvest, that he will send forth laborers into his harvest."

14: What becomes of the converts?

WHEN BILLY GRAHAM is asked, as he repeatedly is: "Will these new converts survive?" he sometimes replies that the same question could just as sensibly be asked, as one looks through the heavy glass windows of a maternity ward, of the newborn infants there. "The answer is 'No, they will not survive—not unless, for a long time, they are cared for, nurtured, and helped to grow.'

"The newly converted person is a newly reborn person. Whether he survives and grows depends on how well he is nurtured. The Bible says, 'As newborn babes, desire the sincere milk of the Word, that ye may grow thereby.'"

The whole purpose of the elaborate follow-up system, a unique characteristic of the Billy Graham meetings, is to insure that nurture. Each person who goes to make a "decision" finds that a counsellor, someone of his own sex and approximate age, has quickly come forward to stand at his side, to walk with him into the Inquiry Room, sit with him there, Bible at hand, to help with what I heard one convert call "my first feeding."

Counsellors are nominated by local ministers from their church membership. They are instructed and qualified or eliminated by members of the Billy Graham team in six intensive, two-hour classes. Their instruction not only includes the paramount business of "spiritual nurture" but reaches to such delicate personal matters as the advisability of deodorants and having handy, for use just before the call for decisions is made, a few mint lozenges.

Each convert is given a packet of pocket-size literature—"Beginning with Christ"—which includes simple questions and answers, well fortified with Biblical quotations; Scripture readings; small cards with Scripture verses for memorizing; suggestions as to how to pray; how to "witness for Christ" in the home, the office, the shop.

Name, address, church connection or preference and other data having been listed by the counsellor, each convert, within thirty-six hours, receives a personal letter of encouragement from Billy Graham. During the next two weeks, he receives two further letters from members of the Graham team, and another packet of literature: "Going On with Christ."

The preliminary work of enlisting the churches not only in this follow-up campaign but also in the matter of providing and training counsellors, the organization of prayer groups, the recruiting of hundreds of ushers and of other hundreds for Cliff Barrows' choir, is in the hands of Mr. Willis G. Haymaker, a former banker and a veteran of the campaigns of Gypsy Smith and Billy Sunday. Mr. Haymaker's integrity and dedication are of the high quality which greatly eases the task of stirring preachers and church people into above-normal activity.

The actual training of counsellors and the meticulous job of directing them during a Crusade are tasks assigned to two other team members: Mr. Lorne Sanny and Mr. Charles Riggs. Like other members of the Graham team—and I have seen them all in operation—Sanny and Riggs are highly effective— a result which, as with the others, seems to me in large part due to the depth of their Christian commitment.

234

How well this carefully prepared and tested "nurture" is continued depends, however, almost wholly on the clergy. Every convert is directed to make immediate contact with some church. The minister of the church of his preference or nearest his residence receives, within thirty-six hours, a duplicate of his Decision Card. Along with that goes a brief form, with postage-prepaid envelope, on which the preacher is expected to report back that he has made contact with the convert and the results. Ministers who do not report or are slow at it are checked on by a committee of their colleagues. "Ours has been the more spectacular, but the less important part," said Billy Graham in a final message to the ministers of one city. "The real Crusade begins now, with you."

In England more than a year after the Greater London Crusade I talked to many of its converts. I read the testimonies of several hundred others. As witnesses to the durability of the faith of those converted in a Billy Graham Crusade, I want to recount in this chapter the testimony of some of those out of the large number I talked to.

It may be said that these stories are exceptional. Perhaps they are. Moreover, out of the more than 38,000 who made decisions for Christ at Harringay they perhaps will not be regarded, percentagewise, as a conclusive representation. If they are an inadequate basis for generalization, this, at least, can be said. The spirit, the dedication, the contagious faith I found in them are typical not of a few, but, with hardly an exception, of all those with whom I had contact.

It should also be emphasized that these stories are more than accounts of religious survival. In fact, their significance chiefly derives from the fact that the persons involved in them are doing so much more than survive. What they got, beginning at Harringay, has not only kept them; it has proved too good to keep. They got a contagious faith. They are spreading the contagion.

I can readily believe that in some places, especially in some churches, the eagerness of these new converts—the face value at which they accept what the church, on a remoter level, teaches, their zeal to let no day, no occasion, no conversation pass without "witnessing for Christ"—must be a little disconcerting, to say the least, and at times, no doubt, downright embarrassing.

A layman, a church official, unexpectedly accosted as he arrived at his office one morning by a convert among his employees, remarked to me later, "It's really a bit out of my line, you know, to talk about the Holy Spirit so soon after breakfast."

I imagine that much the same embarrassment must have accrued from the persistent testifying of the early Christians.

As I have read through my notes and the written testimonies of these converts, I have wondered how many years elapse in the history of most Christian churches which see no Christians of this "exceptional" sort added to their rolls. Yet from some knowledge of the Christian ministry, it is my belief that these are the kind of Christians the average, dedicated minister wishes his ministry to produce, even though it seldom does.

Meanwhile, I point out again, the several hundred converts from whose testimonies I have selected these stories are probably exceptional. Perhaps to some they will seem too few to prove anything. But it is, I think, pertinent to recall that the achievement of the Christians of the first century was due to the fact that their faith was so exceptional as triumphantly to outbalance their numerical insignificance. It is already evident that the infusion into the religious life of Great Britain of even, relatively, a few such exceptional Christians has been a salutary leaven. There is Christian precedent for the possibility that it may prove to be a leaven potent enough—when the reckoning is all in—to leaven the whole lump.

A buyer in one of London's largest stores: On that Saturday night, she went to Harringay "solely out of curiosity and to lay in an extra conversation piece for a buying trip to the U.S."

236

But all through Sunday Billy Graham's text kept recurring: "What shall it profit a man," or, she interpolated, a woman, "if he shall gain the whole world and lose his own soul." Monday night, without a ticket, she returned to Harringay, slipped in with the choir and, at the end of the service, made her decision.

Three days later she sailed for the United States, "the strangest buying trip I ever made." In her purse, "of all things," she carried a newly bought Bible and the packet of instructions, "Beginning with Christ." In New York and Chicago her first after-business move was to find a church and a preacher. Her "conversation piece" became a personal testimony.

The first persons she told, on her return, were the employees of her own department. Her assistant reserved some questions. Does this mean she will get here in the morning in a pleasanter frame of mind? "She does." Will she be more patient with the employees? "She is." Will she be nicer to salesmen and inspectors, and especially to cantankerous Mr. So-and-So, whom we all hate? "They can't believe it—and particularly old Mr. So-and-So."

She told the chairman of the store's board of directors; later asked his permission to invite a Church of England bishop, a staunch Graham supporter, to speak to the employees. It was the first meeting of its kind in the store's history. More than 500 stayed, after hours, to attend. The chairman of the board presided. For the continued spiritual counseling of its employees, the store has now appointed a minister-chaplain. Once a week a group of executives and employees meets for prayer and Bible study.

"I sometimes am impatient," she says, "that out of 5,000 employees, this year's beginning is so small. Then I remember Jesus' story of the mustard seed."

An ex-Communist factory worker: The party secretary in his home city and its best-known agitator, he went to Harringay "to see how Billy does it." The text that night was

"Choose ye this day whom ye will serve." He was not impressed. As for the singing, "I'd heard the Communists, in that same arena, sing 'The Red Flag' with more enthusiasm." Nevertheless, a week later he returned. He did not go forward. But when, the next Sunday evening in a church near his home, the minister, himself stirred by Harringay, asked for decisions, he joined the five others at the altar.

His resignation from the party was a front-page story in the British press: "Due to deep and unsatisfied unrest within, I have decided to resign from the party and rejoin the Christian church. This does not mean that I shall take up a position of treachery and antagonism to comrades whom I respect and esteem, but that I feel belief in Jesus Christ to be incompatible with membership in the Communist party."

Before joining the church, its minister put him through a period of intensive preparation. His first public testimony was in the city square where, for years, he had spoken for the Communists. "The Lord provided a rainstorm and the biggest crowd I ever had." The heckling he got was more than offset when, at his call for decisions, five men stepped forward: "More than I ever got at one time for the Communists."

In his church, "all working at it," are twenty other Harringay converts. After a few months one of them dropped out. But on last New Year's Day this man saw a movie of the news highlights of 1954. One shot was Harringay, the choir singing "Just As I Am, without One Plea." "That night we got a phone call from that fellow. Now he's with us again."

Traveling almost every Sunday by bus and train, he has testified before dozens of workers' groups in many cities. He usually spots some of his former party comrades. At least one of them, a party official in his own city, has been converted and is now in training as a lay preacher.

He does not attempt to refute the continuing bitter attacks that he has "betrayed" the workingman. "I just tell them what Christ has done for one workingman, namely me."

238

A newspaper employee, official of his labor union: "I don't know why I went to Harringay, except that it was my night off and the show was free." Billy's text was from Joshua: "Choose you this day whom ye will serve." "I walked home five miles through the rain, trying to figure out what had happened to me."

Instead of laughing him off, as he expected, his wife went with him to Harringay a few nights later and made her decision.

"She was pretty much of a saint already," he says, "I have to sweat at being a Christian. But the difference it's made is beyond all comparison. That goes for my wife and me and how we get along. It goes for how we get along with our five children. You ought to hear the 'Little Harringay' we have on Sunday evenings after church, singing Crusade songs."

Before the Wembley meetings in the spring of 1955 he reconditioned his automobile—an overage London taxi—and ran a bus service for his neighbors to the stadium. At Wembley, he never sat with his passengers: "I didn't want them to feel under obligation." But eighteen of the thirty-seven he transported made decisions.

"Now," he says, "our Sunday evening gatherings make a houseful."

A London policeman: When the London Crusade started, he was a traffic officer at one of the city's busiest corners in the Strand. Hundreds of busses passed him every day—and from every bus Billy Graham looked down at him from a Crusade poster. One night he said to his wife—a former policewoman and officer in the wartime WAAFS—"Let's go out and see that fellow in person." They were both converted.

"It took me three days," he says, "to find the happiness Billy promised. Then, one day in the poolroom at the police station, it hit me all of a sudden. My wife and I haven't had anything but happiness since."

He told his friends on the police force, expecting to be met with "hoots of laughter." Instead, "they quizzed me: wanted

239

to know what I did, how I felt and what made me so sure." Now he belongs to a prayer group of policemen: eight of them Harringay converts. They go out in pairs to "witness for Christ."

Before Harringay, discontented in his home life and unsatisfied with his job, he planned to take his family to Australia, "looking for the pot of gold." "Now," he says, "I wouldn't leave either London or the job. We've found something better than a pot of gold."

A food manufacturer: His firm, one of the largest makers of meat and fish paste in England, has been in his family 200 years, employs 500 people. When, with a busload of sixty employees, he and his wife went to Harringay, his wife said, "Let's agree we won't make fools of ourselves before our own people. Whatever this thing is, let's not fall for it." He heartily agreed. When Billy Graham made his call for decisions, "fool or not, I knew I'd have to break that promise and go forward." He turned to his wife to explain. She slipped her arm through his: "We're both going."

"We stood there, grown people, yet spiritual infants." In the counseling room, where every convert goes, "we were given a formula for infant feeding: a four-part compound of prayer, Bible reading, witnessing, and Christian fellowship. For nearly a year we have followed that diet and we know it works.

"No one told us, specifically, what to do about the problem of our disunited family. After we'd had a family altar for a few weeks, no one needed to. Billy Graham didn't tell me how to run my business. But after we had settled a troublesome labor dispute an old employee came to my office: 'We'd like to know what's happened to you.' "

Out of a town in Cornwall, his company employs a fleet of twenty fishing vessels. A good place, he decided, to bring his witnessing. Instead of the 100 or so he had expected to hear him there were 2,200 and 45 decisions.

"With those tough-minded fishermen," he says, "it was no

240

passing matter. Later, out of their meager incomes, those 45 sent four of their number as 'return witnesses' to my city."

During one week last February, he, with other converts, helped arrange a Crusade in his city, a "Harringay in miniature," to which I have referred elsewhere. Laymen raised the funds. Harringay converts organized the supporting prayer groups. Churches of all denominations cooperated. One service was presided over by the Church of England Bishop. More than 15,000 attended the meetings; there were 592 decisions.

"We've now been asked by some preachers," he says, "to give them time to catch up. They've already got as many converts as they can handle."

A doctor: His large practice is in a suburban community not far from London. He went to Harringay armed with binoculars: "If this was a circus, I wanted to see all the acts." Billy Graham's text was the First Commandment: "Thou shalt have no other gods before Me." Halfway through the sermon, the doctor put down his binoculars and got out his notebook. That was the first of five successive nights at Harringay: on the fifth he made his decision.

His wife, convalescing from an operation, was at a coastal resort. Strolling along the boardwalk, he "casually" told her, "Two nights ago, at Harringay, I gave my life to the Lord."

"She forgot she was British," he says. "There in that crowd she threw her arms around my neck and kissed me. She said, 'I've been praying for this for seven years.' "

When the London Crusade ended, they began in their own home a Saturday night "Drawing-room Harringay." The number who come has increased during this year, from 10 to 50.

"We start with refreshments, and sing with the Harringay Hymn Book. My wife plays the piano, and if we cannot get a good soloist, we hear a recording of Beverly Shea. We then hear a testimony, usually by someone who came to know the Lord at Harringay. This is followed by a message from a special speaker. We have the backing and prayers of several keen

241

Christians who attend the meetings, and God has blessed them and answered these prayers beyond all that we had hoped for. Recently, bidding good night to a lady I know, I asked her how she enjoyed the meeting. 'Oh, I never enjoy them,' she said, 'but I can't keep away. I hope you don't mind.' "

From this fellowship of "spiritually hungry friends and patients," there have been twenty-five decisions for Christ.

For the 1955 Billy Graham meetings at Wembley Stadium, the doctor organized six busloads of people from his community. There were twelve decisions for Christ among them. Recently, he totaled up his "missionary mileage": to give his testimony he had driven, in the year since Harringay, 7,500 miles, spoken to 20,000 people.

A London bank clerk: "I knew no more about Billy Graham and what he was going to do in this country than anybody else who wasn't actually interested—and I wasn't. Then I heard that the Crusade choir was singing selections from the *Messiah* on April 13, and I thought that might be worth hearing.

"I walked to Harringay from the city. I had been there often to skate and watch ice hockey. It was a changed place. Instead of confusion and a bit of swearing and drinking, there were Bible texts on the walls and a strange quiet among the people. It was the night Billy spoke on the Eighth Commandment, 'Thou shalt not steal.'

"At the end of his address he started asking people to come up front. I didn't know what this was all about. I had never been to a revival meeting, never seen a conversion or any of that sort of thing. But I had a funny feeling I knew this meant me and I had to go.

"When I got into the Inquiry Room a counsellor pointed out those key verses I have since become so familiar with. He prayed with me and asked the Lord to come into my life.

"The next morning in the office I hadn't been there five minutes before a friend appeared who had been there as a counsellor and had actually seen me going into the Inquiry

242

Room. She came up to talk to me about my decision. Then, for the first time, I began to know what Christian fellowship meant. All through that day I had Christians coming up to me and giving me the hand of fellowship. I look back on that as one of the most wonderful days I have ever spent, I think.

"The next thing that happened was that I was put in touch with the secretary of the Christian Union we have at my bank, a very active one of about 100 members. They invited me to all their activities—their monthly meetings, Bible study groups, and every day a prayer meeting at some time or other. That has become very much a part of my life. Since then once a week on Fridays I've got my regular group of friends when a dozen of us go into a small room that the bank has given us to set apart as a prayer-meeting room where we pray for the bank, chiefly our Christian friends in the bank, the activities of the Christian Union.

"Right away I joined a church. I heard one was in need of a bit of help and my wife and I thought that was the place for us to give a hand.

"For months now I've never had a moment's doubt or looking back. The joy of my life has been something I'd never known before. For a year I've not known what it is to be miserable or bored. When it comes to 'witnessing' I've got so much to do I have to run an engagement diary for the evenings in order to fit it all in."

Headmaster of a well-known boys' preparatory school: When three upper-school boys asked permission to go to Harringay, he "reluctantly" said yes. Two days later the three returned. "We posted a notice," they said. "Can ninety go?" They did, and the headmaster went with them.

At Harringay, the "emotional reaction" he had feared would happen happened. From their widely separated seats, fifty of them went forward. He decided the "wearing off" would take a few days, perhaps until Sunday.

In addition to compulsory daily chapel, the school, through

its Christian Union, sponsors a voluntary religious service every Sunday evening. The headmaster speaks. Average pre-Harringay attendance was ten to fifteen boys. The next Sunday evening—deadline for the "wear-off"—there were more than seventy.

Some parents, sure their sons were too young to know what it was all about, said, "Give them a month." At the Sunday evening service a month later, attendance was still more than seventy. After a year the average, despite graduations, is still nearly sixty.

The first week after Harringay, the headmaster received another delegation. "We'd like to form a group for Bible study in our hall." Soon every hall had one. A year later, every hall still had one.

"There's a better climate in the school and evidently a better one in some homes. Parents no longer ask, 'How long do you think it will last?' Some of them are more concerned that it won't."

A Royal Academy drama student: "I was studying the theater. I went to Harringay because it was the best show in town." The text that night was Matthew 12:30: "He that is not with Me is against Me."

She lives with her parents in a flat over her father's pub. They called it a "nine days' wonder" when she told them her decision. A few nights later she came home from her first converts' class. Stairs to the flat led up from the bar. Perhaps she was conspicuous, carrying her Bible, the first she ever owned, under her arm. Perhaps she had what one of her teachers had called "that Harringay look." "In my business," her father told her, "we don't hold with Bible-toting."

Three others from her class were converted at Harringay. "At first we buttonholed almost anybody, almost anywhere: 'You've got to be converted.' Now I think we're wiser and better witnesses." Their group has grown, in eleven months, from four to nineteen. With Billy Graham planning to return

244

to London's Wembley Stadium in May, they had raised among themselves £12 for two busses to take eighty students. By mid-April, they had a waiting list.

"For ten months my parents wouldn't talk to me about what had happened. They just watched. I never missed a day praying for them." Then, one day, her father said, "I hear your Billy Graham is coming to Wembley. You wouldn't have any tickets?" She got six: for her father, her mother, and four patrons. "Now," she said, "I'm praying double."

"So that I can make Christian use of whatever dramatic ability I've got," she plans to come to the United States to study religious drama.

A young woman medical student: I met her exactly a year, to the day, after her "decision" at Harringay: "My re-birthday," she called it. Billy, that night, had preached on Adam and Eve —"I didn't know," she said, "that anybody ever did any more —and sin."

On her way back to the hospital after her "decision" she wondered what she would do about the all-girl house party planned that weekend at her home. What she did was to start it off by telling her story. To her amazement, two others—Harringay converts—had "stories" to tell. By Sunday afternoon, three of her guests had made "decisions." "For a year, now, we've all been in the same prayer group."

Her father, a churchwarden, was a little dubious. When, later, she told him how some of her prayers had been answered he was "positively uneasy."

"But don't you get answers to your prayers?"

"I can't say," he said, "that I do."

In the year since Harringay, the Bible study group in the hospital where she is studying had more than doubled. At the preparatory school where she graduated she has organized another group—"twenty of them and all going strong." On the completion of her medical course, instead of practicing in a community not far from London as she had planned, she has signed up with a church mission board for assignment to a hospital in Africa.

A Scot, former captain of the Argyll and Sutherland Highlanders, blind and partly paralyzed from wounds received at Tobruk. Pre-Harringay, he was a near-alcoholic, "a drifter— frustrated, bored, and with nothing but more of this darkness to look forward to." Billy Graham and the London Crusade were "so much American ballyhoo" until his girl friend was converted. The sudden change in her life jolted him into going to Harringay. He went four nights straight. On the fourth night, a counsellor came and sat at his side:

"Young man, you're in trouble."

"I know it."

"Come along with me"—and he made his way to the Inquiry Room.

In the hotel lobby where he told me his story, he unscrewed the top of his hollow, aluminum crutch where he had kept his reserve supply of gin. "For eleven months now, there's not been a drop in it or in me. And for eleven months, I've not known what it is to be bored."

He had just returned to London from a week's mission—a "miniature Harringay"—in a small city in the Midlands. One fourth of the population of the community had attended these meetings. There were several hundred decisions.

To memorize Bible passages, he reads from his Braille Bible onto a tape recorder, then, over and over, plays them back. He has memorized so many that when he speaks he is sometimes startled to hear himself saying, like an echo of Billy Graham, "the Bible says. . . ."

A free-church clergyman: He did not go forward at Harringay or sign a Decision Card. But this—much like many minister-testimonies I read—is his story.

"When first suggested, I was suspicious of the Greater London Crusade. But I went to Harringay. On the next Sunday I told my folk all about it. I thought it was a great venture

246

of faith when we booked two coaches. Then, the reservations for the first trip were so many, I gave up my seat. From that visit nothing seemed to happen. Then we had another visit. I can't exactly describe what happened or how I felt when I saw first one and then another of my people going forward; then one of my own deacons and then another—tears streaming down their faces—to make the greatest of all decisions; and greatest of all, my own son, then eighteen, went forward.

"Later, when our young people had their annual morning service, an elder deacon said to me, 'You know, we've had these youth services for sixty years. Our young folk have gone up and talked, in a general way, about God and religion. But have you noticed that this year what they have been saying is not general, it is personal. It is: "My Lord, My Saviour and My God."'

"As just a humble, working minister I feel I've had more results from my labours—more lives visibly changed—in the last few months than in the previous twenty years. For me, in my own particular life, Harringay was a reconversion."

An Anglican vicar: "For some days I have felt constrained to write to you. I am the vicar here of a small country town in some of the most lonely country in England. I have been ordained nearly twenty years—and I have only just found Christ for whom I have searched ever since I was little more than a kid of twelve. I want to tell you because I think you have been the mediator of my finding.

"Last year, Billy Graham came to England. Like many others I was skeptical at first. I ended by writing you a letter asking you to come here. But I never posted it. Then came *Souls in Conflict.* I took twenty-seven folk from here. And then something happened to me, the vicar. It's all a chain of events. But now I *know* I have found Christ, that He has even forgiven my sins, the really awful sins, of the past. I seem to have a new life. I *know* He is risen. . . .

"Last Friday night in a friend's house I watched you on TV

and then went back to the church—just to make sure again that I knew. . . . Maybe I'll come down from this mountain. But this time I know that I shall not come down alone. My heart is full of joy and peace. . . ."

In the year after Harringay there sprang up throughout Britain scores of "Drawing-room Harringays"—small groups of converts, growing as new converts were added, which met regularly for Bible study, prayer, testimony, and fellowship. The one I attended one night in London was in its tenth month. There were twenty-two present: stenographers, clerks, young businessmen, a nurse, a medical student, an Oxford graduate student, all but one under thirty. The leader was a young minister, lately a Cambridge University chaplain.

When my mission was explained—"to find what happens after a Billy Graham Crusade"—one of them said, "Your story is all told in the thirteenth chapter of Matthew."

Later that night I read the passage he referred to:

"Behold, a sower went forth to sow. . . . Some seeds fell by the wayside and the fowls came and devoured them up; some fell upon stony places . . . and because they had not root, they withered away. . . . And some fell among thorns; and the thorns sprung up, and choked them. But other fell into good ground, and brought forth fruit, some an hundredfold, some sixtyfold, some thirtyfold. Who hath ears to hear, let him hear."

15: In the wake of the U.S. Crusades

BEGINNING with Los Angeles, in the fall of 1949, through Richmond, Virginia, and Oklahoma City in the spring of 1956, Billy Graham, in addition to scores of single-meeting engagements, has conducted full-fledged Crusades in twenty-two U.S. cities, and one in Toronto, Canada.

It is worth noting that, prior to the Los Angeles Crusade, no large-scale evangelistic meetings had been held in the United States since, in the years before World War I, Billy Sunday was in his prime. From the 1920s through the early 1940s, Protestant gatherings of as many as 10,000 people seldom if ever happened and were rarely attempted.

It was, in large part, the currently unprecedented size of the crowds which made the Los Angeles Crusade front-page news in that city and a news story across the country. And a Protestantism impelling enough to enough people to merit front-page attention was, in itself, a heartening upturn of events for the churches. I have described, in an earlier chapter, how in every Billy Graham Crusade there is, via the press, the same widespread confrontation between the Christian Gospel and a multitude of those who customarily are indifferent to and untouched by religion's conventional appeals. That, perhaps,

249

does not rate among the results of a Crusade. It certainly rates as one of its opportunities.

As for the churches themselves, Dr. John Sutherland Bonnell, minister of the Fifth Avenue Presbyterian Church in New York City, remarked, after seeing in one city the many hundreds of laymen and laywomen who—in prayer and Bible study groups and in counseling classes—were drawn into the work of preparation for a Crusade: "If no meetings were held, just the expectancy has been worthwhile."

But, beginning with Los Angeles, Billy Graham's U.S. Crusades not only made religion front-page news. They tested Billy Graham. They sped his growth. They established his evangelism as no fly-by-night religious extravaganza, but as a sober, constructive, church-centered ministry and they established Billy Graham as no hellfire-and-brimstone ranter but as an evangelist whose personal dedication and integrity merited comparison with the great evangelists of the past. It was such evidence—growing in weight and recognition with every U.S. Crusade—that opened the way for his expanding ministry in Great Britain, on the European continent and in Asia.

In many U.S. cities I have followed—from one to six years later—in the wake of Billy Graham. The evidence I gathered as to the permanence of the results of his Crusades is not statistical. I do not know and I did not make any particular effort to find out just what percentage of the "converts" in those cities are still carrying on. The statistical polls which I have seen for two cities were both made by amateurs obviously critical of Billy Graham. The results of both were somewhat negative.

I am not disputing as I might the accuracy of those results. But I do question their importance. I am quite sure that if Dr. George Gallup had been operating in the first century A.D. and had made a poll in Athens or Ephesus or Philippi or Rome he could have come up with the kind of negative data which would have made it possible to give a similar statistical brush-

250

off to the permanence of the results of the preaching of St. Paul. Dr. Gallup would have been right, statistically. How wrong he would have been historically!

Moreover, if, statistically, a considerable percentage of converts do not survive, some substantial measure of responsibility for that failure must be borne by the ministers and churches to whom—with greater care and insistence than has ever before characterized such an evangelistic effort—their survival is entrusted.

The attitude and climate which, in a few churches, insure a high casualty rate among converts was never more clearly revealed than by the London correspondent of the *Christian Century,* influential nondenominational U.S. church paper, in his account of Billy Graham's meetings in London's Wembley Stadium in May, 1955. These were the meetings hailed by an at-first hostile press as "the phenomenon of the mid-century." Yet this correspondent for a religious paper, himself a minister, made this "phenomenon" a fifteen-line item in his two-column report of British church news. His concluding sentence is, happily, a libel on most members of the British clergy. But it deserves pondering by anyone honestly concerned to know why some converts sent to some churches fail to survive the shock: "All that many of Britain's clergymen ask for now is a quiet summer, free from the unceasing attentions of the Graham publicity machine, and a chance to get on with the humdrum parish work without having to lead parties to the heady delights of gigantic meetings in the rain."

I am aware, of course, that the yearning of the minority of ministers for whom this minister speaks to get shed of Billy Graham and have a "quiet summer" is not, in any important part, due to the fact that a Crusade involves them in more work or exposes them unduly to the elements. It is due, rather, to the fact that, for this limited segment of the clergy, the work it often involves them in is so totally unlike their "humdrum parish work" and the people it often involves them with are

251

so utterly different from the kind such parish work conventionally produces. I can well understand how upsetting, not to say nervously exhausting, it would be for both minister and people if some U.S. churches I know were suddenly to find themselves on the receiving end of a group of eager converts—zealous to test and grow in their new-found faith and, at the drop of a hat, to "bear witness for Christ" to others.

Statistically, the churches of the United States do not need Billy Graham. Statistically, they are doing all right. But spiritually, as J. B. Phillips points out in the introduction to his stirring translation of the Acts of the Apostles, there has been a "deterioration in Christian faith and Christian living. . . . The Church is very rarely making any considerable impact upon the modern pattern of living. It has unquestionably lost power; it has lost vision. . . ."

It is true that statistics—the size of the crowds, the numbers who make "decisions"—figure importantly in the news of every Billy Graham Crusade. But the real test—the payoff, so to speak—is not statistical. It is not whether, adding-machine-wise, the churches have gained great numbers, but whether, altar-wise, they have gained a few great Christians. Beginning in the first century, every triumphant chapter in the church's history is evidence that a few who are Christian enough have always proved to be numbers enough.

In every city I found, as I had found in Great Britain, men and women who, since the Billy Graham Crusade and because of it, were doing much more than carrying on; who had not only caught the Christian contagion, but had made it catching; individuals in the first-century tradition who, beginning with themselves, were turning their worlds—small worlds though they often were—"upside down." I do not know how many Christians of this kind would be required to make a total large enough to constitute "success" in the eyes of the critics of Billy Graham. The New Testament gives the impression that, in the eyes of the Lord, it would not take very many.

252

Out of curiosity and to please Susie, his wife, Stuart Hamblen—Southern California's best-known radio singer and songwriter—attended one Billy Graham meeting. To escape a second, he left Los Angeles on a hunting trip. A storm drove him out of the mountains. The next night he went again with his wife to hear Billy Graham.

"Boy," he said, after he had "successfully" resisted that night's call for decisions, "you made it."

About three o'clock the next morning Billy Graham got a telephone call in his hotel. It was Stuart Hamblen:

"Can Susie and I come over right away?"

They had a prayer meeting there—Billy Graham, Grady Wilson, Susie, and Stuart—kneeling around the bed in Billy's room.

"Lord," Stuart prayed, "You're hearing a new voice this morning. . . ."

Among the more than 5,000 who made "decisions for Christ" during the Los Angeles Crusade, Stuart Hamblen would not add much, percentage-wise, to the evidence of that Crusade's permanent results. Religiously—like so many others I have met—the consequences of his conversion cannot be reckoned by addition, but only by multiplication.

One of the faith-slanted songs written since his conversion, "This Ole House," was at one time at the top of the *Hit Parade*. Another, "His Hands," recorded by Mahalia Jackson for Columbia Records, has been a best seller. So has the recording for Coral Records of "Open Up Your Heart."

To "witness for Christ," by song and personal testimony, Stuart Hamblen, every year, appears at scores of religious gatherings. In 1955, by air and at his own expense, he made more than 100,000 miles of such evangelistic journeyings.

"How about it?" one of his skeptical friends asked him. "Have you still got sawdust on your knees?"

"I sure have," said Hamblen, "and I'm going to die with sawdust there."

In September, 1949, when the Billy Graham Los Angeles Crusade began, Jim Vaus, an electronics expert, was established—and getting rich at it—as chief wiretapper for Mickey Cohen, Southern California's boss gangster. One night, on the eve of his departure on a Mickey Cohen mission to St. Louis, Vaus's wife, Alice, persuaded him—"lacking any good movies in the neighborhood"—to go with her to a Billy Graham meeting "just to see what this fellow's like." That night, Alice says, "Billy preached on God's judgment and God's mercy. When he gave the altar call I prayed, 'This is for me and for Jim, too, Lord, please.' Jim sat there unmoved. I prayed again, 'Lord, if this doesn't touch him, what will . . . ?'

"The crowd rose to sing, 'Almost persuaded, now to believe, almost persuaded, Christ to receive.' Again my heart cried, 'Persuade Jim, Lord, persuade him.'

"A wiry man with spare hair and a determined look on his thin face grabbed him by the arm. Jim glared at him. But he bowed his head to pray and when he raised his eyes, Jim muttered, 'I'll go.' "

To make restitution for electronic and photographic equipment he had stolen—there was some $15,000 of it—Jim Vaus sold his house and his automobile. He wrote, among others, to radio station KFWB, detailing what he had stolen, asking what he could do to make things right: "I want to right things with men that I may be right with God." The station manager's answer was: "Your unusual but courageous letter of December 8 received and we are happy to note your admission and your change of attitude. That in itself is payment in full as far as we are concerned. . . ."

When he turned up at the telephone company with a load of stolen goods, the manager there—instead of calling the police as Vaus expected—offered him a job.

He wrote to the district attorney confessing that, in a recent gangster case, he had committed perjury. He was promptly subpoenaed. The Court warned him: "You don't have to

254

testify if your testimony will incriminate you." Vaus chose to testify and concluded his testimony with the Court's permission by giving his own account of what, as a result of "accepting Christ as my personal Savior," had happened to him. As a result of the evidence he gave, an officer of the Los Angeles police force was freed from charges pending against him. The indictment for perjury, which Vaus was certain would come, never materialized.

Now, Jim Vaus spends several months of every year conducting evangelistic services across the country. His crowds are large and so are the offerings. But all of the latter, save traveling expenses and his own $400-a-month salary, go into his Missionary Communication Service—a non-profit foundation he has established to provide electronic equipment for Christian missionaries in isolated stations around the world—"turning my specialty from crime to Christ's account." *Wiretapper,* a film produced in 1955 which dramatized the story of his underworld career and his conversion, was described by *Time* magazine as one of present-day evangelism's "most potent weapons."

Before World War II, Louis Zamperini was a track star at the University of Southern California. He was a miler on the U.S. team in the 1936 Olympics. In 1943 the plane in which he was a bombardier was shot down in the Pacific. When finally picked up by a Japanese fishing boat he, with one other survivor, had floated forty-seven days in a rubber raft. Worse tortures were visited on him by guards in Japan's prison camps. When, at the war's end—a year after the War Department had declared him dead—he was released, he was rated as one of the half-dozen men "who suffered most in World War II."

Four years after the war's end, the "hero stuff" having worn thin, his marriage was near the rocks, his funds were running out, he had no settled job and "what's worse," he says, "no plan or purpose for my life."

It was his wife, Cynthia, herself a Crusade convert, who

255

persuaded him to "give Billy Graham a one-meeting once-over." He left before Billy had finished preaching. When, on Cynthia's urging, he agreed to go a second time it was on condition "that you will leave with me whenever I ask you to." She promised.

That night Billy Graham's text was: "For what shall it profit a man if he gain the whole world and lose his own soul? Or what shall a man give in exchange for his soul?"

"When he gave the invitation to accept Jesus as our Savior, I would not budge; I could not; I would not.

" 'Don't you want to go forward?' asked Cynthia. . . . The moment had come; I stood at the top of a high wall; at the peak of conviction, I could still jump either way.

" 'Let's leave,' I said and she rose slowly, her face very sad. But halfway down the aisle I stopped fighting and knew what I had to do. Turning around, I made my way to the prayer room. . . ."

Zamperini, too, made restitution: to the guards who, day after day, had tortured him in Japanese prison camps and toward whom, with the passing years, his hatred had not diminished. With friends helping to finance his trip, he went to Japan. He sought out as many of his torturers as he could find—some of them in prison. To each he gave his Christian testimony and offered, with his hand, his friendship.

"The six-year hate was over and I prayed my thanks. . . ."

Back in the United States, Zamperini was offered a lecture contract: $50,000 a year for seven years—the only condition being that when it came to "talking about Christ," he would have to tone down a bit, agree not to "go overboard." Zamperini turned down the contract and "went to work, full-time, for the Lord."

Today the dream which he and Cynthia had after their conversion is a reality: a Christian camp in the mountains not far from Los Angeles for juvenile delinquents, "Victory Boys' Camp." When the first "batch" of boys arrived the camp bank account was down to $50. "Faith," says Zamperini, "opened the camp and miracles have kept it going." Even greater miracles appear to have been worked in the lives of many of the confirmed delinquents he has taken in. The reality of those miracles is, I think, pretty well indicated by the wholehearted endorsement of his work by officials of the government of Los Angeles and of the state of California.

It probably could be figured, in estimating, statistically, the results of the Billy Graham Los Angeles Crusade, exactly how much the conversions of Stuart Hamblen and Jim Vaus and Louis and Cynthia Zamperini added quantitatively to Christianity's lump in that city: an infinitesimal percentage. The item of real significance, however, cannot be reckoned: how much, in Los Angeles and beyond it, their conversions added to Christianity's lump-enlivening leaven.

There are stories like these in every city where there has been a Billy Graham Crusade: of individuals who, as a result of that Crusade, became contagious Christians and for whom life's most important business has become the spreading of that contagion. I have enough such "case histories" in my own notes not merely to fill a chapter, but to make a substantial start toward a book. Yet I know that my inquiries hardly scratched the surface.

In a Midwestern city I had breakfast one morning with a couple—converts in the Billy Graham Crusade in that city more than five years before. At that time he was a member of the State Parole Board. When I met him he had become its chairman. Of the 1,500 convicted criminals then on parole in his state there had not been a single serious case of parole violation—a record probably unmatched in the United States.

"There is no mystery about it," he said. "I told my fellow members of the board what had happened to me. I suggested that we give God a place in our deliberations. They agreed and we have."

Every parole board meeting, thereafter, began with prayer;

257

every case was given not only factual, but prayerful consideration. Through most of that morning he recounted stories —not merely of parolees who had met the requirements of their parole, but of individuals who, helped back to a place in society, had had their lives transformed.

Two invitations had just come to him: one, to accept in New York an executive position with the National Probation and Parole Association of the National Parole Board; the other, to establish, at Wheaton College in Illinois, a department for preparing Christian students to go into the field of correction and social work.

His wife said, "If you have met many people whose lives were changed through Billy Graham's preaching, you will know why we chose Wheaton."

Five years after the Billy Graham Crusade there, I met the mayor of a Deep South city, a successful businessman.

"As a city," he said, "we've never been the same since, and, as a person, neither have I. It has made a difference for the better in the way business is carried on in our city that four groups of businessmen, organized as a result of the Crusade, meet regularly for Bible study and prayer. It has made for better labor-management relations that plant prayer meetings of employees and employers, begun during the Crusade, still meet, some of them daily.

"Today, in our city, interracial good will and cooperation are at an all-time high. Whites and Negroes, we are moving ahead together. When I appointed a Negro—the first—to our school board, the community accepted it, not as the necessary, but as the right thing to do. I don't think that would have happened without the new spirit engendered among our people during the Billy Graham Crusade. And, save for what happened to me, personally, in that Crusade, I doubt if I would have made such an appointment in the first place."

For a young businessman in another city, the night his wife persuaded him to go with her to a Crusade meeting was his first attendance at a religious service in sixteen years. He had made a success of business. Amateur golf champion of his state, "the only god I had was golf."

That night, he went to the Crusade "straight from a gambling session at the club." He had a good seat: "My wife had gone two hours before the doors opened to make sure of it." What he heard "hit me squarely between the eyes." For five nights thereafter, he says, "I weathered the storm of conviction." On the sixth night—the last—"I was patting myself on my back when God took over: 'It's tonight or never.' Then something happened that really shook me. My wife got up, brushed past me, and walked down that long aisle. My last excuse was washed out. The choir was on the fifth verse of 'Just As I Am'—only one more verse to go.

"'All right, Lord,' I said, 'I can't figure it all out. But I'm going to put one foot forward and let you take me the rest of the way. . . .'

"That was six years ago. Our quarrel-riddled home has been made over. We didn't argue with our cocktail-party and gambling friends. We were finding a bigger thrill in our daily devotions. Bible reading, and prayer. It's one of the miracles to us how many of those friends, in the years since, have discovered the same thrill."

Today he still plays tournament golf—on any day but Sunday. Sundays he teaches a men's Bible class through which, in 1955, there were thirty-nine "decisions for Christ." He is chairman of the evangelistic committee of his church, member of the board of directors of a Christian Service Center. He leads a small laymen's group which conducts religious services in the state penitentiary, prison farms, veterans' hospitals, the state university.

"I wouldn't trade one minute of my life in these six years for all the more than thirty years that went before."

There is more such evidence, in high places and low, than I have space to recount:

In Washington, D.C., a Pentagon stenographer has shared a home with several girls—all converts in the Washington Crusade in 1951—in order that they might have "a base from which to witness for Christ.". . . . In Philadelphia, a bank vice-president who, hearing Billy Graham, decided, "I can't fool around the edges of the real thing any longer." Now, three years later, he is chairman of the Philadelphia Christian Business Men's Committee, active in its religious radio program. His country home is "still a place for weekend parties—but now they are Christ-centered parties.". . . . In a Southern city, the editor of a newspaper who, converted in a Billy Graham campaign two years before, gave his first testimony in a signed front-page story in his newspaper, today is active in the church he joined and says today that his conversion "made all the difference." . . . In 1952, a senior at the University of Washington attended—"totally unconcerned, but just for the fun of it"—one of the meetings of the Seattle Crusade. What he got at that meeting he took back to his fraternity house, and soon there was a "Christian cell" meeting regularly in his room for Bible study and prayer. He graduated in 1956 from a West Coast theological seminary—"the last thing on earth I thought I'd be doing." The "cell" he started in his own fraternity house is continuing. As a result, several others, in both fraternity and sorority houses, have since been started.

In the fall of 1955 several young men were ordained for the Presbyterian ministry in Washington, D.C. Every one of these young men, according to Dr. Edward L. R. Elson, pastor of Washington National Presbyterian Church, was "brought to Christian experience in Billy Graham's Washington meeting."

One of the ministers of Southern California's largest Presbyterian church told me, "I personally know of more than a few young men and women who are now in seminaries or in church work here or in the mission field as a result of the 'decision for Christ' they made during the Los Angeles Crusade. Moreover,

260

that Crusade was like a great bridge across the rift between the secular man and the churchman. Today the churches of this area are closer to the man in the street than ever before. That drawing together began with Billy Graham."

I called one day in Los Angeles at the office of one of the city's prominent real estate operators. "But this," he told me, "isn't the biggest thing in my life. The biggest thing in my life comes on Thursday night." Beginning with the Billy Graham Los Angeles Crusade, he had invited a few friends for Thursday evening Bible study. Now, after more than six years, that Bible class—taught by a well-known Los Angeles surgeon—has grown to an average attendance of more than 200. "To handle the crowd," he said, "my wife and I have built an addition to our house. If it continues to grow we'll gladly add another."

Riding through a residential area of Nashville, Tennessee, a friend called my attention to a sign on the front lawn of a lovely home. "There," he said, "is one of the permanent results of the Billy Graham Crusade." The sign read: "Neighborhood Prayer Meeting Here, This Morning." In preparation for the Crusade in 1954, Nashville women organized over 1,600 such neighborhood prayer groups. They met four mornings a week for four weeks. Now, more than two years later, scores of them are continuing to meet once a week. "If we stopped," the leader of one group told me, "every family in this street would be the loser. So would Nashville."

A Chattanooga newspaperman wrote me: "Interest has grown, not lessened since the end of the Crusade four years ago. Chattanooga may be the only city in America where students at the two largest high schools have organized prayer groups. It all began with Billy Graham. As for individuals, I could tick off for you the names of at least a half-dozen young men who made 'decisions' during the Crusade and are now studying for the ministry. Doesn't that sound pretty permanent?"

The minister of Chattanooga's largest Methodist church gave it as his conviction four years after the Billy Graham meetings that "the Crusade created a new spirit and environment in the city. . . . Prayer groups organized during the Crusade are more alive today than when they began. In my own church there are more than 200 prayer cells of from three to seven people each. Stirred by the Crusade many of our Methodist laymen have become lay preachers in small rural churches without pastors."

Two years after the New Orleans Crusade, the minister of the First Baptist Church reported that since Billy Graham's meetings there religion has had "a new lift" to it. The lasting consequence is not only still felt in the churches, but "extends to the whole moral life of New Orleans." In Memphis, says the minister of one of its largest churches, Billy Graham, three years after the Crusade, "is still refreshing to the religious life of the city. He was, and is, like a breeze in the desert. People are talking more about the church since he was here."

Three years after the 1952 Crusade in Pittsburgh, the editors of *Parade* magazine sent two reporters to that city to find the permanent effects of that Crusade, if any. An Episcopal bishop told them that "the general awakening" stirred by Billy Graham was still being felt. The minister of a United Presbyterian church described the lasting results as "formidable"; a Methodist minister, as "tremendous." Among Pittsburgh's churchgoers, "there seems to be little doubt," said these reporters, "that a new spirit, engendered by Graham, is visible. Prayer groups and youth rallies started under the initial Graham enthusiasm, still meet weekly." Among all kinds of people—businessmen, schoolteachers, housewives, students, office workers—they found converts who were effectively and contagiously carrying on. Their conclusion:

"The question—Does Billy Graham's kind of religion 'stick'? —can be answered. The answer is Yes and No, with emphasis on the Yes."

Statistical appraisals of the permanence of the results of Billy Graham's Crusades will, I am sure, continue to be undertaken. The results of some of them, no doubt, will continue to serve as a means whereby the spiritually comfortable will seek to escape discomfiture. But there is another and, for Christians, a more conclusive kind of appraisal from which there is no such easy out:

"Another parable set he before them, saying, the kingdom of heaven is like unto a grain of mustard seed, which a man took and sowed in his field; which, indeed, is less than all seeds; but when it is grown it is greater than the herbs and becometh a tree, so that the birds of the heaven come and lodge in the branches thereof."

16: Revival in our time?

IN THE SUCCESSION of small Nebraska and Wyoming towns where he served, my Methodist-preacher-father, six nights a week for at least two weeks each winter, conducted a revival. In the language of the Methodist Discipline this was called a "protracted meeting" and whatever results accrued were duly reported to the Presiding Elder at the next Quarterly Conference. In the lower echelon of churches, such as ours, such meetings were common Methodist practice. But my father faithfully followed that practice not so much because such evangelism was prescribed by the Discipline as because his own convictions were "soundly evangelical."

With so much rousing singing of Gospel songs and so much rousing Gospel preaching to listen to, these protracted meetings were a stirring time for the minister's family and, in, I am sure, a somewhat lesser degree, for others of the faithful. But therein lay the distressing thing about them: that they were so seldom attended by any but the already saved.

Mornings, at family devotions, and each night in church, it was the burden of my father's prayers that somehow, someway, God would bring the unsaved within reach. He did not doubt that God had entrusted to him a Gospel needful and sufficient for the sinner's salvation. What he longed and prayed for was access to the sinner. Like prayers, I am sure, must have besieged the Throne of Grace from countless other altars such as ours.

In this generation in the United States that prayer is being answered: "abundantly," as my father would have expressed it, "above all ye are able to ask or think." Whether they are still called sinners or by some pleasanter, if less definitive, name, the church's problem with the unevangelized is no longer one of inaccessibility. This is perhaps the most religiously accessible generation in American history. The present problem is not how to bring in the unreached, but, rather, how to deal with a generation that is almost too reachable.

In proportion to total population, more Americans than ever before belong to some church; more attend church regularly; more send their children to Sunday school. They give a greater proportion than ever before of their disposable income, i.e., income after taxes, to religious causes; build more and more beautiful churches; read more religious and pseudoreligious books and articles; sing and dance to more songs which have near-religious lyrics; attend more movies on religion or quasi-religious subjects; hear and see more religious radio and TV.

In fact, by every quantitative measurement and by all the external manifestations, religion in the United States is booming. Its marks and signs were never so visible; its spokesmen never so widely, so often or, in many instances, so gladly heard; its conventional appeals never so readily responded to. Observing all this, as he could hardly fail to, the Apostle Paul would almost certainly say of mid-twentieth-century Americans what he said of the first-century Athenians: "Men of Athens, I perceive that in every way you are very religious."

Many secular observers agree with the historian Arnold J. Toynbee that the saving of the West and the restoring of the spirit of Western man require "the revival of religion." Impressive as they are, the facts of revived religious interest in

266

the United States do not indicate that such a religious revival as yet is under way. From this great abundance of religious manifestations, there is still no like abundance of authentic religion. Religion, as yet, is not making a deep enough difference to a large enough number of people in a significant enough number of ways.

What these stirrings do indicate is that vast numbers of people have now come within reach of those whose calling it is to take such inadequate gropings and so deal with them that if a revival is to come at all, this will be its time.

They have not been generally dealt with that way. Though the openness to religion which now prevails is a consummation long and earnestly prayed for, its advent has not been received, at least among Protestantism's so-called liberals, as answered prayers presumably are. Whether or not this is due to consternation at being confronted with an answer—and a challenge—of such proportions, these stirrings have not been welcomed in these quarters so often as they have been decried; discounted as "fad" or "vogue" or "passing fancy"; "The New Look," as the heading in one religious journal put it, "in American Piety."

Preachers who have seen a religious opportunity in this situation and whose preaching, as a result, has won a popular following have been widely, sometimes intemperately, attacked by fellow clergymen for fostering a "cult of reassurance," variously described as "dangerous," "sinister," "very nearly blasphemous."

In *Look* magazine, the president of the National Council of the Churches of Christ thought he discerned in the present "religious boom" certain signs which he feared might make it a "spiritual bust." What, in his opinion, is being revived in America is not the "righteous and living God" but "the old tribal gods." Chief among them, he says, are "Mammon, the god of industrial prosperity and worldly success"; the god of "escapist religion"; god in the guise of "Healer."

267

A professor in Union Theological Seminary, progressive Protestantism's most influential theological school, has reduced "today's religious revival" to an expression of "culture religion" with these its distinguishing features: "The tendency to reduce Christianity to a Gospel of happiness and success. . . . The loss of any basis of criticism of our culture as a whole and the close alliance with the forces of nationalism. The capitalizing on the fact that communism is atheistic and the strong suggestion that because we are against communism God must be on our side. The close cooperation between many of the leaders of this movement and the forces of social reaction."

A writer in the *Christian Century,* which is progressive Protestantism's most influential journal of opinion, has defined the "new piety" as the ascendancy in our midst of three dubiously religious "cults." The "cult of peace of mind," "which readily turns into religious narcissism," is described as "piety concentrating on its own navel." The "cult of the Man Upstairs" is "Gospel boogie replete with masters of ceremonies, Gospel quartets, popcorn and soda pop." The "cult of We versus They" which assumes that "the God of judgment is dead" and his place taken by a "god who fights on the side of his chosen people, supporting their racial, economic or national interests."

Few will deny the measure of truth in some of these warnings or doubt that the religion of some of those who have been caught up in today's religious boom and of some of those who are riding its crest may have something to be desired and something, no doubt, to be feared. The unfortunate fact about these often salutary words of warning is that they are so generally the only words that are authoritatively spoken. In the midst of this vast upsurge, the clearest call is not "take over," but "watch out."

By every visible prospect, "the harvest, indeed, is plenteous." Yet, so far, "the laborers are few."

This is not because of a shortage of Christian workers or a

lack of energy in their pursuit of Christianity's good works. There are no figures for it but, from considerable observation I am sure that, currently, a greater proportion of church members go more busily than ever before about the church's business. The activities listed in the Sunday bulletin of the average congregation are a record of the unpausing pursuit of things worthwhile. It does not minimize their importance to say that they also seem to reflect what sometimes appears to be a peculiar genius of the modern church: to make several organizations grow where previously one seemed to suffice.

With so many mechanisms to man, to guide, to fuel and lubricate, it is not remarkable that the functions of the minister have become less those of shepherd than of overseer. If what was once his study is now his office, that fact is a mark of what the present business of the church demands and of his undeniable diligence in it.

But underneath this ceaseless religious bustle there is an ominous fact. That fact is that for more than a generation, the theology which has widely prevailed among Protestant clergy and the Gospel widely preached in the churches have been such as to prepare organized religion to meet almost any contingency save the kind that now exists; to speak, with authority, on almost any kind of need save the present kind. A large part of the lukewarmness with which these present religious phenomena are received must be due less to skepticism and indifference than, simply, to unfamiliarity with phenomena of such sort and lack of preparation in how to deal with them.

The preparation which, for the present situation, has left so much of the church unprepared was a natural, perhaps the necessary, product of the almost totally different religious situation of a generation ago. At that time, compared to the present, organized religion in the United States was in the doldrums and religious belief was widely—and, in some quarters, to the point of panic—on the defensive.

Protestantism, in that period, had yet to benefit from the

269

dynamic apologetics of Reinhold Niebuhr or Catholicism from those of Fulton Sheen. Bertrand Russell declaring that "omnipotent matter rolls on its relentless way" and Henry Mencken describing man as "a sick fly taking a dizzy ride" on a flywheel cosmos spoke for more people than the theologians. Humanism—"religion without God"—was a rising tide. Modern man, said one secular survey, "knows almost nothing about the nature of God, almost never thinks about it and is complacently unaware that there may be any reason to."

Such religious unconcern was probably an inevitable product of the times. In the wake of the discoveries and industrialism of the nineteenth century had come twentieth-century mass production, and almost every American home was or was about to become a shrine to house its benefits. God's face was obscured by the accumulation of man's handiwork. Things were the ultimate good; the struggle to get them was becoming our way of life.

"The general tendencies toward the secularization of life," wrote a distinguished theologian, "have been consistent enough to prompt its foes to predict religion's ultimate extinction as a major interest of mankind."

In such a period of religious depression the concerns of the spokesmen for religion were not—perhaps they could not be—theologically selective; their doctrines not dogmatic; their prescriptions not too hard to take. Man had too much that was too visibly to his material credit and he was too satisfied with its enjoyment to have time or patience for such apparently discrediting, prehumanistic notions as the Christian doctrines of Satan and Savior, Hell and Heaven, Sin, Repentance, and Salvation. The most popular preachers were those who gave such doctrines the widest berth.

Theology, necessarily perhaps, was tailored to the times. That was the heyday of modernism whose "reduced Christianity" doubtless was as strong stuff, religiously, as, in view of the prevailing appetites, there was any stomach for. Since it seemed

270

futile to try to make God spiritually real, modernism undertook to make Him intellectually respectable. If God could not be pleased, man, at least, might be placated.

What dynamism there was then in the churches was largely supplied by the so-called social Gospel which found in the amelioration of social conditions and the betterment of racial and international relations the chief purpose of the Christian revelation and the chief means for its validation.

That it was sometimes preached with authentically prophetic voices, that it greatly extended the boundaries of Christian concern, that it added and continues to add significantly to Christianity's this-worldly contributions does not alter the fact that the social Gospel was, in considerable measure, a product of the spiritually indifferent times in which it arose. Many people to whom, on the personal level, such Christian doctrines as I have mentioned above—Sin, Repentance, Salvation —were repugnant were readily stirred when those doctrines were expounded on a level that was impersonal and collective. No doubt, also, some people found in the social Gospel the means by which, temporarily at least, they could sublimate their need for a personal Gospel. Knowing, as Bishop Sheen has pointed out, that something was "wrong on the inside," they attempted "to compensate for it by righting the wrong on the outside."

Religion, thus, was widely, often effectively prepared to speak to men's minds and to their social consciences, but with much less assurance to their hearts and their wills.

However great their contributions were and continue to be, it seems clear that if good works, modernist theology, and a social Gospel had in them the materials for a religious revival, such a revival, long before now, would have been upon us. There has been, in those vineyards, no shortage of laborers. It is not, I think, for the fruit of those vineyards that today's seekers are most earnestly looking.

Though the quest may be only haltingly under way, the level

271

of today's seeking is not so much social, as personal; its difficulties not so much intellectual as of the heart and will; the changes which, however hesitantly, are being sought are not, first, in the world, but, first, in "me"; the life plan which is being reached for, however clumsily, is not first for society's life, but first for "mine."

Religion has, so generally, become a common American concern because of the personal problems which have become common to so many Americans.

Countless people are turning to religion for precisely the same reasons of inner stress and conflict which are leading an unparalleled number of others to turn to barbiturates. Are these expecting too much from a religion whose Founder said, "Peace I leave with you, my peace I give unto you: not as the world giveth, give I unto you"?

A religious answer is being sought by countless people for the same reasons of inner disturbance and fear which have led so many others to seek escape in alcoholism. Is it promising too much to say that there is such an escape in the religion whose Founder also said, "Let not your heart be troubled: neither let it be afraid" . . . ?

Many are looking to religion for a plan and purpose for life for precisely the same reasons of frustration and meaninglessness which have helped make mental health our country's most serious health problem. Are these people fooling themselves to expect such plan and purpose from a religion which declares: "For God hath not given us the spirit of fear; but of power, and of love, and of a sound mind"?

There may be, there no doubt are better religious answers than those sometimes offered by the so-called "cult of reassurance." But the very fact that there is such a cult and that it has grown to such proportions is in itself evidence of how large the number is of men and women who feel, within themselves, the need to be reassured and who acknowledge that, of themselves, that need is not being met.

272

Who were most of those who sought out Jesus, if not men and women seeking, each for his own particular distress, re-assurance? And is there any single theme other than one of reassurance—"Glad Tidings," "Healing," "Hope," "Light," "Peace," "Salvation," "Eternal Life"—which runs so clearly through the whole of the New Testament?

This present looking to religion for these personal answers is not a religious revival. But if it is not revival material, then, it seems to me, there is little to guide us in the teachings of Jesus Christ and little of meaning for us, as individuals, in the lives of history's triumphant Christians. In that case the best and most that Christian leadership will have to offer will be a pious smattering of amateur psychiatry and, that failing, a roster of accredited psychiatrists.

Here, I think, is the quality which above all else most notably distinguishes the preaching of Billy Graham and constitutes the most portentous fact about his ministry. To him today's turn to religion is revival material and constitutes a challenge such as the churches and their leadership have not faced in generations. His life and ministry are staked on the belief that this bewildered but unquestionably seeking generation is re-vival tinder which, for the kindling of a revival's fire, requires only the preaching of an authentically compelling Gospel.

In this, it seems to me, he stands in the Pauline Succession. Whatever the Apostle Paul would find missing from today's un-precedented interest in and openness to religion, one thing he would almost certainly find present: an unprecedented oppor-tunity. From having seen in Athens the marks and signs of religion Paul went on to preach to the Athenians the sermon on Mars Hill:

"Whom therefore ye ignorantly worship, him declare I unto you."

There is such assurance in the preaching of Billy Graham. That assurance is rooted in Christian experience, the kind of experience which transpired for Paul on the Damascus Road.

Whether or not Billy Graham proves to be the human instrument of revival in our time, one thing, I think, is certain: such a revival will come from the preaching of no other or no lesser Gospel.

ABOUT THE AUTHOR

Stanley High was raised in a Methodist parsonage, his father serving for many years as a minister of that church in Nebraska and Wyoming. After his graduation from Nebraska Wesleyan University, service as an Air Force pilot in World War I, and a year traveling in China with a study commission of the Methodist Church, he entered Boston School of Theology. Graduating there in 1923, Mr. High was not ordained, but joined the staff of *The Christian Science Monitor.*

After four years—during which, as a correspondent, he made several trips abroad—Mr. High made a world tour for the Methodist Church as assistant secretary of its Board of Foreign Missions. From that position he went to the *Christian Herald* as its editor.

For a number of years, in addition to his editorial work, he had a regular radio program, *Religion in the News,* over the NBC network. Beginning in 1937, he was a regular contributor to *The Saturday Evening Post,* his first article in that magazine resulting in a break with President Roosevelt, of whose speech-writing staff Mr. High had been a member during the 1936 election. He was a member of the staff of Governor Thomas E. Dewey in the 1948 Presidential campaign and that of General Eisenhower in the campaign of 1952.

In 1940, Mr. High became a Roving Editor of *The Reader's Digest* and, in 1952, a Senior Editor. His *Reader's Digest* assignments have taken him to many parts of the world, and many of his articles have been on religious subjects. It was on an assignment from *The Reader's Digest* that he first met Billy Graham, and on subsequent assignments he covered his Crusade in various cities in America and abroad.